AF840697

Property and Trust Law in Croatia

Property and Trust Law in Croatia

Tatjana Josipovic

This book was originally published as a monograph in the International Encyclopaedia of Laws/Private International Law.

Founding Editor: Roger Blanpain
General Editor: Frank Hendrickx
Volume Editors: Alain Verbeke & Vincent Sagaert

Wolters Kluwer

Published by:
Kluwer Law International B.V.
PO Box 316
2400 AH Alphen aan den Rijn
The Netherlands
E-mail: lrs-sales@wolterskluwer.com
Website: www.wolterskluwer.com/en/solutions/kluwerlawinternational

Sold and distributed by:
Wolters Kluwer Legal & Regulatory U.S.
920 Links Avenue
Landisville, PA 17538
United States of America
E-mail: customer.service@wolterskluwer.com

DISCLAIMER: The material in this volume is in the nature of general comment only. It is not offered as advice on any particular matter and should not be taken as such. The editor and the contributing authors expressly disclaim all liability to any person with regard to anything done or omitted to be done, and with respect to the consequences of anything done or omitted to be done wholly or partly in reliance upon the whole or any part of the contents of this volume. No reader should act or refrain from acting on the basis of any matter contained in this volume without first obtaining professional advice regarding the particular facts and circumstances at issue. Any and all opinions expressed herein are those of the particular author and are not necessarily those of the editor or publisher of this volume.

ISBN 978-94-035-2366-8

e-Book: ISBN 978-94-035-2676-8
web-PDF: ISBN 978-94-035-2686-7

© 2022 Kluwer Law International BV, The Netherlands

All rights reserved. No part of this publication may be reproduced, stored in a retrieval system, or transmitted in any form or by any means, electronic, mechanical, photocopying, recording, or otherwise, without the prior written permission of the publisher.

Permission to use this content must be obtained from the copyright owner. More information can be found at: www.wolterskluwer.com/en/solutions/legal-regulatory/permissions-reprints-and-licensing

The Author

Prof. Dr Sc. Tatjana Josipović is a professor of civil law at the Faculty of Law, University of Zagreb. She teaches courses in Civil Law, European Private Law and Land Registry Law. Before she joined the University in 1987, she practised in the legal office. She acted as a member of the working groups that drafted the Inheritance Act (IA), Property Act, Land Registry Act and Agricultural Land Act. She has written many scholarly and professional papers and several books on civil law and European private law and presented papers at numerous national and international conferences and seminars. Professor Josipović was a vice dean of the University of Zagreb School of Law. She is an arbitrator with the Croatian Chamber of Commerce Permanent Arbitration Court. Prof. Dr Tatjana Josipović is a member of a number of scholarly and professional associations. She is a fellow of the Academy of Legal Sciences of Croatia, an associate member of the International Academy of Comparative Law, a member of: Academia Europea; the Croatian Society for Civil Law Science and Practice; the Society of European Contract Law (SECOLA); European Law Institute; and the Civil Law Forum for South East Europe. Prof. Dr Tatjana Josipović was the head of the task force preparing Croatia's accession negotiations in the chapter Right of Establishment and Freedom to Provide Services and was also a member of the task force preparing accession negotiations in the chapter Free Movement of Capital. She was awarded a research grant at the *Max Planck Institut für ausländisches und internationales Privatrecht*, Hamburg, on several occasions.

The Author

Table of Contents

List of Abbreviations

ABOR	Act of Basic Ownership Relations
ABGB	Allgemeines Bürgerliches Gesetzbuch
ALA	Agricultural Land Act
APPCG	Act on the Protection and Preservation of Cultural Goods
ASSRPC	Act on State Surveying and Real Property Cadastre
BA	Bankruptcy Act
CA	Concessions Act
CdA	Act on State Surveying and Real Property Cadastre /Cadastre Act
CHA	Cultural Heritage Act
CLA	Commercial Lease Act
CPA	Civil Procedure Act
EA	Enforcement Act
ECHR	European Convention on Human Rights
EDP	Electronic Data Processing
EEAA	European Economic Area Agreement
EU	European Union
ExA	Expropriation Act
FINA	Financial Agency
FsA	Forests Act
HRK	Croatioan *kuna*
IGZ	*Opći građanski zakonik*
IsA	*Island Act*
Lat.	Latin
LRA	Land Register Act
LRR	Land Register Rules
MDPA	Maritime Domain and Ports Act
NATO	North Atlantic Treaty Organization
NPA	Notaries Public Act
NtPA	Nature Protection Act
OA	Obligations Act

List of Abbreviations

OG	Official Gazette of the Republic of Croatia (*Narodne novine*)
OGZ	*Opći građanski zakonik*
PA	Act on Ownership and Other Property Rights/Property Act
PA/2008	Act on Amendments to the Act on Ownership and Other Property Rights Property of 2008
PPPA	Public-Private Partnership Act
PF	Provident Fund
RA	Roads Act
Register Act	Act on the Register of Secured Transactions Established in Movables and Patrimonial Rights before a Court or Notary Public
RC	Republic of Croatia
RLA	Residential Lease Act
RwA	Railway
SECOLA	Society of European Contract Law
SFRY	Socialist Federal Republic of Yugoslavia
UN	United Nations
WA	Waters Act
WTO	World Trade Organization
WWI	World War I
WWII	World War II
ZIS	*Zajednički informacijski sustav*

General Introduction

§1. General Background of Croatia

1. The Republic of Croatia (*Republika Hrvatska*) is a Central European country along the Adriatic Sea, forming an important intersection between Central Europe and the Mediterranean on the one hand and between Central and South-eastern Europe on the other. Croatia borders Slovenia and Hungary in the north, Serbia in the east, and Bosnia and Herzegovina and Montenegro in the south. The country covers a total of 88,073 square kilometres. The land area amounts to 56,594 square kilometres, the sea area stretches over 31,479 square kilometres, and there are 1,185 islands (47 of them inhabited). The Republic of Croatia has a population of 4,437,460 (2011 census). The official language is Croatian, and the official script is Latin. The Republic of Croatia is territorially and administratively divided into twenty counties, while the City of Zagreb forms a special administrative unit. There are altogether 128 towns and 428 municipalities. The capital of Croatia is Zagreb, with approximately 790,017 (2011 census) inhabitants. Zagreb is the country's economic, cultural and political centre. The City of Zagreb is connected to other Croatian towns with more than 1,310 kilometres of highways.[1] The main economic activities in Croatia are agriculture; food processing; textiles; wood processing; the metal, chemical, petroleum, and electrical industries; construction; trade; shipbuilding; marine engineering; and tourism. The monetary unit is the Croatian *kuna* (HRK).

2. The Republic of Croatia has been a sovereign, autonomous and independent state since 1991. On 8 October 1991, the Parliament of the Republic of Croatia (*Hrvatski Sabor*) adopted a decision whereby, on that very day, the Republic of Croatia severed all the constitutional ties by which, together with the other republics and provinces, it had constituted the Socialist Federative Republic of Yugoslavia.[2] This decision was passed on the basis of the Constitutional Decision on the Sovereignty and Independence of the Republic of Croatia and the Declaration on the Establishment of the Independent and Sovereign Republic of Croatia on 25 June 1991.[3] The Republic of Croatia is a multiparty parliamentary republic. The first Constitution of the Republic of Croatia was proclaimed on 22 December 1990. The

1. Data from 'Statistical Yearbook of the Republic of Croatia 2018', pp. 44,45,59,60,107,352 https://www.dzs.hr/Hrv_Eng/ljetopis/2018/sljh2018.pdf (29.4.2021).
2. OG 53/1991.
3. Both decisions published in OG 31/1991.

highest values of the constitutional order of the Republic of Croatia are freedom, equal rights, national and gender equality, peace-making, social justice, respect for human rights, inviolability of ownership, conservation of nature and the human environment, the rule of law and a democratic multiparty system.[4] The government is organized on the principle of the separation of powers into legislative (the Parliament), executive (the President of the Republic, the Government) and judicial authority. The Croatian Parliament is a unicameral body with a maximum of 160 deputies elected by popular vote for a term of four years. The government (*Vlada*), headed by the Prime Minister, is politically responsible only to the Croatian Parliament (*Sabor*), which is comprised of the House of Representatives (*Zastupnički dom*). Members of the Parliament serve four-year terms. The President of the Republic of Croatia (*Predsjednik Republike Hrvatske)* is the head of state, directly elected for a term of five years. The President is also Commander-in-Chief of the Armed Forces and represents the Republic of Croatia in foreign relations.

3. The Republic of Croatia has been a member of the United Nations (UN) since 22 May 1992, of the North Atlantic Treaty Organization (NATO) since 1 April 2009, and of the World Trade Organization (WTO) since 30 November 2000. The Stabilisation and Association Agreement between the Republic of Croatia, on the one hand, and the European communities and their Member States, on the other, was signed on 20 October 2001.[5] The accession negotiations between the EU and Croatia started on 4 October 2005. On 30 June 2011, the Republic of Croatia closed all thirty-five negotiating chapters and thus formally concluded the negotiations on Croatia's accession to the European Union. The Treaty concerning the accession of the Republic of Croatia to the European Union (Accession Treaty) was signed on 9 December 2011.[6] After fulfilling the conditions concluded in the Accession Treaty, Croatia will become the EU's Member State on 1 July 2013.

---

4. Article 3 of the Constitution of the Republic of Croatia, OG 56/90, 135/97, 8/9, 113/00, 124/00, 28/01, 41/01, 55/01, 76/10, 5/14.
5. The Republic of Croatia signed the Stabilisation and Association Agreement with the European Communities and their Member States on 29 Oct. 2001 in Luxembourg. The Act on the Adoption of the Stabilisation and Association Agreement between Croatia and the European Communities and their Member States was published in the OG/IA 14/01. The Implementation Act of the Stabilisation and Association Agreement between the Republic of Croatia and the European Communities and the Temporary Agreement on Trade and Other Related Matters between the Republic of Croatia and the European Community was published in the OG/IA 15/01. The Stabilisation and Association Agreement entered into force on 1 Feb. 2005 (OG/IA, 1/05).
6. Treaty between the Kingdom of Belgium, the Republic of Bulgaria, the Czech Republic, the Kingdom of Denmark, the Federal Republic of Germany, the Republic of Estonia, Ireland, the Hellenic Republic, the Kingdom of Spain, the French Republic, the Italian Republic, the Republic of Cyprus, the Republic of Latvia, the Republic of Lithuania, the Grand Duchy of Luxembourg, the Republic of Hungary, the Republic of Malta, the Kingdom of the Netherlands, the Republic of Austria, the Republic of Poland, the Portuguese Republic, Romania, the Republic of Slovenia, the Slovak Republic, the Republic of Finland, the Kingdom of Sweden, the United Kingdom of Great Britain and Northern Ireland (Member States of the European Union) and the Republic of Croatia concerning the accession of the Republic of Croatia to the European Union (Official Journal of the European Union, L 112, vol. 55, 24 Apr. 2012).

§2. INTRODUCTION TO PROPERTY LAW

I. A Historical Overview and Property Law Reform

A. *Property Law Before 1991*

4. The development of contemporary law in Croatia started with the introduction of the Austrian Civil Code (ACC) and other Austrian regulations (land register, cadastre, etc.). Since then, Austrian property law has had the most important impact on the development of Croatian property law. The ACC was applied as the main source of legislation for Croatian civil law norms ever since it was introduced in certain Croatian territories [7] and was applied up until the end of World War II (WWII). With the entry into force of the ACC and other Austrian rules, the then medieval Croatian-Hungarian law ceased to be applied as separate law in the territory of Croatia.[8] With its entry into force, conditions were created for the development of a new Croatian legal and liberal society, a new judiciary and modern procedural law through which the ACC provisions were to be applied in practice. The ACC continued to exist as Croatian law even after the Croatian-Hungarian Agreement of 1868, by which, among other things, the legislative autonomy of Croatia was recognized. However, the ACC remained in force in the Croatian territories, which were not connected to the Hungarian Crown but were a part of the Austrian portion of the Austro-Hungarian Empire. The ACC remained an important source of property law even after World War I (WWI) when Croatia became part of the Kingdom of Serbs, Croats and Slovenes (in 1929, it became the Kingdom of Yugoslavia). The land register, civil proceedings, ex parte proceedings, the service of notaries public and a number of other services were also organized on the model of Austrian law. They remained in force until the end of WWII. The Kingdom of Serbs, Croats and Slovenes and the Kingdom of Yugoslavia never passed their own civil codes with validity in the entire territory of the state. The ACC therefore remained the most important source of property law regulation in all the territories in which it had existed as a property law source before WWII.

5. After 1945, the Croatian private law system was no longer part of the sphere of continental European legal orders and became a component of the legal circle of socialist countries. The socialist legal order was aimed at the development of a socialist society based on workers' self-management. The main features of the legal system at the time were collective social ownership, a planned economy and so-called associated labour in socially owned enterprises. Property law significantly

7. The Austrian Civil Code (*Allgemeines Bürgerliches Gesetzbuch/ABGB),* which is called *Opći građanski zakonik (OGZ),* was gradually introduced in certain Croatian territories from 1812 to 1853. It was introduced in the territory called the 'Croatian Military Border' in 1812, in Istria in 1815, in Dalmatia in 1816 and in other particle of Croatia in 1853. For further details, *see* Gavella, *Die Rolle des ABGB in der Rechtsordnung Kroatiens* (The Role of the ACC in the Croatian Legal Order, Zeitschrift für Europäisches Privatrecht, 4/94), 603.
8. For more details on medieval property law based on feudal principles, *see* Margetić et al., *Hrvatska pravna povijest u europskom kontekstu* (Croatian Legal History in the European Context, Zagreb, 2005), pp. 125–141.

departed from the continental European standards governing property law. The individualistic regulation of ownership based on protection of individual property rights was abandoned. Ownership was regulated on the basis of a collectivistic concept. There were two diverse general property law models of regulation concerning the appurtenance of things: social and private ownership. A special form of ownership was developed – social ownership. This was based on wholly different principles from ownership relations in continental Europe. Many things, particularly estate, were socially owned (e.g., building lots, agricultural land, forests, buildings, flats, and so on). There was no ownership right to socially owned things. Various legal entities had only some specific subjective rights to such things (the right to use, dispose of and manage them), which appear to have been absolute and protected by law. In practice, those rights were frequently referred to as 'new property rights' with *erga omnes* effect on socially owned things.[9] Along with the abandonment of the individualistic regulation of ownership, other principles were also discarded: the uniformity of the right to ownership, the equality of all legal entities and the uniform treatment of all objects of ownership, as well as other property rights. The principle of legal unity of real property (*superficies solo credit*) was also abandoned. It was abandoned in the regulation of legal relations arising when a privately owned building was built on a socially owned plot. The building was then legally separated from the land, the owner being a private person, and the building was in private ownership, whereas the land continued to be socially owned. The owner of the building was entitled only to use the land. The different parts constituting a piece of real property (the plot, flats, common areas of the building) were subject to different rights belonging to different persons. This dualism in the regulation of property constituted a serious obstacle to the development of a market economy. Legal transactions involving property (and particularly real property) were undeveloped, non-transparent and slow and were performed under the strict control of public authorities. Many things and goods were not subject to any transactions, and even in cases where they did exist, they were restricted. Modern institutions of secured transactions appropriate to a market economy did not exist at all.

6. For a long time in the socialist period, there was no positive regulation providing for property. In the beginning, the only source of property law was the ACC. After WWII, with the Act on the Invalidity of Regulations Adopted Prior to 6 April 1941 and during the Occupation (1946), all regulations adopted prior to 6 April 1941 and during the Occupation were derogated. The ACC, which was, until the end of WWII, a very important source of property law in Croatia, also lost its legal force. Nevertheless, despite the fact that the ACC was not in force, its provisions in reality continued to be applied. Because of the lack of valid regulations in the area of property law, the ACC provisions became an indirect source for the regulation of property law. The ACC provisions were no longer applied as positive law but only as 'legal rules'. Their application was permitted in the case of legal relations not

9. For more details on the types of rights on socially owned things, *see* Borić, *Eigentum und Privatisierung in Kroatien und Ungarn* (Ownership and Privatisation in Croatia and Hungary), Berlin, 1996, pp. 64–75; Gavella in *Property Law I*, 347, 814–816.

provided for in the positive regulations, namely where existing gaps in the legislation had to be filled. Property law relations that were not provided for in the positive body of law were regulated in accordance with the content of the ACC provisions. The ACC provisions were applied to property relations as 'legal rules'. However, the ACC norms – as legal rules – could be applied only in a very limited sense. Their application was manifested only in the property relations that belonged to the so-called private ownership segment, which was limited to a narrow circle of legal subjects of ownership and other property rights, and only to objects which could be privately owned.[10]

7. The first property act, the Act on Basic Ownership Relations (ABOR) (*Zakon o osnovnim vlasničkopravnim odnosima*) [11] was enacted in 1980. The Act provided only basic provisions governing possession and some individual property rights. Its importance in property regulations at the time was quite marginalized. The provisions of the ABOR were applied only in a very limited way, that is, only to property relations between legal subjects (who were holders of the ownership and other property rights) and the objects based on which such rights could exist. The Act provided only basic provisions governing possession and some individual property rights. Some property law segments remained unregulated. The provisions of the ABOR were applied only in a very limited way, that is, only to the property relations between legal subjects (who were holders of the ownership right and other property rights) and the objects based on which such rights could exist. All other property relations not provided for by this Act continued to be governed by the ACC norms as 'legal rules' (personal easements, neighbourhood law).

B. *Reform of Property Law after 1991 until Today*

8. After the independence of Croatia and the introduction of a market economy, the development began of modern private law that would correspond to such an economic system. The Croatian private law system, including property law, was reintegrated into that of Continental Europe (in particular, Central Europe, i.e., its German circle). Croatian property law is one of the areas of private law which, after transition to a market economy, went through the most radical changes. The basis for property law reform had already been laid in the new Constitution of the Republic of Croatia[12] of 1990. The Constitution proclaimed the inviolability of ownership as one of the highest values of the constitutional order of the Republic of Croatia[13] and guaranteed the right of ownership as one of the fundamental rights.[14] The current Croatian Constitution recognizes only one type of ownership, based on an individualistic concept and on the doctrine of the social function of ownership.

---

10. For more details, *see* Gavella et al., *Das ABGB in Kroatien* (Österreichs Allgemeines Bürgerliches Gesetzbuch, Band III, Berger/Hrsg), Berlin, 2010, 174–177.
11. OG SFRY 6/80, 36/90, OG 53/91.
12. The Constitution of the Republic of Croatia, OG 56/90, 135/97, 8/9, 113/00, 28/0176/10,5/14 .
13. Article 3 of the Constitution of the Republic of Croatia.
14. Article 48/1 of the Constitution of the Republic of Croatia.

9. Property law reform in Croatia was carried out through the adoption of the Act on Ownership and Other Property Rights/Property Act (PA)[15] and the Land Register Act (LRA),[16] which entered into force on 1 January 1997. The PA is considered to be the fundamental and main source of the new property law in Croatia. It is based both on an individualistic concept of the right to own and on the traditional principles of the regulation of property rights and is thus closer to other contemporary European legal orders. The most important steps in property law reform have been the final abolishment of social ownership and its transformation into private ownership, as well as the return to traditional and fundamental continental European principles of property law regulation (the principles of *superficies solo cedit,* the protection of bona fide purchasers in legal transactions, and the social function of ownership). The most important features of the new Croatian regulation on property law are the following: a return to the principle of the legal unity of real property,[17] an extension of the closed number of property rights,[18] increased protection of trust in legal transactions,[19] a new regulation of secured transactions,[20] transformation of social ownership, the establishment of unity of real property in former social ownership[21] and the separate regulation of the transition period (a transitory regime) for the things previously socially owned.

10. The PA, developed on the model of Austrian property law,[22] provides for the traditional principles of property law (the principles of a closed number of property rights, absoluteness and publicity),[23] types of property rights (ownership/co-ownership/joint ownership/condominium, personal and real easements, real encumbrances, liens, the right to build), acquisition, termination and protection of individual property rights, restriction of property rights, and the concept of things and their division into movables (chattels) and immovables. The PA does not make any distinction between the regulation of movables and immovables (it does so only when this is necessary for some particular types of things where it provides for some specific characteristics (e.g., conditions for the acquisition of ownership by contract *inter vivos*). The PA has detailed provisions for some property rights, particularly when it comes to conditions for acquisition, protection of trust and the legal foundations for the termination of property rights. The PA also contains very detailed

15. OG 91/96, 68/98, 137/99, 22/00, 73/00, 114/01, 79/06, 141/06, 146/08. 38/09, 153/09, 143/12, 152/14.
16. OG 91/96, 68/98, 137/99, 114/01, 100/04, 107/07, 152/08, 126/10, 55/13, 60/13, 108/17 .
17. For more details, *see* Part I, Ch. 1, §2. Legal Unity of Real Property.
18. For example, the right to build that had not existed in Croatian property law was introduced. For more details, *see* Part I, Ch. 1, Ch. 5, §3. Right to Build.
19. For more details, *see* General Introduction, §2. IV. E. Principle of Bona Fide Protection in Legal Transactions.
20. For more details, *see* Part VI. Security Rights.
21. For more details, *see* General Introduciton, §2. VI. B.3.c. Transformation of Social Ownership to Private Ownership and Part I, Ch. 1, §2. III. Return to the Principle of Legal Unity of Real Property.
22. The new Croatian property law is still largely regulated on the model of the Austrian property law provided for in the ACC and other Austrian regulations such as the Austrian Condominium Act, the Right to Build Act and the LRA.
23. For more details, *see* General Introduction, §2. IV. Principles of Croatian Property Law.

rules on the legal position of foreigners in legal transactions concerning property[24] and very complex rules on transition to the new property regulation after the transformation of social ownership and the establishment of the legal unity of an immovable (the principle of *superficie solo cedit*).[25] However, although there are a lot of similarities with Austrian property law, there are some deviations from Austrian property law that result from a different approach to the regulation of individual property law institutions. The Croatian PA has adopted an objective concept of possession[26] and has taken over the rules of the German Civil Code on the acquisition of movables from non-owners[27]

11. Besides the PA, as the main legal source of property law, many other regulations important for property rights relations have been adopted or amended. Among these, the new Enforcement Act (EA) was adopted (1996),[28] which introduced new types of securities. The reform of security rights was continued with the adoption of the Act on the Register of Secured Transactions Established in Movables and Patrimonial Rights before a Court or Notary Public/Register Act,[29] introducing registered liens against movables and patrimonial rights. The service of notaries public was reintroduced;[30] litigation proceedings were reformed, and digitization of the land register began. A large number of separate regulations were adopted regarding specific legal property.[31] The process of reform of property law continues and is aimed both at adjustment to the market economy and harmonization with the law of the European Union.

II. Sources of Property Law

A. The Constitution of the Republic of Croatia

12. The Constitution of the Republic of Croatia (*Ustav Republike Hrvatske*) lays down the basic principles for the regulation of property rights relations in the Republic of Croatia. The right of ownership is considered a constitutional right within the framework of economic, social and cultural constitutional rights. In the Constitution, the inviolability of ownership is enshrined as one of the highest values of the constitutional order of the Republic of Croatia.[32] Further, the Constitution contains an express provision guaranteeing the right of ownership.[33] A person

24. For more details, *see* Part I, Ch. 8. The Position of Foreign Persons in Transactions with Immovables.
25. For more details, *see* General Introduciton, §2. VI. B.3.c. Transformation of Social Ownership to Private Ownership and Part I, Ch. 1, §2. III. Return to the Principle of Legal Unity of Real Property.
26. For more details, *see* General Introduction, §2. VIII. Possession.
27. For more details, *see* Part III, Ch. 2, §3. III. Acquisition of Ownership from Non-owners.
28. OG57/96, 29/99, 42/00, 173/03, 194/03, 151/04, 88/05, 121/05, 67/08, 139/10, 154/11, 70/12.
29. OG 121/05.
30. Notaries Public Act, OG 78/93, 29/94, 162/98, 16/07, 75/09. 120/16, 57/22
31. For more details, *see* Part I, Ch. 7. Special Legal Regimes Regulating Immovables.
32. Article 3 of the Constitution of the Republic of Croatia.
33. Article 48/1 of the Constitution of the Republic of Croatia. The constitutional guarantee of ownership applies to all citizens of the Republic of Croatia. The Constitution guarantees equality of all

who believes that his right of ownership has been violated by an act of a state body (e.g., by a court decision), a body of local and regional self-government, or a legal person with public power, deciding on his rights and obligations, may lodge a constitutional complaint with the Constitutional Court of the Republic of Croatia.[34,35]

13. The Constitution expressly provides that ownership implies obligations. Holders of the right of ownership and its users contribute to the general welfare.[36] In the interest of the Republic of Croatia, ownership may be restricted or rescinded by law, subject to indemnification equal to the market value of the pertinent property.[37] Property rights may exceptionally be restricted by law for the purposes of protecting the interests and security of the Republic of Croatia, nature, the human environment and human health.[38] Ownership may also be restricted in order to protect the sea, seashore, islands, waters, air space, mineral resources and other natural assets, land, forests, flora and fauna, other components of the natural environment, real property and items of particular cultural, historical, economic or ecological significance which are specified by law to be of interest to the Republic of Croatia and enjoy its special protection.[39] Separate laws provide for the manner in which assets of interest to the Republic of Croatia may be used and exploited by holders of the rights thereto and by their owners. When ownership is restricted in order to protect the assets of interest to the Republic of Croatia, the owners are entitled to compensation which must be regulated by law.[40]

B. Legislation

14. The main legal sources of property law in the Republic of Croatia are the Act on Ownership and Other Property Rights/ PA,[41] the LRA,[42,43] the Enforcement

---

people. Art. 14(1) of the Constitution lays down that every person in the Republic of Croatia shall enjoy rights and freedoms regardless of race, colour, gender, language, religion, political or other beliefs, national or social origin, property, birth, education, social status or other characteristics. Pursuant to Art. 14(2) of the Constitution, all citizens are equal before the law. In the Republic of Croatia, equal rights are guaranteed for the members of all national minorities (Art. 15).

34. The protection of constitutional rights and freedoms by way of a constitutional complaint is provided for in Arts 62–80 of the Constitutional Act on the Constitutional Court of the Republic of Croatia, OG 49/2002.
35. On the constitutional guarantee of ownership, *see* Gavella in *Property Law I*, 354.
36. Article 48/2 of the Constitution of the Republic of Croatia.
37. Article 50/1 of the Constitution of the Republic of Croatia.
38. Article 50/2 of the Constitution of the Republic of Croatia.
39. Article 52/1 of the Constitution of the Republic of Croatia. Any restriction of property right shall be proportionate to the nature of the need for restriction in each individual case (Art. 16/2 of the Constitution to the Republic of Croatia.
40. Article 52/2 of the Constitution of the Republic of Croatia. For more details, *see* General Introduction, §2. VI. E. 3.b. Limitations of Ownership.
41. OG 91/96, 68/98, 137/99, 22/00, 73/00, 114/01, 79/06, 141/06, 146/08, 38/09,153/09, 143/12, 152/14.
42. OG 63/19.
43. Several bylaws have been passed that are important for the implementation of LRA, such as the Ordinance on the internal structure and maintenance of land registers and the execution of other tasks

Act/EA,[44] and the Act on the Register of Secured Transactions Established in Movables and Patrimonial Rights before a Court or Notary Public/Register Act.[45] The PA has been in force since 1 January 1997. The LRA of 2019 has been in force since 6 July 2019. The PA is, however, the main source of property law in the Republic of Croatia. It is based both on an individualistic concept of the right to own and on the traditional principles of the regulation of property and is thus closer to other contemporary European legal orders. The PA lays down the general rules on property regulation, the concept of the thing, the concepts of immovables and movables, ownership and other property rights, the concept of property rights, and the establishment, acquisition, protection and termination of property rights. The most important provisions of the PA deal with the regulation of ownership and its most important types (individual ownership, co-ownership, joint ownership, condominium or freehold division), including types of acquisition, protection and termination. All other property rights are defined in separate chapters (easements, real burdens, the right to build, security rights). The PA provisions on ownership apply to these rights accordingly unless otherwise specified in other legislation. The LRA provides for the connection between land register and the cadastre, the composition of land register, the subject of entries, the types and conditions of land register entries, the land register procedure, and the establishment of land register books and their digitization. The LRA is based on and ensues from the PA. The EA and the Act on the Register of Secured Transactions Established in Movables and Patrimonial Rights before a Court or Notary Public provide for particular types of security rights whose establishment is governed accordingly by the rules of the law on enforcement.

15. There are also numerous regulations laying down a separate legal regime for special types of immovables[46] or particular legal relations concerning immovables, such as the Roads Act (RA),[47] Agricultural Land Act (ALA),[48] the Water Act,[49] the Forest Act (FsA),[50] the Nature Protection Act (NtPA),[51] the Islands Act,[52] the Act on Lease and Sale of Business Premises,[53] the Flat Leases Act,[54] the Act on State

in court land registry departments – Land Register Rules (OG 81/97, 109/02, 123/02, 153/02, 14/05, 60/10, 55/13, 63/19), the Ordinance on forms used in land registry proceedings (OG 123/04, 63/19), the Ordinance on the structure and function of the land registry database in the Republic of Croatia (OG 90/04, 63/19), the Ordinance on integrating the book of deposited contracts and the land register (OG 60/2010), The Ordinance on electronic business operations of users and authorised users of the Land Registry system (OG 108/19).

44. OG 112/12, 25/13, 93/14, 55/16, 73/17, 131/20 .
45. OG 121/05.
46. For more details, *see* Part I, Ch. 7. Special Legal Regimes Regulating Immovables.
47. Roads Act/RA, OG 84/11, 18/13, 22/13, 54/13, 148/13, 92/114, 110/19, 144/21,114/22
48. Agricultural Land Act/ALA, OG 20/18, 115/18, 98/19, 57/22
49. Waters Act/WA OG 66/19, 84/21.
50. Forests Act/FsA OG 68/18, 115/18, 98/19, 32/20, 145/20.
51. Nature Protection Act/NtPA OG 80/13, 15/18, 14/19, 127/19.
52. Islands Act/IsA OG116/18, 73/20, 70/21.
53. Act on Lease and Sale of Business Premises OG 125/11, 65/15, 112/18.
54. Flat Leases Act OG 91/96, 48/98, 66/98, 22/06, 68/18, 105/20.

Surveying and Real Property Cadastre /Cadastre Act (CdA),[55] the Physical Planning and Construction Act,[56] the Act on Compensation for, and Restitution of Property taken During the Yugoslav Communist Regime,[57] the Expropriation Act (ExA)[58] and others. Concerning property regulation, particular importance is given to the rules providing for civil procedure[59] and enforcement proceedings, the legal rules of non-contentious proceedings, the rules on notaries public[60] and many other regulations in the area of obligations,[61] commercial law,[62] family law,[63] administrative law,[64] tax law[65] and other areas of law.

C. International and Bilateral Conventions

16. A very important source of property law includes international and bilateral conventions to which Croatia is a signatory.[66] One of the most important international sources for Croatian property law is the European Convention on the Protection of Human Rights and Fundamental Freedoms,[67] which entered into force in Croatia on 5 November 1997. Particularly significant is Article 1 of the First Protocol to the Convention on the Free Enjoyment of Possession.[68] The Convention is directly applied in the Republic of Croatia. Pursuant to Article 141 of the Constitution of the Republic of Croatia, international treaties, if concluded and ratified in accordance with the Constitution and published, are a component part of its domestic legal order. As for their legal force, these international treaties take precedence over domestic laws. The European Convention has special importance for the protection of ownership and other property rights in cases when all the available

55. Act on State Surveying and Real Property Cadastre /Cadastre Act/CdA OG 112/18, 39/22.
56. Physical Planning Act, OG 153/13, 65/17, 114/18, 39/19, 98/19; Construction Act OG 153/13, 20/17, 39/19, 125/19.
57. Act on Compensation for, and Restitution of Property taken During the Yugoslav Communist Regime OG 92/96, 92/99, 39/99, 42/99, 43/00, 131/00, 27/01, 65/01, 118/01, 80/02, 81/02, 98/19.
58. Expropriation Act/ExA OG 74/14, 69/17, 98/19.
59. Civil Procedure Act/CPA, OG 4/77, 36/77, 6/80, 36/80, 43/82, 69/82, 58/84, 74/87, 57/89, 20/90, 27/90, 35/91, 53/91, 91/92, 112/99, 88/01, 117/03, 84/08, 123/08, 57/11, 25/13, 89/14, 70/19, 80/22
60. Notaries Public Act, OG 78/93, 29/94, 162/98, 16/07, 75/09, 120/16,57/22.
61. Obligations Act/OA, OG 35/05, 41/08, 125/11, 78/15, 29/18, 126/21.
62. Companies Act, OG 111/93, 34/99, 52/00,118/03, 107/07, 146/08,137/09, 152/11, 111/12, 68/13, 110/15, 40/19, 34/22 .
63. Family Act, OG 103/15, 98/19.
64. Act on General Administrative Procedure, OG 47/09, 110/21; Act on Administrative Disputes, OG 20/10,143/12, 152/14, 94/16, 29/17, 110/21.
65. Act on the Tax on Sales of Immovables, OG 115/16, 106/18.
66. However, in the Republic of Croatia, the international agreements entered into and acceded to by the former SFRY (before 8 Oct. 1991) are also in force. Such international treaties are applicable in the Republic of Croatia on the basis of international law provisions regarding the succession of states, provided they are not contrary to the Constitution and the legal order of the Republic of Croatia. Point 3 of the Constitutional Decision on the Sovereignty and Independence of the Republic of Croatia of 25 Jun. 1991.
67. Act on the Ratification of the Convention for the Protection of Human Rights and Fundamental Freedoms and its Protocols 1, 4, 6, 7 and 11 (OG/IA 18/97).
68. *See* http://www.echr.coe.int/ECHR/EN/Header/Basic+Texts/The+Convention+and+additional+protocols/The+European+Convention+on+Human+Rights/.

domestic legal remedies for the protection of ownership have been exhausted. Persons whose ownership and other property rights have been infringed may bring an action to protect their rights before the European Court of Human Rights.[69]

17. There are very many international multilateral and bilateral[70,71] agreements signed by the Republic of Croatia which are highly important for property rights

---

69. For more details on the importance of the protection of ownership in Croatian law, *see* N. Gavella: Art. 1 for the First Protocol to the European Convention for the Protection of Human Rights and Fundamental Freedoms in N. Gavella, et al., *Europsko privatno pravo* (European Private Law), Zagreb, 2002, pp. 43–78; Bodiroga, N. Vukobrat, *Zaštita prava vlasništva u europskom pravu* (Protection of the Right of Ownership in European Law), *Zbornik PF Rijeka* (Collected Papers of the Faculty of Law in Rijeka), 2002, pp. 201–214.
70. *See*, for example, the Agreement between the Government of the Republic of Croatia and the Government of the Republic of Macedonia on the Regulation of Property Relations made on 18 Nov. 1998 in Zagreb and entered into force on 12 Aug. 1999 (OG/IA, 9/1999, 5/00). The Agreement between the Republic of Croatia and the Republic of Slovenia on the Regulation of Property Relations made in Ljubljana on 8 Oct. 1999 and entered into force on 23 Feb. 2000 (OG/IA 15/99, 4/00). With these agreements, the parties bound themselves to respect ownership and other property rights on immovables and movables acquired in the territory of the other contractual party until the establishment of state sovereignty (Art. 2/1 of the Agreement with the Republic of Macedonia, Art. 2/1 of the Agreement with the Republic of Slovenia). The parties to the agreements bound themselves to make acquisition possible for the nationals and legal persons of the other contractual party who, before the date of the establishment of state independence, had acquired a valid legal basis for the acquisition of ownership and other property rights as if they had been domestic entities (Art. 4/1 of the Agreement with the Republic of Macedonia, Art. 4/1 of the Agreement with the Republic of Slovenia). As for other international agreements of significance for legal transactions involving immovables, particularly important is the Agreement on Succession Issues signed on 29 Jun. 2001 by Bosnia and Herzegovina, the Republic of Croatia, the Republic of Macedonia, the Republic of Slovenia and the Federal Republic of Yugoslavia in Vienna (OG/IA 2/04, 5/04) and above all Annex G to that Agreement (Private Property and Acquired Rights). The provisions of Annex G stipulate that private property and acquired rights of citizens and other legal persons of the former SFRY shall be protected by successor States in accordance with the provisions of this Annex (Art. 1).
71. Croatia has also entered into a series of bilateral agreements with many countries on enhancement and mutual protection of investments aimed at promoting economic cooperation and the creation of favourable conditions for foreign investments and has thus assumed an obligation to encourage, allow and protect investments in its territory for investors of other contracting parties in accordance with its legislation. Within the framework of these measures, special incentives are foreseen for investments in immovables which take precedence in implementation with regard to general real property regulations. Agreements on the enhancement and protection of investments have been made with the Republic of Albania (OG/IA 2/94, point 4, Proclamations 1/97, 3/10), the Republic of Argentina (OG /IA 4/96, point 5, Proclamation 1/97), the Republic of Austria (OG/IA 19/97, Proclamation 11/99), Azerbaijan (OG/IA 2/2008, Proclamation 4/08), the Republic of Belorussia (OG /IA 5/05, Proclamation 5/05), the Republic of Bosnia and Herzegovina (OG /IA 8/97, Proclamation 7/01, Amendment 13/02), the Republic of Bulgaria (OG/IA 1/14/96, Proclamation 4/98), the Czech Republic (OG/IA 6/97, 7/09), the Republic of Chile (OG/IA ents 5/96, point 12, Proclamation 1/97), the Kingdom of Denmark (OG/IA 14/00, Proclamation 1/02), the Arab Republic of Egypt (OG /IA 8/98, Proclamation 13/99), the French Republic (OG/IA 1/97, Proclamation 11/99), the Hellenic Republic (OG/IA 6/97, Proclamation 13/98), the Republic of India (OG/IA, 13/01, Proclamation 7/02), the Islamic Republic of Iran (OG/IA 15/00), the Italian Republic (OG/IA 4/97, Proclamation 10/98), Israel (OG/IA 14/00), the Kingdom of Jordan (OG/IA 3/00, Proclamation 8/00), the Federal Republic of Yugoslavia (OG/IA1/02, Proclamation 3/02), the Kingdom of Cambodia (OG/IA9/01, Proclamation 7/02), Canada (OG/IA 12/97, Proclamation 3/01), the People's Republic of China (OG/IA, 2/94), the State of Korea (OG/IA 4/06, Proclamation 1/08), the State of Kuwait (OG/IA 11/07, Proclamation 11/98), Lithuania (OG/IA 5/08, Proclamation 1/09), the Republic of Hungary (OG/IA

relations and, in particular, for the regulation of the legal status of foreigners acquiring and using immovables in Croatia. The most important are those entered into with the Member States of the European Union, providing for Croatia's accession to the EU, since the obligation to liberalize the legal transactions between Croatia and the EU countries involving immovables ensues from these agreements. In 2001, Croatia signed the Stabilisation and Association Agreement with the European Communities.[72] Apart from the general obligation to harmonize its legislation with that of the European Union, Croatia has expressly bound itself to adjust its legislation on the acquisition and use of immovables as part of its obligations regarding the freedom of establishment and free movement of capital and alignment with the corresponding provisions of EU law.[73] In 2011, Croatia signed the EU Accession Treaty, which provided for further liberalization of property transactions with nationals and legal persons from the Member States of the EU following Croatia's accession.[74]

D. *Additional Sources*

1. Legal Rules of the Former Property Law

18. The rules of the former property law,[75] which were in force in the territory of the Republic of Croatia during specific periods, are often an important additional source for the resolution of property cases in practice. Although these rules have lost

---

1/97, Proclamation 7/02), the Republic of Macedonia (OG/IA 10/95), Malesia (OG/IA 1/7/96), the Republic of Moldova (OG/IA 3/07, Proclamation 4/07), the Kingdom of the Netherlands (OG/IA 10/98, Proclamation 5/99), the Federal Republic of Germany (OG/IA 12/98, Proclamation 18/97), Romania (OG/IA 6/95, Proclamation 10/11), the Russian Federation (OG/IA 1/13-96), the United States of America (OG/IA 6/97), the State of San Marino (OG/IA 3/05, Proclamation 1/07), the Socialist People's Lybian Jamahiriya OG/IA 5/06, Proclamation 9/06), the Republic of Slovakia (OG/IA 1/97, Proclamation 19/97, 8/09), the Kingdom of Spain (OG/IA 11/98, Proclamation 13/98), the Kingdom of Sweden (OG/IA 8/01, Proclamation 8/02), the Swiss Confederation (OG/IA 6/97), the Kingdom of Thailand (OG/IA 7/00, Proclamation 2/08), the Republic of Turkey (OG/IA 16/97, Proclamation 7/98), the United Kingdom of Great Britain and Northern Ireland (OG/IA 12/97, Proclamation 7/98), Ukraine (OG/IA 4/01), the Republic of Zimbabwe (OG/IA 7/00), Finland (OG/IA 11/02, Proclamation 13/02), the Economic Union of Belgium and Luxembourg (OG/IA 7/02), Malta (OG/IA 5/02, Proclamation 11/02), the State of Qatar (OG/IA 5/02).

72. The Republic of Croatia signed the Stabilisation and Association Agreement with the European Communities and their Member States on 29 Oct. 2001 in Luxembourg. The Act on the Adoption of the Stabilisation and Association Agreement between Croatia and the European Communities and their Member States was published in the OG/IA 14/01. The Implementing Act of the Stabilisation and Association Agreement between the Republic of Croatia and the European Communities and the Temporary Agreement on Trade and Other Related Matters between the Republic of Croatia and the European Community was published in the OG/IA 15/01. The Stabilisation and Association Agreement entered into force on 1 February 2005 (OG /IA 1/05).
73. Articles 49, 60 of the Stabilisation and Association Agreement.
74. For more details, *see* Part I, Ch. 8. The Position of Foreign Persons in Transactions with Immovables.
75. For more details, *see* the rules of the Austrian Civil Code, rules of the ABOR (1980), the rules of the Act on Ownership of Flats (1973) etc.

the force of positive regulations,[76] they are still applied in practice. They regulate property rights relations that had emerged prior to the entry into force of the PA (1 January 1997). The PA expressly lays down that the acquisition, change and termination of property rights, acquired prior to its entry into force, are regulated according to the rules applied at the time of their acquisition, change or termination.[77] This means that property rights relations that were in effect prior to 1 January 1997 are regulated by the rules which were valid at the time of their emergence. Therefore, numerous provisions of the ACC and other former property rules are still very much present in practice and are applied to the regulation of property law relations that were in effect prior to the entry into force of the new property law legislation.

19. The application of the rules of the former property law depends on when the disputed property right relation emerged, as well as on whether that particular relation was provided for by the then-positive regulations. Property relations which were in effect prior to the entry into force of the ABOR (1980) were provided for by the paragraphs of the ACC as the applicable law. The courts applied the ACC paragraphs as 'legal rules' on the basis of the Act on the Application of Regulations adopted prior to 6 April 1941[78] (1991). By virtue of this Act, it is permitted to apply, as legal rules, the regulations that had been in force on 6 April 1941 (including the ACC) if pursuant to separate regulations, they had already applied in the Republic of Croatia until the day of the entry into force of the mentioned Act.[79] Such application was possible regarding the relations that were not provided for by the valid regulations of the Republic of Croatia and if the rules were in accordance with the Constitution and the law of the Republic of Croatia.[80] Property relations that emerged after the entry into force of the ABOR (1980) were governed by the provisions of those regulations. However, even then, the application of the ACC provisions was possible for the relations that were not provided for in the ABOR (1980), such as personal easements and neighbourhood rights.

2. Case Law

20. In the Republic of Croatia, court decisions in property cases have the importance of an additional source of property law. They do not have the character of

76. The ACC lost its legal force as a result of the Act on the Invalidity of Regulations Adopted Prior to 6 Apr. 1941 and During the Occupation (1946). The ABOR (1980) and the Act on Ownership of Flats (1973) lost their legal force when the PA entered into force on 1 Jan. 1997 (Art. 394).
77. Article 388/2 PA.
78. The Act on the Applications of Legal Regulations Adopted Prior to 6 Apr. 1941 (OG 73/91).
79. Before the entry into force of the Act on the Application of Regulations Adopted Prior to 6 Apr. 1941 of 1991, the provisions of the ACC had been applied as legal rules on the basis of several different regulations: the Act on the Invalidity of Regulations Adopted Prior to 6 Apr. 1941 and During the Occupation (1946), the Act on the Adoption of the ABOR (OG 53/1991), and the Act on the Adoption of the Obligations Act (OG 53/1991).
80. For more details on court practice, *see* T. Josipović, '*200 Jahre der ABGB-Anwendung in Kroatien – 135 Jahre als Gesetz und 65 Jahre als "Rechtsregeln"*' (200 Years of ACC Application in Croatia – 135 Years as a Law and 65 Years as Legal Rules, *Festschrift 200 Jahre ABGB, Band II, Hrsg. Fischer-Czermak, C., G. Hopf, G. Kathrein, M. Schauer*) Wien 2011, pp. 157–174.

precedents, as is the case in the Anglo-Saxon legal system. Numerous court decisions rendered in property cases represent a very useful source of interpretation of property law provisions in practice, particularly in cases where the legal positions are incomplete or where they contain specific legal standards that have to be interpreted in individual cases. Case law, as an additional source of law, is particularly important for the harmonization of case law dealing with property cases in the implementation of new property regulations.[81] However, even the more dated case law regarding the implementation of former law regulations is of importance for property law adjudication. Former regulations are still frequently used in the resolution of property disputes that had emerged before the entry into force of the new property regulations. A very extensive and rich case law, the legal understanding of the courts and the published collections of judicial decisions are the most significant sources of information on the interpretation and implementation of former regulations. Therefore, former case law can offer very important guidance when applying the new provisions of property law. In most of its parts, the new property law is based on the same principles as the old one, particularly the rules that were in force before the transition to the socialist system.[82]

III. Courts Administering Property Law

21. The resolution of disputes in the area of property law is under the jurisdiction of regular courts (municipal courts, county courts, and the Supreme Court of the Republic of Croatia).[83] Judicial protection of property rights is obtained in litigation proceedings defined in the Civil Procedure Act (CPA).[84] First-instance protection is obtained from municipal courts,[85,86] and second-instance adjudication is conducted before county courts.[87] The Supreme Court of the Republic of Croatia decides on extraordinary legal remedies (e.g., revision) in property law cases.[88] In

81. Court decisions are placed on the Internet and are accessible to the public free of charge. For the Supreme Court of the Republic of Croatia, for example, *see* http://sudskapraksa.vsrh.hr/*supra*/; for the Constitutional Court of the Republic of Croatia, *see* http://www.usud.hr/default.aspx?Show=c_praksa_ustavnog_suda/m1=2/m2=0/Lang=hr.
82. For more details on the role of case law, *see* Gavella in *Property Law* I 47, Klarić/Vedriš in *Civil Law*, 23.
83. The organization of courts is provided for in the Courts Act, OG 28/13, 33/15, 82/15, 82/16, 67/18, 129/19, 130/20, 21/22.
84. OG 53/91, 91/92, 58/93, 112/99, 88/01, 117/03, 88/05, 02/07, 84/08, 123/08, 57/11, 148/11, 25/13, 89/14, 70/19, 80/22.
85. Articles 3/2 18 of the Courts Act; Art. 34 of the Civil Procedure Act.
86. The municipal court in whose territory the claimant has permanent residence has territorial jurisdiction over disputes concerning ownership and other real rights on movables (Art. 47 CPA). For disputes concerning ownership and other real rights on an immovable, and for disputes on interference with possession, territorial jurisdiction lies with the municipal court in whose territory the immovable is located (Art. 56/1 CPA).
87. Article 34 a CPA.
88. Article 20 of the Courts Act and Art. 34 d CPA.

some cases, protection is obtained in non-contentious proceedings before municipal courts[89] (e.g., dissolution of co-ownership, regulation of boundaries, establishment of freehold division, and the like).

22. The protection of ownership and other property rights may be obtained from the Constitutional Court of the Republic of Croatia (*Ustavni sud Rrepublike Hrvatske*) as well because ownership (including other property rights) is considered one of the constitutional rights guaranteed by the Constitution.[90] In order to protect his property right, the holder may lodge a constitutional complaint before the Constitutional Court of the Republic of Croatia. A constitutional complaint may also be lodged when the holder of a property right deems that an individual act of a state body, a body of local and regional self-government, or a legal person with public authority, which decided on his property rights, has violated his property right guaranteed by the Constitution.[91] If some other legal remedy is provided against the violation of constitutional rights, a constitutional complaint (*ustavna tužba*) may be lodged only after this remedy has been exhausted.[92] This means that in cases where the protection of property rights has been sought before regular civil courts, the holder of a property right must have availed himself of all regular and extraordinary legal remedies, and only then can he lodge a constitutional complaint. A constitutional complaint may be submitted within thirty days of the day the decision was received.[93]

IV. Principles of Croatian Property Law

A. Principle of the Universal (contra/erga omnes) *Effect of Property Rights*

23. Property rights are absolute rights because they have an effect on all third persons (*contra omnes, erga omnes, načelo apsolutnosti*). Everyone is obliged to refrain from acts violating another person's property rights. Property right holders are authorized to exclude others from unauthorized encroachment or restriction of exercising their property rights. They are entitled to protect their rights against anyone who illicitly restricts these rights or prevents them from exercising them.[94] In order for property rights to be absolutely effective, they must be publicized accordingly, i.e., they must be 'visible' to all third persons. The publicity of property rights on movables is achieved by possession,[95] while the publicity of property rights on immovables is achieved exclusively by an entry in the land register.[96]

---

89. Article 18 of the Courts Act.
90. Article 48 of the Constitution of the Republic of Croatia.
91. Article 62/1 of the Constitutional Act of the Constitutional Court of the Republic of Croatia.
92. Article 62/2 of the Constitutional Act of the Constitutional Court.
93. Article 64 of the Constitutional Act of the Constitutional Court.
94. Gavella, in *Property Law I*, 25, Klarić / Vedriš in *Civil law*, 190.
95. Article 11/3 PA.
96. For more details, *see* General Introduction, §2. IV. D. Principle of Publicity.

B. *Principle of the Closed Number* (Numerus Clausus) *of Property Rights*

24. The number, types and essential content of property rights, as well as the basic conditions of acquisition, protection and their termination, are determined by law (*načelo zatvorenog broja stvarnih prava*). Only property rights which are specified by law may be established on movables and immovables (the principle of the closed number of property rights).[97] The parties may not establish a new property right by contract if it is not specified by law; they may not agree on removing its universal effect; and they may not change the core content of rights specified by law. Based on the PA, the following rights exist in the Croatian legal order:[98] ownership,[99] easements,[100] real burdens,[101] the right to build[102] and liens.[103] The PA lays down the core content of every property right, as well as the types and conditions for its acquisition, realization, protection and termination. If there is nothing specifically established by law for a particular property right and it does not ensue from its legal nature, whatever is prescribed for ownership applies accordingly to all other property rights.[104]

C. *Principle of Speciality*

25. Every individual property right may be established on a particular, individually specified thing (movable, immovable) with a precisely defined content (*načelo specijaliteta*). These are the basic conditions for a property right to have an absolute effect and to be respected by every person.[105] The object of a property right is always a particularly specified and individualized thing.[106] Another aspect of the principle of speciality, determining the content of property rights, is derived from the principle of the closed number of property rights. Every property right has its core content defined by law.

97. Gavella in *Property Law I*, 25, Klarić / Vedriš in *Civil Law*, 191.
98. Articles 174–245 PA.
99. Articles 30–173 PA.
100. Articles 174–245 PA.
101. Articles 246–279 PA.
102. Articles 280–296 PA.
103. Articles 297–353 PA.
104. Article 1/6 PA.
105. Gavella, in *Property Law I*, 28, Klarić / Vedriš in *Civil Law*, 191.
106. In property law, as opposed to the law on obligations, the principle of dispositivity does not apply in such a wide scope. The parties may not establish property rights in a contract that are not provided for in the law, and they may not agree on changing the essential content of particular property rights prescribed in the law. Dispositivity in the regulation of individual property relations is allowed only to the extent to which it is expressly allowed by the law. As a rule, the parties may agree on the modification of some unimportant aspects of a particular property right (e.g., they may lay down some limitations, the duration, the conditions of termination, and the like). It must be emphasized, however, that such agreed modifications of the content of property rights are primarily effective against the parties. They are effective against third persons only if they are aware of their existence and only if they are publicized in a proper way.

D. Principle of Publicity

26. For property rights to have an absolute effect on all third persons and for such persons to be able to observe them, every property right must be visible, published and publicized (*načelo publiciteta*).[107] This is the basic condition for property rights established on a thing to be observed. By publicizing property rights, an obligation is created for all third parties to observe another's property rights. After this has been done, no one may claim that he was unaware or could not know that such a right existed.

27. The way in which property rights are publicized primarily depends on the type of thing on which such rights exist. Sometimes it also depends on the type of right that is established on a particular thing, as well as on the legal basis on which rights are established. In most cases, publicizing property rights are connected with the fulfilment of some of the necessary conditions for their acquisition or establishment (e.g., delivery/tradition of possession, registration in public registers and the like).

28. As a rule, property rights on movables are made public by way of direct possession.[108] Therefore, in a large number of cases, surrendering possession or taking possession of a movable is a condition for the acquisition of a property right on a movable.[109] In some cases, property rights on movables are publicized by registration in a special public register, which is a prerequisite for the acquisition of a property right.[110,111] Property rights on immovables are publicized by their entry in the land register.[112] It is thus prescribed that all property rights on immovables, acquired by contract *inter vivos*, are acquired by entry in the land register, and they terminate by being deleted from the land register.[113] Even when entry in the land register is not a condition for acquisition, every property right holder may request his property right to be entered in the land register so that it is publicized and, as a result, it has an absolute effect.[114]

107. Gavella in *Property Law I*, 34.
108. For more details on possession, *see* General Introduction, §2. VIII. Possession.
109. *See*, for example, Art. 116 PA (acquisition of ownership of a movable by contract *inter vivos*), Art. 131 PA (acquisition of ownership of a movable not owned by anyone by taking it into possession), Arts 159, 160 (acquisition of ownership of a movable by prescription), Art. 222 (acquisition of easements on movable by contract *inter vivos*), Art. 308 of the PA (acquisition of voluntary liens on movable).
110. *See*, for example, Art. 6 of the LRA.
111. Property rights on vessels and aircrafts are also acquired with their entry into special public registers. For more details, *see* Baretić in *Property Law III*, 669–815, Marin in *Property Law III*, 580–665.
112. For more details on land registers, *see* Registration of Immovable Property.
113. *See*, e.g., Arts 111–121 PA (ownership), Arts 220, 239/5, 240/3, 241/5, 242/5, 245/4 PA (easements), Arts 263, 274/5, 275/2, 276/3, 279/2 PA (real burdens), Arts 288, 292/2 PA (right to build), Arts 309, 344/5, 351/2, 352/2 PA (liens).
114. *See*, e.g., Arts 127, 130 PA (acquisition of ownership on the basis of a court decision or on the basis of law).

29. The legal effects of publicizing property rights by way of possession or registration in a public register are important for all legal transactions. They are regulated by separate statutory presumptions. For the possessor of a movable, it is a statutory presumption that he is the owner of the movable – presumption of ownership.[115] For the person who is entered in the land register as the holder of a particular property right, it is a statutory presumption that he is the holder of the property right registered in his favour.[116] These statutory presumptions constitute the necessary prerequisites for the absolute effects of all property rights, their proof, protection and exercise against all third persons. They are also important for the creation of legal security and trust in legal transactions and serve as tools for the realization of the protection of third persons who have acted in good faith in legal transactions, relying on the fact that the persons who are in possession of movables and in whose favour property rights are registered are the real holders of these rights. The effects of publication are regulated by the principle of bona fide protection in legal transactions.

E. Principle of Bona fide Protection in Legal Transactions

30. Publication of property rights has particularly important effects on bona fide third persons who have participated in legal transactions by having confidence in the accuracy of the publicized legal status (*načelo zaštite povjerenja*). Even when a person in whose favour a particular property right on a thing is publicized is not a real holder of that right, bona fide third persons will be protected. Any person who did not know or could not have known that the publicized legal status is not accurate because its possessor is not the owner or because the person entered in the land register as the owner of an immovable is not actually the owner is protected in legal transactions. When the publicized property status regarding a movable or an immovable is not correct, the legal effects of the protection of trust come into play.[117] Bona fide third persons will be protected although they have acquired a property right from a person who is not its holder (the property right is only publicized in favour of that person). Such protection means that, under certain conditions, they will be able to acquire property rights from persons who are not the actual owner of a particular thing (acquisition from non-owners).[118,119]

F. Priority Principle

31. The priority principle (*načelo prvenstva*) regulates the legal relations among the holders of several property rights on the same thing or among several acquirers

115. Article 11/3 PA.
116. Article 122/1 PA; Art. 8/2 LRA.
117. Articles 11/3, 122 PA; Art. 8/3 LRA.
118. For more details, *see* Arts 118, 123, 124, 127/2, 130/2, 227, 230, 243, 264, 31, 318 PA.
119. For more details on the acquisition of ownership and other property rights from non-owner, *see* Part III, Ch. 2. Acquisition by Contract *Inter Vivos*.

of mutually excluding property rights. The main rule is that the priority of property rights established on the same thing is determined according to the order of acquisition or establishment. If several property rights are established on the same thing, which may exist in parallel, the order of their acquisition is established on the basis of the sequence of establishment.[120] Priority will be given to the property right which was established earlier.[121,122] However, separate rules apply in cases of multiple disposals of the same thing in such a way that property rights which exclude each other are established in favour of different persons.[123] In such a case, priority is given to the person who first acquired a property right. When the owner of a movable sells one and the same movable to several persons, the owner is the person into whose possession the movable was surrendered first.[124] When the owner of an immovable sells it to several persons, the owner is the person who first registered as its owner in the land register.[125,126,127]

V. Objects of Property Rights

A. General

32. An object of property rights may be individually specified things, some types of rights, as well as everything else that is by law equated with things.[128] An object of the right of ownership is an individually specified thing (*stvar*).[129] Things are the corporeal parts of nature, different from people and are used by people.[130] All individually specified things may be objects of ownership, except those which cannot belong to an individual as a result of their natural characteristics or by

120. The order of acquiring property rights on immovables is determined by the order of submitting the applications for entry in the land register. The order of priority of registration is established at the moment when an application is submitted to the court (Art. 50/1 LRA).
121. For example, in the case where several liens are established on the same thing, the lien that was established first has priority in enforcement procedure (Art. 302/2 PA).
122. Holders of property rights on immovables may, under special rules, dispose of the order of priority (rank) of their rights entered in the land register (Art. 302/4 PA). The conditions for a change of the order of priority of rights entered on the same immovable are laid down in Arts 51-56 LRA.
123. Sometimes, the order of priority of property rights on the same thing will be important in order to access whether the conditions for the establishment on new property right on the same thing have been fulfilled. For example, when the land on which the right to build is established is already encumbered by a property right which would be harmed by the right to build subsequently established (e.g., by mortgage), the right to build may be established only if the holder of the limited property right established earlier has agreed to it (Art. 288/2 PA).
124. Article 117/1 PA.
125. Article 125/1 PA.
126. For more details, *see* Part III, Ch. 2, §4. II. Multiple Conclusion of Contracts on the Alienation of the Same Thing.
127. The relationship between the alienator and other persons who have not become owners are regulated by the rules of the law on obligations (Arts 117/2, 125/3 PA).
128. Articles 2/1, 2/6, 5 PA.
129. Article 5/1 PA.
130. Article 2/2 PA.

operation of law.[131,132] The owner of an individually specified thing also owns all its appurtenances unless provided otherwise by law.[133] The appurtenances of a thing are: (a) all its parts;[134] (b) everything that is joined with the thing on a relatively permanent basis (accretion); (c) fruits (*plodovi*) derived from the thing[135] until parted from it;[136] (d) everything appurtenant to it (*pertinencije*).[137,138,139]

B. Movables: Immovables – Patrimonial Rights

33. All movables or immovables may be objects of ownership or other rights, except for those which cannot belong to anyone because of their natural characteristics or by operation of law.[140,141] Some types of patrimonial rights may also be objects of ownership.[142] Immovables (*nekretnine*) are parcels (*katastarske čestice*) of the earth's surface together with everything that is permanently affixed to the land, on or below the earth's surface (Articles 2/3, 9/1 PA).[143,144] Movables (*pokretnine*) are things that can be moved from one location to another without jeopardizing their substance (Article 2/4 PA).[145,146] In case of doubt whether a thing is a movable or immovable, it is deemed as movable. Patrimonial rights (*imovinska prava*), which may be objects of property rights, are in legal transactions equated with movables.[147] The rules on property rights on movables apply accordingly to

---

131. Article 3/2 PA.
132. Such things are called things belonging to the public domain. There can be no ownership or property rights on things belonging to the public domain. For more details, *see* General Introduction, §2. V. D. Public Domain.
133. Article 5/2 PA.
134. Article 6 PA.
135. Article 8 PA.
136. Fruits of a thing are products that a thing yields naturally or as a result of someone's work, as well as everything else the thing yields in view of its purpose (Art. 8/2 PA). Fruits are also contributions that a thing or right yields by mediation of a legal relationship, such as rentals, leases and interests (Art. 8/4 PA). Benefits belong to whoever the thing or right that yields them belongs, unless they belong to someone else based on a particular legal title (Art. 8/5 PA).
137. Article 7 PA.
138. Appurtenances are movables whose purpose as designated by the owner is to serve the purpose of the main thing on a permanent basis (Art. 7/1 PA). An appurtenance is not a part of the main thing but an independent thing separated from the main thing.
139. In the case of some movables, the PA expressly provides that they are considered as appurtenances of particular immovables. Machines and similar devices intended for the permanent purpose of a business building, i.e. a building which is permanently used for some production or craft, are considered as appurtenances of that particular building (Art. 7/4 PA). Machines and cattle intended for further agricultural production, and agricultural products and seeds needed for further agricultural production are considered as appurtenances of the immovable permanently intended for agricultural production (Art. 7/5 PA).
140. Article 2/1 PA.
141. Forces of nature are regarded as things if they are subject to human control (Art. 2/5 PA).
142. Article 2/6 PA.
143. For more details, *see* Gavella in *Property Law I*, 79–93.
144. For more details on immovables as objects of property rights, *see* Part I, Ch. 1.
145. For more details, *see* Gavella in *Property Law I*, 78–79.
146. For more details on movables as objects of property rights, *see* Part II, Ch. 1.
147. Article 2/7 PA· For more details on property rights as objects of property rights, *see* Part II, Ch. 2.

property rights on patrimonial rights. A patrimonial right is regarded as an immovable only if it is connected to the ownership of an immovable, if it is its encumbrance, or if it is proclaimed to be an immovable by law (Article 2/6 PA). The rules on property rights on immovables then apply accordingly to property rights on such a right.[148]

C. Public Goods

34. Things, movables and immovables owned by public bodies or the Croatian state, bodies of local government or regional self-government or other legal persons governed by public law are called public goods (*javna dobra*).[149] They can be objects of ownership or other property rights. The Republic of Croatia and other public law entities, as holders of the right of ownership of public goods, are equated with private owners unless otherwise provided by law.[150] Disposal, administration and use of particular publicly owned immovables are regulated by separate acts (e.g., acts on agricultural land, forests, waters, and the like). Regarding their purpose, public goods in common use (*javna dobra u općoj uporabi*) are things owned by the Republic of Croatia and other bodies governed by public law that are intended to be used by all.[151] Everyone has the right to use them in a way to achieve such purpose and in the scope determined thereby. Public goods in public use (*javna dobra u javnoj uporabi*) are things intended for the direct exercise of the rights and duties of legal persons governed by public law, i.e., by the Republic of Croatia and its bodies and institutions.[152] Things considered public goods in public use are used by the bodies and institutions responsible for their administration in line with their purpose. Things that are publicly owned and that are not intended for either common or public use are deemed to be financial assets (*financijska imovina*). They are also owned by the Republic of Croatia or other public law entities and are used in accordance with the purpose determined by the body responsible for the determination.[153] The right of ownership of these things is exercised by the body responsible for the determination of their purpose unless it has delegated this to another body, institution or person.[154] Immovables owned by local self-government units may be alienated or otherwise disposed of only on the basis of a public tendering procedure and subject to the compensation established on the basis of the market value of property unless provided otherwise by law.[155]

148. Thus the rules on the establishment of liens on immovables will apply accordingly to liens on the right to build which is equated with the immovable by operation of law (Art. 280/2 PA).
149. For more details, *see* more Gavella *Property Law I*, 140–142.
150. Article 35/1 PA.
151. Article 35/4 PA.
152. Article 35/5 PA.
153. Article 35/6 PA.
154. Article 35/6 PA.
155. Article 391/1 PA.

D. *Common Goods*

35. Things belonging to common goods (public domain, *opća dobra*) are those that are not capable of being objects of ownership or of other property rights.[156,157] Some things are considered common goods because of their natural characteristics and others because it is so established by law. Common goods include things which, as a result of their properties, may not be individually owned by a natural or legal person, although they may serve to satisfy public needs, i.e., to be used by all (e.g., the air, water in rivers, lakes and the sea, the sea shore).[158] Common goods may be used by everyone. Unless otherwise laid down by law, the Republic of Croatia cares for them, administers them and is responsible for them.[159] Economic exploitation of immovables within the regime of common goods is carried out by concessions provided for in separate laws.[160] By virtue of a concession on immovables, the concessionaire may own a building or another facility of public domain, but only for the duration of the concession.[161]

VI. Property Rights

A. *Concept*

36. Property rights (*stvarna prava*) are rights which entitle their holders to have full or partial and direct legal power over a particular thing.[162] They are different from other property rights in that a particular thing (a movable or an immovable) is their direct object and in that they have an absolute effect on all third persons. Their special characteristic is that they are 'externally visible', i.e., they are made public in a particular way for all third persons to be aware of them. An additional characteristic is that their main content is always regulated by law so that the parties may not change it. The rights and obligations of holders arising from particular property rights are expressly provided for by law. The law also provides for their acquisition/establishment, protection and termination. All property rights may be limited by a time limit or a condition based on the parties' agreement, but these time limits and conditions are effective against third persons only if they are publicized in a particular way (e.g., by being entered in the land register).

156. Article 3/2 PA.
157. For more detail, *see* Gavella *Property Law I*, 136–140.
158. Article 3/2 PA.
159. Article 3/3 PA.
160. For more details on concessions, *see* Part I, Ch. 6, §3. Concessions.
161. Articles 3/4, 9/4 PA.
162. For more details, *see* Gavella in *Property Law I*, 100.

B. Types of Property Rights

1. Ownership: Limited Property Rights

37. Depending on their content and the powers held by their holders, property rights are divided into two main groups: ownership (*vlasništvo*) and limited rights (*ograničena stvarna prava*), e.g., easements, real burdens, the right to build, liens. Ownership gives the holder unlimited (integral) legal power over a thing. Limited property rights give their holders only limited (partial) legal power over another person's thing. According to their main content, limited property rights are classified as property rights entitling their holders to use another's thing in a particular way (easements, right to build) and as property rights authorizing their holders to secure their claims and their settlement against the value of the thing (securities, liens).[163]

2. Legal Interests: Equitable Interests

38. In Croatian property law, property rights are not divided into legal interest and equitable interest. Namely, Croatian property law belongs to the family of European civil law (the continental legal order) and developed mostly under the influence of Austrian and German law. There is no system of property rights in Croatian property law that is typical of common law orders. Therefore, equitable interests do not exist in the Croatian property system. Based on the principle of a closed number of property rights, they are all regulated by law.

3. Ownership

a. Concept

39. The right of ownership (*vlasništvo*) is a property right on a particular thing authorizing its holder to use the thing and any benefits arising from it as he sees fit and to exclude any person from it unless that is contrary to such a person's rights or any limitations imposed by law.[164,165] The owner has, *inter alia*, the right to the possession, use, utilization and disposition (factual and legal) of the thing he owns.[166] An object of ownership may be any – movable or immovable. The holder of the right of ownership may be a single person (individual ownership), or several persons (co-ownership, joint ownership, freehold division or condominium).[167] Ownership may be acquired by contract *inter vivos*, by inheritance, on the basis of a court decision or a decision of another body or on the basis of law.[168]

---

163. For more details, *see* Gavella in *Property Law I*, 129.
164. Article 30/1 PA.
165. For more details, *see* Gavella *in Property Law I*, 341.
166. Article 30/2 PA.
167. For more details, *see* Part I, Ch. 3, and Part III, Ch. 1.
168. For more details on the acquisition of ownership, *see* Part III.

b. Limitations of Ownership

40. There are different types of limitations of ownership (*ograničenja prava vlasništva*) in Croatian law. Some are imposed by law and are of a statutory nature (*zakonska ograničenja vlasništva*). Depending on whether such statutory limitations are valid for all or only for the owners of particular things, we distinguish general statutory limitations (*opća zakonska ograničenja*) or particular statutory limitations (*posebna zakonska ograničenja*) of ownership.[169] Ownership may also be limited in expropriation proceedings by the establishment of limited property rights on a thing (*nepotpuno izvlaštenje*). Finally, an owner may limit his ownership voluntarily by virtue of a contract (*ograničenja vlasništva na temelju pravnog posla*).[170]

41. In exercising his powers, the owner is limited by the so-called general statutory limitations of ownership.[171] General statutory limitations are valid and effective in relation to every owner of individual things. In order to exercise his powers, the owner is bound to be considerate of general interests and other people's interests that are not in contradiction with his right.[172] General limitations particularly oblige the owner not to use his right with the purpose of harming or bothering another person (prohibition of misusing the right of ownership). The owner is not authorized to prohibit another person's interventions or works on his thing if they are necessary to remove the damage directly threatening another person, which would be disproportionally greater than the damage the owner would suffer as a result of the works. The owner is also not authorized to prohibit works by another person at a height or depth at which he has no justified interest to exclude them.[173]

42. In exercising his ownership rights, the owner may also be limited by particular statutory limitations laid down in separate laws. Particular statutory limitations bind only owners of particular things. The owners of such particular things may exercise their ownership rights only within some limitations based on a particular piece of legislation with the aim of protecting the interests and security of the state, nature, the human environment and health.[174,175] Particular statutory limitations of ownership are also laid down in order to protect things proclaimed to be of interest to the Republic of Croatia. The owners of such things may then be bound by law to use them in a strictly prescribed way.[176,177] If the owner does not act in

169. Articles 31 and 32 PA.
170. Article 34 PA.
171. The constitutional basis for the general limitations of ownership is Art. 48/2 of the Constitution of the Republic of Croatia which lays down that ownership implies obligations, and that the holder of ownership rights and their users are bound to contribute to public welfare.
172. Article 31 PA.
173. For more details, *see* Gavella in *Property Law I*, 409.
174. The constitutional basis for the introduction of special limitations is Art. 52 of the Constitution of the Republic of Croatia which lays down which things are regarded as things of special interest for the Republic of Croatia.
175. Article 32/1 PA.
176. Article 32/2 PA.

accordance with the obligations imposed by local self-government bodies, these bodies may take temporary control of the thing by applying the rules on temporary custody (sequestration).[178]

43. In the interest of the Republic of Croatia, ownership may be taken away by law (complete expropriation, *potpuno izvlaštenje*), or it may be limited by the establishment of a right (easement, lease) on the owner's thing (incomplete expropriation, *nepotpuno izvlaštenje*). In such a case, the owner is entitled to compensation in line with the regulations on expropriation, i.e., in accordance with the ExA.[179,180,181]

44. The owner may also limit his ownership voluntarily by contract *inter vivos* (*ograničenja vlasništva na temelju pravnog posla*). He may impose limitations on his ownership in favour of other persons by establishing their limited property rights or obligations; he may prohibit alienation or encumbrances established on the thing he owns; he may lay down a condition for the termination of ownership by the fulfilment of requirements or time limits, or he may obtain or retain ownership of a thing in order to secure a claim.[182,183] Such limitations are effective against third persons only if they are entered in the land register.

c. Transformation of Social Ownership to Private Ownership

45. When Croatia was part of the socialist legal circle, ownership was regulated on the basis of a collectivistic concept. There were two diverse general property law models of regulation concerning the appurtenance of things: social ownership (*društveno vlasništvo*) and private ownership (*privatno vlasništvo*). Many things, and in particular immovables, were socially owned (e.g., building lots, agricultural land, forests, buildings, flats, and the like). Unlike the right recognized in legal orders characterized by a market economy, there was no ownership right to socially owned things. Nevertheless, various legal entities did have some specific subjective rights to such things (the right to use, dispose of and manage them), which appear to have been absolute and protected by law. After transition to a market economy, Croatia started developing a modern property law that would correspond to such an economic system. A process of privatization and denationalization was conducted,

177. On special limitations of ownership of particular immovables of interest for the Republic of Croatia which enjoy its special protection such as agricultural land, forests and forest land, maritime domain, cultural goods and the like, *see* Part I, Ch. 7: Special Legal Regimes Regulating Immovables.
178. Article 32/3 PA.
179. OG 74/14, 69/17, 98/19.
180. Article 33/1 PA.
181. For more details on expropriation, *see* Part III, Ch. 3, §2. II. Acquisition of Ownership by Expropriation.
182. Article 34 PA.
183. For more details, *see* Gavella in *Property Law I*, 420.

and the system of social ownership was abolished. Based on the Croatian Constitution, only one type of ownership, i.e., private ownership, is recognized.[184] The establishment of a property system based on only one type of ownership (private ownership) demanded special regulation in order to carry out the transition of the existing social ownership to a new property system.

46. The transformation of social ownership over certain things had been carried out by virtue of many acts even before the PA entered into force. It was conducted in such a way that social entities, as holders of the rights to socially owned things, changed their status and became private enterprises.[185] The transformation from social to private enterprises affected the rights that social entities had over socially owned things. These rights were thus transformed into ownership rights of persons who, prior to the process of privatization, had had the right to use the same things. In the case of certain immovables (e.g., agricultural land, forest land), social ownership ceased to exist on the basis of various separate acts setting forth that those things would *ex lege* come under the ownership of the Republic of Croatia. The process of transformation was also carried out by restitution/denationalization, whereby the things that had been subject to nationalization and confiscation were returned to their former owners.[186,187]

47. The transition to private ownership was finalized by the entry into force of the PA. The legal effects of the transition were established *ex lege*, i.e., by the entry into force of the transitional and final provisions of the PA (1 January 1997). Rights on socially owned things that had not been transformed by a special law before the entry into force of the PA were transformed into the right of private ownership. The transformation was carried out on the basis of the transitional and final provisions of the PA.[188] The rights over socially owned things were transformed into the right of ownership whose holder became known. The owners of things that used to be socially owned (*ex lege*) now had rights on these things, as did their heirs and other legal successors. All holders of such transformed rights were able to protect and prove such rights acquired through the process of transformation in accordance with the general rules on the protection of ownership. After the transformation, these rights kept their previous order of priority.[189,190]

---

184. Article 48/1 of the Constitution of the Republic of Croatia.
185. For example, the Act on the Transformation of Socially Owned Enterprises (OG 19/91, 83/92, 94/93, 2/94, 9/95, 42/95, 21/96, 118/99, 90/03, 145/10).
186. For example, the Act on the Compensation for the Assets Seized during the Yugoslav Communist Rule (OG 92/96, 39/99, 42/99, 92/99, 43/00, 131/00, 27/01, 34/01, 65/01, 118/01, 80/02, 81/02, 98/19).
187. For more details, *see* Josipović, *Immobiliarsachenrecht in Kroatien* (Property Law in Croatia) Vienna, 2002, pp. 4–6. Gavella, Josipović, Transformation of Rights of Use and Disposition on Real Property after the Transformation of Rightholders into Companies as a Precondition of the Croatian Legal Order to the European Legal Order, Zbornik Pravnog fakulteta u Rijeci, Suppl. no. 3, 2003.
188. Articles 354–365 PA.
189. Article 389/2 PA.
190. For more details, *see* Gavella in *Property Law I*, 116–127.

4. Limited Property Rights

48. Limited property rights are property rights on another's thing authorizing their holders either to use another person's thing in a particular way or to settle their claims against the value of the encumbered thing (securities). In line with the principle of the closed number of property rights, Croatian property law recognizes four types of limited property rights: easements, real burdens, right to build and liens. The PA expressly provides for the content and the conditions for the acquisition, protection and termination of these limited property rights.

49. Easements (servitudes) are limited property rights over the property of another, authorizing the holder to use the property in a specific manner, regardless of who the owner might be, while its everyday owner is bound to sufferance or omission as a result.[191,192] Easements are classified into real and personal easements. Real easements (*stvarne služnosti*) are the property rights of the everyday owner of a particular property (dominant property, *povlasna stvar*) to use the property of another in a specified manner (servient property, *poslužna stvar*) for the purposes of his own property, while the everyday owner has to endure sufferance or omit to take certain actions regarding his property that he would otherwise be entitled to take.[193] Personal easements (*osobne služnosti*) are property rights granting a specific person the right to use the property of another in a specific manner (servient property, *poslužna stvar*) and obliging the everyday owner to sufferance of such use.[194] Personal easements are usufruct, right of use and habitation.[195]

50. Real burdens (*stvarni tereti*) are property rights over another's immovable, authorizing its holder to repeatedly receive things or to have acts done as a charge on its value, that are the content of the real burdens.[196,197] Real burdens are divided into real burdens in favour of an immovable (*predijalni stvarni tereti*), real burdens in favour of a person (*osobni i stvarni tereti*) and public law real burdens (*javnopravni tereti*). A real burden in favour of an immovable (dominant property, *povlasna nekretnina*) is a limited property right on another's immovable, authorizing the everyday owner of the dominant tenement to repeatedly receive things or to have acts done that are the content of the real burden.[198] A real burden in favour of a person gives that person a limited property right on another's immovable, authorizing its holder to repeatedly receive things or to have acts done that are the content of the real burden.[199] Public law real burdens are established by operation of law upon the fulfilment of the conditions laid down by law.[200,201]

191. Article 174/1 PA.
192. For more details, *see* Stipković in *Property law II*, 8–47.
193. Article 186/1 PA.
194. Article 199/1 PA.
195. For more details on easements, *see* Part I, Ch. 5, §1. Easements.
196. Article 246 PA.
197. For more details, *see* Gavella in *Property Law II*, 47–73.
198. Article 256/1 PA.
199. Article 259/1 PA.
200. Article 266/1 PA.

51. The right to build (*pravo građenja*) is a limited property right on someone's land, authorizing the person holding the right to have his own building on the surface of the land or below it, while the everyday owner of the land is bound to sufferance.[202,203] With the right to build, the plot is legally separated from the building that is erected on it. When the right to build is established on a piece of land, the building erected by the holder of the right to build is not considered part of the piece of land, and it does not share its legal destiny. It is considered to be an appurtenance of the right to build which is equated with the immovable.[204]

52. A lien (*založno pravo*) is a limited property right on a particular thing (liened property), authorizing the holder (lienor, *založni vjerovnik*) to have a particular claim settled against the value of the thing if the claim is not settled on maturity, while its everyday owner (lienee, *založni dužnik*) is bound to sufferance.[205,206] With the lien, the lienor secures the enforcement of his claim if the debtor does not settle it upon maturity. Immovables, movables and patrimonial rights may be the objects of liens. Depending on the legal basis of the acquisition of the lien, we distinguish voluntary liens, judicial/notarial voluntary liens, compulsory judicial liens and statutory liens.[207]

VII. Holders of Property Rights

53. Any natural or legal person may be the holder of the right of ownership or other property rights.[208] The Republic of Croatia and other bodies governed by public law, which are holders of the right of ownership or other property rights, have the same position with respect to ownership in legal relations as private owners unless provided otherwise by law.[209] Foreign natural and legal persons are in principle equated with domestic persons as holders of property rights. They may own movables and be holders of any limited property rights on movables or immovables under the same conditions that apply to domestic persons. The only difference compared to domestic holders is when it comes to the acquisition of immovables. Foreign nationals and legal persons from countries that are not members of the EU must meet some additional conditions to the general conditions for acquisition to be fulfilled by domestic persons.[210] Separate laws also lay down that foreign natural and

201. For more details on real burdens, *see* Part I, Ch. 5, §2. Real Burdens.
202. Article 280/1 PA.
203. For more details, *see* Gavella in *Property law II*, 73–99.
204. For more details on the right to build *see* Part I, Ch. 5, §3. Right to Build.
205. For more details, *see* Gavella in *Property Law II*, 119.
206. Article 297/1 PA.
207. For more on liens, *see* Part I, Ch. 5, §4. Mortgage and Part VI Security Rights.
208. Article 1/1 PA.
209. Article 35 PA.
210. Articles 354–358 PA.

legal persons may not own particular immovables in the Republic of Croatia specified in law and may not acquire them on any legal basis.[211]

VIII. Possession

54. Possession (*posjed*) is the actual control, factual power of a thing (Article 10/1 PA). Possession of a right (*posjed prava*) is the factual enforcement of the content of real easements regarding a particular immovable.[212] A person having factual power over a thing is regarded as a possessor (*posjednik*).[213] Factual enforcement of the content of real easement is considered to be the possession of the right of real easement (*posjednik prava stvarne služnosti*).[214] Possession is not a property right but a fact. This is a factual status protected by law.[215] A possessor may, but does not need to, have the right to possession, i.e., the right from which authorization is derived to enforce factual power over a thing. Due to the very fact that someone exercises factual power over a thing, he is deemed to be the possessor, regardless of whether he has any right to the particular thing or not. In Croatian law, we must distinguish possession as the factual power over a thing from the right to possession (*pravo na posjed*) derived from a property or personal right (i.e., the right of ownership, easement, lease, rental, and the like). Croatian law has accepted the so-called objective conception of possession (*objektivna koncepcija posjeda*). In order for someone to be the possessor, it is sufficient that he exercises factual power over a thing, while the intention of the possessor to own the thing (*animus possidendi*) is not required.[216] Possession, regardless of it being only a fact, has very important functions in the Croatian property system. Surrendering possession of an immovable is a way for someone to acquire property rights on immovables by contract *inter vivos*,[217] and sometimes taking possession of a thing is a condition for the acquisition of ownership on the basis of law[218] (acquisitive function of possession).[219] Possession of a thing during a certain period of time, provided it is of a particular quality, leads to the acquisition of ownership by acquisitive prescription[220] (the continued function of possession).[221] The possessor of a movable is presumed to be its owner, which results in very important effects in legal transactions in terms of

211. For more details on the acquisition of ownership of immovables in favour of foreigners, *see* Part I, Ch. 8. The Position of Foreign Persons in Transactions with Immovables.
212. Article 10/5 PA.
213. Article 10/4 PA.
214. Article 10/5 PA.
215. For more details, *see* Gavella in *Property Law I*, 151.
216. For more details, *see* Gavella in *Property Law I*, 156.
217. Articles 116, 222, 308 PA.
218. Articles 131, 141, 142, 143 PA.
219. For more details, *see* Gavella in *Property Law I*, 228.
220. Articles 159 and 160 PA.
221. For more details, *see* Gavella in *Property Law I*, 233.

the protection of bona fide acquirers of property rights over movables and the acquisition of property rights over movables from non-owners[222] (publicity function of possession).[223]

55. Objects of possession may be any movable or immovable, including things over which ownership may normally not exist (e.g., public domain). Parts of things may also be objects of possession, although such parts may not be independent objects of property rights (e.g., a room or any other space in a flat).[224] The right of encumbrance may also be an object of possession.[225] The rules on the possession of things apply accordingly to the possession of the right of encumbrance unless this is contrary to the nature of the right or contrary to statutory provisions. The possession of a thing or a right may belong to a single person or to several persons. When several persons possess the same thing or the same right, they are considered to be co-possessors.[226]

56. Depending on how the factual power over a thing is exercised, Croatian property law distinguishes direct possession (*neposredni posjed*) and indirect possession (*posredni posjed*). A direct possessor is a person who directly enforces factual power over a thing. Direct possessors may enforce their factual power personally or through an assistant (*pomoćnik u posjedovanju*). [227,228] Indirect possessors are persons who exercise their possession through another person who has been given direct possession of a thing on the basis of a legal transaction authorizing the direct possessor to possess the thing for a certain period of time.[229] The legal relationship authorizing a direct possessor to hold possession may be a lease contract, a rental contract, a contract on usufruct, pledges on movables, and the like. In such cases, the lessor, the owner of the thing encumbered by usufruct, or the owner of the pledged movable is considered to be an indirect possessor.[230,231]

57. Depending on whether someone possesses a thing as if he was its owner or was not its owner, Croatian property law distinguishes independent possessor (*samostalni posjednik*) and non-independent possessor (*nesamostalni posjednik*). A

222. Article 11/3 PA.
223. For more details, *see* Gavella in *Property Law I*, 230.
224. Article 10/4 PA.
225. Article 10/5 PA.
226. Article 10/6 PA.
227. An assistant in possession does not have possession because he does not exercise his factual power. An assistant in possession is a person who is employed or has a similar kind of relationship or acts complying with someone else's instructions (Art. 12/2 PA). Such a person exercises the power of the person issuing orders of acting. In such cases, direct possession belongs to the person who gives orders on how to act with regard to a particular thing. *See* Gavella in *Property Law I*, 167.
228. Article 10/2 PA.
229. Article 10/3 PA.
230. The relationship between direct and indirect possession exists until there is a legal relationship authorizing a particular person to have direct possession over a particular thing.
231. For more details, *see* Gavella in *Property Law I*, 169.

possessor who possesses a thing as if he was its owner is considered to be an independent, proprietary possessor.[232] He is an independent possessor because, during his possession, he does not recognize any superior power of another person over the same thing. For example, an owner who owns his thing is an independent possessor because he does not recognize anybody's superior power. A person who finds a lost thing and takes possession of it is also independent possessor of that thing because he possesses it as its owner, without recognizing the superior power of another person. A non-independent (non-proprietary) possessor is someone who possesses a thing by recognizing the superior power of another person. For instance, a person who rents a flat is a non-independent possessor because he recognizes the superior power of the landlord – the owner of the flat – who is an independent possessor. The distinction between independent and non-independent possessors is of particular importance for the acquisition of ownership over a thing by acquisitive prescription. Only an independent possessor, i.e., a person who possesses a thing as if its owner, may, if other conditions are met, acquire ownership of the thing by acquisitive prescription.[233] In addition, the concept of independent possession is also important for the protection of trust in legal transactions involving movables. In order to exercise the publicity function of possession, the PA expressly lays down the presumption that possession is considered independent unless proven otherwise. An independent possessor of a movable is presumed to be its owner.[234] Therefore, a bona fide acquirer, who did not know that the independent possessor was not the real owner of the thing, is protected and may acquire ownership of a movable from a non-owner.[235,236]

58. In terms of quality, possession is divided into lawful or unlawful, truthful or untruthful, and fair or unfair possession. Lawful possession (*zakoniti posjed*) is where the possessor has a valid legal basis for possession.[237] Unlawful possession (*nezakoniti posjed*) is where the possessor does not have a valid legal basis for possession. Truthful possession (*istiniti posjed*) is possession acquired in a valid manner. Untruthful possession (*neistiniti posjed*) is possession acquired by force, fraud or misuse of trust.[238] A distinction between fair possession (*pošteni posjed*) and unfair possession (*nepošteni posjed*) is important in cases where the possessor is not entitled to possession. A fair possessor is one who does not know and has no valid reason to doubt that he is not entitled to possession. An unfair possessor is one who knows or should know that he is not entitled to possession.[239,240] Fairness of possession is presumed. Anyone who claims that possession is unfair must prove this.[241] Possession becomes unfair as soon as the possessor finds out that he is not

232. Article 11/1 PA.
233. Articles 159, 160 PA.
234. Articles 11/2,3 PA.
235. Article 118 PA.
236. For more details, *see* Gavella in *Property Law I*, 446.
237. Articles 159 and 160 PA.
238. Article 18/2 PA.
239. For more details, *see* Gavella in *Property Law I*, 221.
240. Article 18/3 PA.
241. Article 18/5 PA.

entitled to possession. The distinction of the quality of possession is important for the establishment of the acquisitive function of possession. Only fair possessors may acquire ownership over a thing by acquisitive prescription. If possession is both lawful and truthful, less time will be needed for the acquisition of ownership by prescription. However, the fairness of a possessor is important for the establishment of his legal position after he has returned the thing at the owner's request. The possessor's fairness will be taken into account when deciding whether he has to pay compensation to the owner for using the thing and whether he is entitled to compensation of costs for the maintenance of the thing.[242]

59. Possession is acquired by the establishment of factual power over a thing.[243] The factual power over a thing may be established by a unilateral act without the will or against the will of the former possessor (original acquisition of possession). The act must be such so as to enable the acquirer to gain factual power over the thing by excluding the former possessor (e.g., by collecting fruits, taking the thing away from another's possession, changing the lock of a door, and the like). Possession may also be acquired by the will of the former possessor (derivative acquisition of possession), i.e., by surrendering (*traditio*) the thing itself or the means by which the acquirer has power over the thing (e.g., surrendering the keys to the flat, letting a person into the flat in order to exercise factual power over the flat, and the like).[244]

60. Possession, although it is not a right, is protected from unlawful interference.[245,246] Interference of possession occurs when the possessor is deprived of his possession without his will or when his possession is obstructed. The possessor is then entitled to protection of his possession. This right terminates upon the expiry of a time limit of thirty days from the day when the obstructed person learned about the act of obstruction and of its perpetrator and not later than a year from the act of obstruction.[247] The right to the protection of possession is enforced in special civil proceedings by bringing an action against obstruction before the court[248] or through self-help.[249] In court proceedings initiated by an action against obstruction, the court decides on the basis of the last possession and of the obstruction which has taken place regardless of the right to possession, the legal title of possession, the fairness of the possessor, or whether the obstruction serves any social, public, or any other interest.[250] Possession may be protected through self-help if necessary and if judicial assistance would be too late, and if the danger is imminent. However, the applied force must not be greater than required under the circumstances.[251]

242. Articles 164 and 165 PA.
243. Articles 13–17 PA.
244. For more details, *see* Gavella in *Property Law I*, 233–261, Klarić / Vedriš in *Civil Law*, 219–225.
245. For more details, *see* Gavella in *Property Law I*, 183–214, Klarić / Vedriš in *Civil Law*, 207–215.
246. Articles 19–27 PA.
247. Article 21/3 PA.
248. Articles 22–26 PA.
249. Article 27 PA.
250. Article 22/2 PA.
251. Article 27 PA.

61. Possession terminates when the thing is destroyed or lost, and there is no prospect that it will be found or when the possessor has abandoned the thing of his own free will.[252] The possession of a right terminates when the immovable, on which the content of the right was exercised, is destroyed or when the possessor waives the possession of such right.[253] [254]

IX. Trust and Fiduciary Mechanism

62. In Croatian law, trust is not regulated as a specified legal institution. The Republic of Croatia is not a party to The Hague Convention on the Law Applicable to Trusts and their Recognition of 1 July 1985. In Croatian law, there are, however, some forms of fiduciary transfer of ownership and property rights to other persons, and they are laid down in the PA and the EA. They have particular property law effects because the fiduciary transfer of ownership is publicized and has absolute effects against all third persons. The purpose of such fiduciary transfers of ownership or rights is mostly the security of claims and is therefore laid down in separate laws specifying the ways creditors' claims are settled against the values of the transferred things or rights.[255]

63. A fiduciary relationship when transferring ownership for security may be established on the basis of the general rules of obligations. Such fiduciary transfer of ownership does not have any special property law effects which is the case when fiduciary transfer takes place by virtue of the provisions of the PA or EA. The owner may transfer ownership of his thing to a person, while the parties may at the same time agree, on the basis of the general rules on obligations, that the transfer is performed to secure a claim, and the acquirer is bound to return the thing when the claim is settled. The owner is bound to transfer the ownership of a thing to the creditor, and all the conditions must be fulfilled that are normally required for the acquisition of ownership on the basis of a legal transaction. The transfer of ownership to the creditor has an absolute effect against all third persons, and the creditor is considered an unconditional owner. The creditor, as the new owner of the thing, is authorized to dispose of the thing in accordance with the general rules of property law. The fiduciary relationship contracted under the rules of the law on obligations is effective only relatively, i.e., between the parties (*inter partes*). If the claim, for which the fiduciary relationship has been established, is settled, the transferor is entitled to request that the creditor returns the ownership of the thing. However, the creditor will be able to meet this obligation only if, at the time, he is still the owner of the thing. If the creditor continues to dispose of the thing (he is authorized to do so by being the owner), the transferor is entitled to request from the creditor only compensation for damage caused by the violation of the obligation arising from the

252. Article 28/1 PA.
253. Article 29/1 PA.
254. For more details, *see* Gavella in *Property Law I*, 263–273, Klarić / Vedriš in *Civil Law*, 216–217.
255. For more details, *see* Part VI. Security Rights.

fiduciary relationship.[256] For all these reasons, fiduciary transfer of ownership, based solely on the rules of the law on obligations, is not frequently done in practice. This is particularly the case because there are forms of fiduciary transfers with property law effects which offer much greater protection to all parties to the fiduciary relationship.

256. For more details, *see* Gavella in *Property Law II*, 474, 475.

Part I. Immovable Property

Chapter 1. General Classification

§1. The Concept of Immovable Property

64. The real property or immovable property (*nekretnine*) concept is used to denote a plot of land (*zemljište, zemljišna čestica, katastarska čestica*) together with everything that is more or less permanently connected to it on or underneath the land surface unless differently determined by law.[257,258] In transactions, pieces of land are marked by cadastral numbers of plots or cadastral units. A cadastral plot (*katastarska čestica*) is a piece of land marked with a special number and the name of the cadastral municipality (*katastarska općina*) where it is located.[259,260] The shape and the surface of a cadastral unit are depicted by the geometrical division of the earth's surface according to a unique method determined by law. The numbers of cadastral plots and the names of cadastral districts are established in a cadastral map made on the basis of official cadastral land surveying and are entered in the cadastre.[261]

65. Real property, as an object of legal relations in real property transactions, may consist of one or several plots. When real property consists of several plots, it is legally merged into one land register body (*zemljišnoknjižno tijelo*) and is entered in the same land register file (*zemljišnoknjižni uložak*).[262] Several cadastral plots may be merged into one land register body and entered in the same land register file if they belong to the same owner or to the same co-owners if they are not encumbered with different charges, if no differences exist in terms of the restriction on title, or if, at the time of merging, all possible obstacles to such integration have been eliminated.[263] All cadastral plots of the same land register body constitute a

257. Articles 2/3, 9/1 PA.
258. Gavella in *Property Law I*, 79; Klarić / Vedriš in *Civil Law*, 76.
259. Article 2/1 LRA.
260. Josipović in *Land Registration Law*, 93.
261. For more details on the relationship between the land register and cadastre, *see* Josipović in *Land Registration Law*, 93–97.
262. For more details on the content of a land register entry, *see* Josipović in *Land Registration Law*, 104–107.
263. Article 19/3 LRA.

unified object of property relations regarding ownership, its limitation, encumbrances and the like. As a whole, they have the same legal destiny in legal transactions: they may all be subjects to disposal, i.e., the entire land register body, or they may be an ideal part of all cadastral plots or an ideal part of the land register body. In order to establish a different legal status for an individual cadastral plot (for the purpose of selling only one cadastral plot or creating mortgage), the composition of the land register body must be changed in accordance with special rules on the removal or addition of land register plots.

§2. Legal Unity of Real Property (The Principle of *Superficies Solo Cedit*)

I. A General Overview

66. In accordance with the principle of the legal unity of real property (the principle of *superficies solo cedit, načelo pravnog jedinstva nekretnine*), the PA expressly provides that real property consists of land and whatever is reasonably and permanently attached to it either on its surface or below it.[264] Whatever is built on the surface of a plot, above it or below it, and is meant to remain there on a permanent basis, or is built in the real property, on it, or is in any other way permanently attached to it, is considered to be a part of the real property until detached from it.[265] Grass, trees and fruits, as well as all other usable things produced on the land surface, are considered a part of the real property until they are separated from it.[266] Buildings or other objects erected on the plot for some temporary purpose (e.g., kiosks, stalls, booths, etc.) are not considered as its parts.[267,268]

67. The regulation of legal relations concerning real property on the basis of its legal unity comes into play in any real property relations. This principle must be observed in the case of acquisition of ownership when building on somebody else's land.[269] The regulation of all property rights on immovables is based on the principle of the legal unity of real property. For example, the regulation of condominiums is now in Croatian property law also based on the principle of the legal unity

264. Article 9 PA.
265. Article 9/3 PA.
266. Article 9/2 PA.
267. Article 9/3 PA.
268. For more details, *see* Gavella in *Property Law I*, 82, Klarić / Vedriš in *Civil Law*, 76.
269. Thus the principle of the legal unity of real property is also clearly manifested when acquiring ownership by erecting a building on the land of another, *in aedificatio*. A building erected without the knowledge and will of the owner of the land becomes the possession of the owner of the land (Art. 152/1 PA). The same rule applies if the owner of the land had known of the construction, but had failed to ban it without delay and the constructor acted dishonestly (Art. 154 PA). The principle of the legal unity of real property comes into play when somebody adds to, builds on or reconstructs somebody's building, builds additions to it, builds something into it, or otherwise invests in it. The only situation in which the principle of the legal unity of real property does not come into play is when the constructor has been honest, and the owner of the land dishonest. An honest constructor who did not know, or could not have known, that he was building on the land of another becomes

of real property. Condominium is defined as a special form of co-ownership over the whole real property (the plot and the building on it) whereby the co-ownership share is connected with the individual part of the real property (a flat, business premises, and so on).

68. From the entry into force of the PA, the principle of legal unity of real property is valid in any legal relations whose object is a piece of land on which a building is erected.[270] Any legal transaction in which the principle of legal unity of real property is not observed does not have any legal effect.[271] The statutory provisions that provide for the legal status of buildings and their parts differently from the legal status of land must be interpreted and applied only in accordance with the principle of legal unity of real property.[272] The rules, which strictly define the concept of real property and the principle of legal unity and its legal effects on any legal transaction, were more than necessary at the time when the PA was adopted. In such a way, the legislature wanted to eliminate possible dilemmas and different interpretations of the concept of real property in judicial and business practices. It was particularly important to eliminate the interpretation of the concept of real property according to previous regulations in which the principle of legal unity of real property was not observed. Therefore, exceptions from the principle of the legal unity of real property have been expressly stated in the PA.[273]

69. The introduction of the principle of *superficies solo cedit* had a significant impact on legal transactions involving real property. Since the entry into force of the PA, legal transactions involving real property have become much simpler because of its unified character: one can dispose of a unified piece of real property because whatever is connected with any land or is added to it on or underneath its surface must share its legal destiny.[274] An object permanently connected with the land is considered to be a component part of the real property, thus constituting a legal unity which is an object of legal relations until it is detached. In such a way, legal transactions involving real property have become both faster and safer, and the preconditions have thus been created for reaffirming the role of the land register in legal transactions. The land register can potentially now easily fulfil its functions in legal transactions (the functions of publicity, acquisition and protection of trust) whenever the plot of land is registered and the building erected on it might not by then have been registered.[275,276]

---

the owner of the land by the act of having erected a building on the land of another, provided the owner of the land knew about the construction but had failed to immediately ban its continuation, or provided that the owner let the construction continue so that the building could be finally erected on the plot (Art. 153 PA). For more details, *see* Gavella in *Property Law I*, 82–90.

270. Article 366/1 PA.
271. Article 366/3 PA.
272. Article 395/2 PA.
273. The legal separation of the land from the building is possible on the basis of the right to build and on the basis of a concession. In both cases, these are rights authorizing their holders to own a building erected on the land of another.
274. Article 4/2 LRA.
275. Because of the principle of the legal unity of real property, all land register entries concerning land relate to whatever is relatively permanently attached to it, regardless of the fact that it is not entered

II. Exceptions from the Principle of Legal Unity of Real Property

70. Exceptions from the principle of the legal unity of real property, namely cases where a construction that is relatively permanently connected to the plot is not considered as its part but as a separate immovable property, are expressly determined by law.[277] The rule of legal unity of real property is not valid for:

- buildings and other objects connected to the plot only for a temporary purpose, such as prefabricated huts, kiosks, camper vans and the like.[278] In legal transactions, such objects are considered movable property;
- buildings put up on somebody else's land by a person having a separate property right – the right to build.[279] The building is then legally separated from the plot of land and is considered to be separate real property. The owner of the plot of land and the owner of the building are not the same. The owner of the building is the holder of the right to build because the right to build authorizes its holder to own a building or some other construction on somebody else's plot.[280] The holder of the right to build exists in the person who owns the building as long as the right to build exists. When it ceases to exist, the owner of the plot of land becomes the owner of the building, and the unity of real property is thus re-established;[281]

  buildings and other types of construction built on a plot (which is a public good or common good) by a concessionaire. When a concessionaire, on the basis of a concession which allows him to own a building or any other construction on a plot which is subject to a concession, puts up a building or any other type of construction, he is considered the owner of that construction.[282] During the validity of the concession, the building is considered to be separate real property independent of the plot, and its owner is a concessionaire. When the concession ceases to exist, the unity of the plot and the building is re-established so that the same legal relations valid for the plot are also valid for the building; and

  buildings and fixtures that the owner of immovable has put up on the neighbouring immovable on which there is easement in respect of part of the building or the fixture on another person's immovable.[283]

---

into the land register and regardless of whether and when it will be entered into it. For example, a registered owner of land is considered the owner of the building, even though the building is not entered into the land register. A lien encumbers the land with the building even if the building is not registered.

276. With regard to the principle of the legal unity of real property, it is considered that real property is not entered in the land register (non-registered real property) only when the parcel (cadastral plot) is not entered in the land register. In the case of non-registered real property, ownership and other rights in rem are acquired by depositing with a court a verified document sufficient for registration of the right in the land register (Arts 120/4, 121/5, 220/3, 263/3, 309/3 PA).
277. For more details, *see* Gavella in *Property Law I*, 90.
278. Article 9/3 PA.
279. Articles 280–296 PA.
280. Article 9/4 PA.
281. For more details on the right to build, *see* Part I, Ch. 5, §3. The Right to Build.
282. Articles 3/4, 9/4 PA.
283. Article 196 PA. For more details on real easements, *see* Part I, Ch. 5, §1. Easements.

III. Return to the Principle of Legal Unity of Real Property

71. Until the entry into force of the PA, the legal unity of real property had, in many cases, been abandoned. Buildings and their separate parts were then legally separated from the land on which the building was erected, and each of them was subject to a different legal regime. The legal unity of real property was abandoned in legal relations, which arose when a privately owned building was erected on a plot of land that was socially owned.[284] When the PA became effective, in all cases where the plot, buildings and their separate parts were legally separated, the principle of the legal unity of real property was established by law.

72. The establishment of the legal unity of real property also required special transition in all cases in which the land and the building had previously been legally separated.[285] On the basis of special transitional and final provisions governing real property, legal unity, having been abandoned in the socialist regime, was now *ex lege* re-established through the transitional and final provisions of the PA. With the entry into force of the PA (1 January 1997), the legal unity of real property was established in such a way that the land and the building erected on it became unified real property.[286] The owner of the building erected on socially owned land prior to the entry into force of the PA, at the same time, became the owner of the plot on which the building was erected. Due to the fact that the principle of legal unity was also abandoned in the regulation of ownership on individual parts of a building (condominiums) when the PA entered into force, the condominium also regained its legal unity. When the PA became effective, the owners of flats became the co-owners of the entire real property (land + building), and their legal position was also governed by the provisions of the PA governing condominiums.[287]

---

284. A building was legally separated from the plot underneath it, and it was privately owned while the plot was socially owned, and the owner of the building was only entitled to use the land. The ownership of individual parts of a building (flats) was also legally separated from the plot, from other individual part and from common parts of the building and of the land. The owner of a flat was co-owner of all common parts of the building, as well as co-owner of the plot on which the building was erected, if it had been built on a privately owned plot. He had the right to use the common part of the land when a building in social ownership was built on a socially owned plot.
285. For more details, *see* Gavella in *Property Law I*, 86–88.
286. Articles 366–373 PA.
287. Articles 66–99 PA.

Chapter 2. Registration of Immovable Property

§1. The Concept and Characteristics

73. The land register (*zemljišne knjige*) constitutes public books into which data on the legal status of immovables are entered.[288] It contains information on immovables, property rights and personal (obligatory) rights relating to immovables and specific relations and facts of particular importance for real property transactions.[289]

74. The land register is a special kind of record on immovable property containing all the relevant data concerning its legal status. In the Republic of Croatia, the land register is the basic and the only registration system concerning the legal status of immovables which is relevant for legal transactions involving immovable property. Property rights over immovables which may be subject to legal transactions are entered, and they are aimed to achieve particular legal effects regarding publication, protection, realization, acquisition, change and termination of such rights, as well as protection of trust. Where the legal status of an immovable involved in legal transactions is concerned, the only relevant data are those contained in the land register and not those that may be found in any other information system. The statutory organization of the land register, as well as its functions, characteristics, content and the procedure of registration of the rights over immovables and the legal consequences, are set forth in the LRA, the PA, the Land Registry Rules (LRR)[290] and many other acts such as the CPA, the EA, the Notaries Public Act (NPA) and the Family Act (FA).

75. The land register, as a special means of registering immovables and the rights over immovables, has specific characteristics by which it is distinguished from any other system of registration of immovable property. It is based on the cadastral surveying of land. By being public books, it enjoys public trust. It consists of a main (land) register and a collection of documents (a land register in the narrower sense), as well as auxiliary lists and cadastral maps, which all together make up what is called the land register in the wider sense.

76. The land register is based on the data collected by way of a cadastral survey of land.[291] The cadastre office keeps a record of all plots of land, buildings and parts of buildings, as well as other constructions permanently located on plots of land or under their surface unless otherwise provided by law.[292] The data collected by way of cadastral survey are important for the identification and individualization of plots

288. Article 3/1 LRA.
289. Josipović in *Land Registration Law*, 89–90.
290. OG 81/97, 109/02, 123/02, 153/02, 14/05, 60/10, 55/13, 63/19.
291. Article 10 LRA.
292. Article 1 of the Cadastre Act/CdA. The cadastre of real property is regulated by the CdA (OG 112/18, 39/22). The tasks of organizing, keeping and maintaining the real property cadastre are carried out by the State Geodetic Authority in its Central Office in Zagreb and in its field offices (Art. 123 of CdA).

in the land register and for the establishment, renewal and supplementation of the land register. The cadastre of real property is kept by administrative bodies called cadastre offices (*katastarski uredi*) which operate in accordance with the rules of administrative procedure. The land register is kept by municipal courts (their land register departments) in accordance with the rules on extra-judicial proceedings. The land register is competent, among other things, for keeping records of the numbers of cadastral units, their surface area, shape, buildings and other constructions built on the plots or under their surface (data on the build-up areas). The land register also contains data in relation to the property rights on immovables, the holders of such rights and all other data concerning the legal status of immovables of importance for legal transactions. The plots of land contained in the land register are marked by their numbers, i.e., the parts of the earth's surface are marked in the cadastre by special numbers and by the names of the cadastral municipality where they are located. The data regarding the numbers of cadastral units, their surface area and the buildings and other constructions permanently located on the land or underneath its surface (build-up areas) must correspond to the identical data in the cadastre.[293] However, the cadastre data are not relevant for the legal status of immovable. They only show the data regarding the cadastral units, their size, shape and the construction on and under the land surface. An excerpt from the cadastre is not proof of the ownership of immovable, and it does not reflect its legal status or the existence of charges on it (liens, easements and the like) or limitations on the disposal of rights over immovables. In order to establish who owns the immovable, what rights exist on it, or what encumbrances or limitations to its disposal are registered, it is necessary to look into the land register.

77. The land register is open to the public.[294] Any person may request to inspect land register and all the supporting lists and obtain land certificates, listings or transcripts therefrom.[295] The right to inspect the land register is unlimited because no legal or any other interest needs to be proved for its realization.[296] The inspection may be carried out by actual insight into the land register with the land register court or by having insight into a land register excerpt (*zemljišnoknjižni izvadak)* issued by the land register court verifying the legal status of immovable registered in a particular land register file. A verified land register excerpt may be issued by any land

293. Article 11/1 LRA. Therefore, the data on cadastral units, their number, shapes, areas and built constructions kept in the cadastre and land register must permanently be harmonized and any change of such data in the cadastre must also be recorded in the land register. In order to maintain permanent harmonization between the cadastre and the land register courts, dissemination of relevant information regarding any changes of data on cadastral units, important for both registers, must take place regularly (Articles 11,12 LRA). The cadastre office is obliged to submit without delay, on a registration form, any modifications in the numbers, shape, or in the surface area of cadastral plots or in the construction on it to the land register. On the basis of such a registration form, the land register court enters the corresponding changes in the land register. If the data on the existing plots in the cadastre and in the land register are different, the legal status of the immovable will be established on the basis of the data in the land register (Art. 11/4 LRA).

294. Article 7/1 LRA.

295. Article 7/2 LRA.

296. Access to the land register dana is possible by Internet. *See* http://e-izvadak.pravosudje.hr/home.htm or http://www.uredjenazemlja.hr/web/cms/en/home.

register court, regardless of its jurisdiction, by a notary public, an attorney or a cadastral office. Such a verified land register excerpt may also be issued through the e-Citizens system (e-Građani).[297] A land register excerpt is a public document proving the legal status of immovable at the moment of its issuance.[298] The rule that every person is entitled to have insight into the land register means that it is every interested person's duty to be informed of the state of affairs of the land register. Failure to be informed of the land register's state of affairs does not excuse anyone, and every person's knowledge of the *status quo* in the land register is always presumed. No one may claim or prove the absence of the necessary knowledge regarding the situation in the land register. It cannot be used as an excuse because whatever is recorded in the land register is directed at everyone, regardless of whether they have become familiar with it or not.

78. Land registers enjoy public trust. It is believed that the land register fully and accurately reflects the factual and legal state of affairs of immovables.[299] In addition, all rights existing on immovables are considered to have been entered in the land register, and there are no rights that have not been entered. Persons registered as holders of rights are really considered as the holders of these rights, and the registered rights exist for the benefit of registered persons. Any acquirer acting in good faith in legal transactions and having confidence in what is written in the land register is protected, and his acquisition cannot be challenged on account of the data in the land register being incomplete or inaccurate. A bona fide acquirer will thus acquire the right on an immovable unencumbered with any rights, charges or limitations if, at the moment of applying for the registration of his right, they were not entered in the land register.[300] An acquirer acting in good faith will acquire the right on immovable from a person who, although entered in the land register, was not the holder of that right after the time limits for the removal of the registration of a bona fide acquirer's predecessor have expired.[301]

79. The land register is kept by courts. The keeping of the land register and the resolution of land register cases are within the jurisdiction of courts. The land register is kept by a land register department of the municipal court for the immovables located in the area where the municipal court has territorial jurisdiction.[302]

80. The land register is kept in accordance with the system of real folios. The land register is kept according to the existing immovable. An entry in the land register is determined on the basis of a legal object – immovable, and not on the basis

297. Article 27 LRA.
298. Article 8/1 LRA.
299. Article 8/2 LRA.
300. Article 8/4 LRA.
301. Article 8/5 LRA. For more details on the protection of trust in the land register, *see* Part I, Ch. 2, §2. III. The Protection of Trust.
302. Article 5 LRA.

of the subjects of rights on such immovable. Any entry relating to the same immovable and of relevance for its legal status are recorded in the same place in the land register, i.e., in the land register file (*zemljišnoknjižni uložak*) established for particular immovable.[303]

81. The land register is kept by way of electronic data processing (EDP) in the Joint Land Register and Cadastre Information System (*Zajednički informacijski sustav*/ZIS).[304] Entries in the EDP are made exclusively by storing data in the land register database because the main register, as part of the EDP, is kept only as electronically processed data.

§2. Functions of the Land Register

I. General Overview

82. The land register has several important functions. The rights over immovables involved in legal transactions are entered in the land register with certain legal effects for the publication, protection, realization, acquisition, change and termination of property rights over immovables or for the protection of trust. With entry into the land register, the property rights are acquired on the basis of a contract (the so-called acquisitive function of the land register). An entry in the land register makes the information public, stating that, on particular immovable, some property rights are registered in favour of particular subjects (the so-called public function of the land register). With registration in the land register, the legal status of immovables becomes transparent and accessible to the public, and the most important function of the land register is derived from it: the protection of trust in the legal transaction of immovables. As for third parties acting in good faith and having acquired rights over immovable by relying on the data contained in the land register and its public function, these data are considered accurate, authentic and complete.

II. Acquisition of Property Rights

83. An entry in the land register is a precondition (modus) for the acquisition, change and termination of property rights when such rights over immovables are acquired, changed or terminated on the basis of a contract *inter vivos* (the acquisitive function of the land register). Then, apart from the corresponding right of a predecessor, i.e., his power to dispose of the right in the appropriate way and a valid contract (*titulus*), a corresponding modus of acquisition, change or termination of

303. Therefore, in order to find out the legal status of an individual immovable, it is generally necessary to have an insight into a land register file where the immovable is registered.
304. Article 6 LRA.

the right is also required (the principle of causal tradition).[305] The modus of acquiring property rights is achieved by a corresponding entry in the land register.[306] A change or termination of property rights on the basis of a contract is also achieved with an entry in the land register.[307] Removal from the land register is a precondition for the termination of property rights in certain cases when the rights are extinguished on another basis different from the contract.[308]

84. When property rights are acquired, changed, limited or terminated on the basis of a court decision or a decision of another competent authority, on the basis of law or by inheritance, an entry in the land register is not a precondition for acquisition, change or termination of these rights. They are acquired without being entered in the land register, and if such acquisition is entered, it has only a declaratory effect or one of publicity. An acquirer of a property right on the basis of a court decision, of a decision of another competent authority, or by inheritance has the right to apply for its entry in the land register.[309] Such an entry gives publicity to the property right over an immovable which is acquired even without being entered in the land register. This is important for the achievement of an absolute effect of such a right and for its subsequent disposal. By entering it in the land register, the holder is protected from the possibility of its loss due to the existence of the legal effects of the protection of trust regarding the integrity of the land register data with respect to third acquirers.[310]

III. The Protection of Trust

A. *The Protection of Trust in the Completeness and Accuracy of the Land Register*

85. Registration in the land register provides an external picture of the legal status of real property. With the help of these entries, all the information relevant to the legal status of real property subject to legal transactions is made public (*publicitetna funkcija upisa*).[311] By entering the property rights in the land register, one

305. For more details, *see* Part III, Ch. 2, §2. Principle of Causal Tradition.
306. Articles 119/1, 120/1, 121/1-4, 220/1-2, 263/1-2, 288/1-4, 309/1-2 PA.
307. Articles 119/2, 220/4, 263/4, 288/5, 309/4 PA.
308. Removal from the land register is a precondition for the termination of a property right: when its holder has renounced the right (Arts 172, 239/5, 274/5, 293, 344/4 PA); when the time limit for which it was established has expired, or when the termination condition is met under which it was established (Arts 240/3, 275/2, 293, 345/1 PA); when the property right is terminated by default (Art. 241/5 PA); and when it was terminated by a court decision or a decision of an administrative authority (Arts 242/5, 276/3, 294/4, 351/2, 245/4, 279/3, 293, 352/2 PA). A mortgage also ceases to exist only by being removed from the land register regardless of the reason for the termination of the mortgage claim (Art. 347/1 PA). The same applies for the termination of a compulsory mortgage or a statutory mortgage entered in the land register (Art. 353 PA).
309. Articles 127/1, 128/2, 130/1, 223/2, 228/2, 265/2, 289/2, 311/3, 312/4, 314/2 PA, Art. 15/3 LRA.
310. Articles 124, 127/2, 130/2, 227, 230, 243, 277, 289/2, 349 PA, Art. 8/4 LRA.
311. Gavella in *Property Law I*, 291; Klarić / Vedriš in *Civil Law*, 313.

of the basic property law principles is fulfilled – the principle of publicity.[312] Due to the fact that the land register enjoys public trust,[313] it is believed that the land register fully and accurately reflects the factual and legal status of immovables.[314] It is also believed that property rights are entered in the interest of the registered persons and that the content, scope and order of priority are also registered.[315] The land register is deemed to contain all the rights existing over particular immovables, as well as any encumbrances or limitations. Indeed, there are no rights concerning the same immovable or any personal relations not entered in the land register, although, in order for them to have an absolute effect, they should be entered.[316]

86. With regard to bona fide third persons who have acquired property rights over an immovable by relying on the content of the land register, the data contained in it are considered accurate, reliable and complete. Persons who did not know or did not need to know that the state of affairs in the land register was different from the real legal status of an immovable for a reason not registered would be legally protected if it came to the harmonization of the situation in the land register and the real legal status. The rights acquired by bona fide acquirers by relying on the accuracy and completeness of the land register cannot be challenged so that those who have acquired an immovable in good faith are protected. They enjoy the protection of trust in the completeness of the land register and the protection of trust in its accuracy.

87. When the land register data are incomplete because not all the rights existing on particular immovables have been entered, and they can be entered, then the legal effects of the protection of trust in the completeness of the land register set in favour of an acquirer who has acted in good faith (*zaštita povjerenja u potpunost zemljišnih knjiga*). A bona fide acquirer, having trusted the completeness of the land register data, which, however, have turned out to be incomplete, acquires his land register rights unencumbered by any rights, charges or limitations which, at the moment of seeking entry in his favour, were not registered, and the land register did not contain any information that their registration had been requested.[317] In such a situation, it will not be possible to defy an acquirer acting in good faith and trusting the completeness of the land register by claiming unregistered rights over an immovable, the rights acquired by a court decision, by some another authority, or by virtue of law if such rights have not been entered in the land register, or their

---

312. For more details, *see* General Introduction, §2. IV. D. Principle of Publicity.
313. Article 8/1 LRA.
314. Article 8/2 LRA.
315. Article 122/1 PA, Art. 8/2 LRA – the presumption of accuracy of the land register.
316. Article 122/1 PA, Art. 8/2 LRA – the presumption of the completeness of the land register data. The presumption of the completeness of the land register data does not relate only to the rights over an immovable which have absolute effect by virtue of the law, without being entered in the land register. For example, public law real burdens are not entered in the land register because they have an absolute effect by law (Art. 266/2PA). The statutory right of pre-emption is also not entered in the land register because it is also effective towards all third parties by virtue of law (e.g., Art. 44 of the Residential Lease Act).
317. Cf. Art. 8/4 LRA, Arts 124/1, 127/2, 130/2, 227, 230, 243, 277, 293, 349 PA.

registration has not been sought.[318,319] Therefore, a bona fide acquirer acquires an immovable with the legal status which is recorded in the land register at the moment of seeking registration. The legal effects of the protection of trust in the completeness of land register are set in their entirety immediately upon the registration made in favour of an acquirer acting in good faith.[320]

88. When the data in the land register are inaccurate because of a false entry, and a bona fide acquirer has obtained land register rights by relying on such an entry, the legal effects of the protection of confidence in the authenticity of the land register data become effective in his favour (*zaštita povjerenja u istinitost zemljišnih knjiga*).[321] In such a situation, it will not be possible to challenge the acquisition of a bona fide acquirer even though the registration in favour of his legal predecessor had been invalid.[322] On the basis of the legal effects of the protection of confidence in the authenticity of data in favour of a bona fide acquirer, an acquisition of the property right takes place by a person who is not its actual holder, although such a status was entered in the land register.[323] By virtue of the principle of the protection of confidence in the authenticity of land register data, a bona fide acquirer acquires his right regardless of the right of the predecessor because the statutory prerequisites for the protection of confidence have been fulfilled. At the same time, when the legal effects of the protection of confidence in the authenticity of data in favour of a bona fide acquirer set in, the actual holder of the land register right affected by the lack of authenticity and by a false registration loses his right. Unlike the legal effects of the protection of confidence in the completeness of the land register data, the legal effects of the protection of confidence in authenticity do not become effective at the moment of registering the acquisition in favour of a bona fide acquirer. The effectiveness of the legal effects of the protection of confidence in the authenticity of the land register data and the acquisition of the property rights on the basis of the principle of protection of confidence in relation to the bona fide acquirer is conditioned by the expiry of the time limit within which it is possible to file a cancellation claim against the predecessor's false registration and restore the former land registry state of affairs.[324,325]

---

318. However, it is possible to defy such a situation by any unregistered rights, encumbrances and limitations which exist on the basis of law and which are deemed to have absolute effect even without being entered in the land register (e.g., public law real burdens, the statutory right of pre-emption and the like, Art. 124/2 PA).
319. Unregistered holders of property rights may successfully realize their right to seek registration of the right acquired outside the land register before the legal effects of the protection of trust in the completeness of the land register data become effective to the benefit of a bona fide acquirer. After that, their rights cease to exist, and they can no longer be entered in the land register.
320. For more, *see* Josipović in *Land Registration Law*, 246.
321. Article 122/1 PA, Art. 8/3,5 LRA.
322. Article 122/1 PA, Art. 8/3,5 LRA.
323. Articles 123, 221, 264, 288/5, 318 PA.
324. Article 129/2 LRA. If the holder of the land register right which has been violated by false registration has received a decision on the registration in favour of the predecessor, he must, within the time limit for a claim, request an entry that the registration is disputable and file a cancellation claim within sixty days from the expiry of that time limit against the bona fide acquirer (Art. 123/2 PA, Art. 129/2/al.1 LRA). If the aggrieved holder of the land register right has not been served the decision on the predecessor's registration, a cancellation claim against the bona fide acquirer may

89. In order for the legal effects for the protection of confidence in the completeness and authenticity of the land register data to become effective, some preconditions must be fulfilled. The legal effects of the principle of confidence will set in when the land register state of affairs is different from the one existing outside the land register or from the actual or the real legal status of the immovable because the one contained in the land register is incomplete, false or invalid.[326] These legal effects will become effective only in favour of the bona fide acquirer who acted in good faith and did not know or who, due to the circumstances, did not have sufficient grounds for suspicion that the land register data were incomplete and different from the actual state of affairs outside the land register.[327] A bona fide acquirer will be legally protected when it comes to the acquisition of the land register right only if he, by acting in good faith, has entered his right in the land register on the basis of a valid legal ground which can also be a legal ground for a derived acquisition of property rights. An acquirer must act in good faith both at the moment of entering into a legal transaction, as well as at the moment of seeking registration in his favour.[328]

B. The Protection of Trust in the Interim Period

90. At the time when the PA and LRA entered into force, the then-existing state of affairs in the land register concerning immovables was largely not harmonized with the actual status of real property. This lack of coordination between the land register and the actual status was particularly obvious when immovables under former social ownership were at issue because of the transformation of social ownership into private ownership. Therefore, the application of the rules on the protection of confidence was postponed for a certain period of time until the land register was finally harmonized with the actual legal status of immovables in former social ownership. For immovables which on 1 January 1997 were registered as socially owned, the protection of confidence was postponed until 1 January 2015.[329]

§3. The Structure of the Land Register

91. Each land register consists of the main land register (*glavna knjiga*) and a collection of documents (*zbirka isprava*), in addition to which necessary auxiliary lists (*pomoćni popisi*) and cadastral plans (*katastarski planovi*) are maintained.[330]

---

successfully be filed unless three years have elapsed since the registration in the predecessor's favour was requested (Art. 123/2 PA, Art. 129/2/al.2 LRA).

325. For more, *see* Josipović in *Land Registration Law*, 248.
326. Article 8/3 LRA, Art. 122/1 PA.
327. Article 8/3 LRA, Art. 122/2 PA. The good faith and honesty of an acquirer is presumed, and the burden of proof lies with the person who claims that the acquirer had not acted bona fide.
328. Josipović in *Land Registration Law*, 248.
329. Article 388/5 PA.
330. Article 13 LRA.

The main land register[331] is a part of the land register which serves for the registration of registered immovables and changes therein, as well as ownership and other property rights. The main land register is maintained for all immovables located within a particular cadastral municipality.[332] The main land register consists of land registry files (*zemljišnoknjižni ulošci*).[333]

92. A land register file is part of the main land register, which is related to one land registry body (one piece of real property, one immovable), the property rights related to the real property and changes therein.[334] Land register files serve for the registration of only one registered land unit. A registered land unit (*zemljišnoknjižno tijelo*) consists of one or more cadastral plots.[335] Each registered land unit constitutes a single legal entity.[336]

93. A collection of documents[337] consists of documents based on which entry into the land register has been allowed. Original or certified documents serving as a basis for entry in the land register are enclosed with the collection of documents, with numbers according to which the entries have been made in the general register.

94. A collection of cadastre maps[338] consists of all maps prepared by the cadastre authority, showing the position and shape of all cadastral plots and buildings or other structures permanently located on such cadastral plots or underneath their surface. Cadastral maps are maintained electronically within the Joint Information System.

95. Supporting lists[339] differ depending on the data according to which they are maintained. For each general register, a list of cadastral units (*popis zemljišta*) and personal auxiliary lists and a list of owners (*popis vlasnika*) are maintained.

---

331. Articles 17–24 LRA.
332. Article 17/1 LRA.
333. Article 18/1 LRA.
334. Articles 18/2,3 LRA.
335. Several cadastral plots may be integrated into a single registered land unit provided that more plots are located in the same cadastral municipality, if they belong to the same owner or co-owners, and if there are no differences in the limitations of ownership, in charges and encumbrances (Art. 19/3 LRA).
336. Article 19/4 LRA. A land register unit consists of three particles: part A – cadastral land data (*posjedovnica*) serves for the registration of all land parcels which constitute one land registry body; part B – ownership rights (*vlastovnica*) serves for the registration of ownership titles, i.e., data on the owners; part C – charges register (*teretovnica*) serves for the registration of charges encumbering registered land body (Art. 20 LRA).
337. Articles 29,30 LRA.
338. Article 32 LRA.
339. Article 33 LRA

§4. Land Register Entries

A. Preconditions for Entries

96. Land register entries are made in a separate land register procedure. They are made upon an authorized person's proposal. In order for a land register entry to have specific legal effects, certain substantive and procedural preconditions must be fulfilled.

97. There are two basic material preconditions for an entry – a registered predecessor (*knjižni prednik*) and a land register document/deed (*tabularna isprava*). An entry may be allowed only against a registered predecessor. A registered predecessor[340] is a person who, at the time of the submission of a request for entry in the land register, is registered as holder of land register rights for which an entry is requested or who is concurrently registered or conditionally registered as holder of land register rights.[341,342] A land register entry is not allowed against a person who is not registered as a holder of the land register right for which an entry is requested. In that case, an entry is allowed only if all the preconditions have been fulfilled so that this person will concurrently be registered as a holder of that right.[343] Another material precondition for an entry is a land register document. An entry is allowed on the basis of an appropriate land register document. Such documents may be private or public and may be made in an electronic form. [344] Private land register documents are those by which legal entities independently and without any public authority regulate their private law relations. Public documents are issued in a prescribed form by government bodies within their area of competence or by legal or natural persons within the performance of their public authority entrusted to them by a law or a regulation.[345,346]

---

340. Article 45 LRA.
341. Article 45 LRA.
342. Josipović in *Land Registration Law*, 182–188.
343. If some immovable has been transferred successively to more persons without a land register entry, the last acquirer may request the entry only if he is able to prove uninterrupted succession of acquisition of non-registered rights from the registered predecessor (Art. 46 LRA).
344. Article 49/4 LRA An electronic document, a document transposed into an electronic form or an excerpt from an electronically maintained register are considered to be original documents (Art. 112/2 LRA). Authorised users of the information system (e.g. notaries public) verify such documents to be identical to those on paper (Art. 112/5 LRA).
345. A document is appropriate for entry if the following preconditions have been fulfilled: (a) the document is made in a form prescribed as valid (Art. 48/1 LRA); (b) legal grounds for the acquisition, modification or termination of rights are made evident in the relevant document (Art. 48/2 LRA); (c) the document contains all the data on persons against whom and in whose favour an entry is requested, so there is no danger of their being confused with other persons, no matter when these documents were complied, te isprava sadržava osobni identifikacijski broj stranaka (Art. 49/2 LRA); (d) the document does not contain any apparent fault which would be bring its authenticity into doubt (Art. 49/1 LRA); (e) the document contains the name of the place, date, month and year when it was made (Art. 49/3 LRA).
346. For more, *see* Josipović in *Land Registration Law*, 188–190.

98. The procedural (formal and legal) preconditions for registration are provided for in the provisions of the LRA prescribing the land register procedure. In order for the legal effects of an entry to ensue, it is necessary for an authorized person to submit a proposal for an entry.[347] The documents on which the proposal for an entry is based and which are necessary for the land registry court to allow it must be attached to the proposal.[348] After reviewing the proposal for entry and after examining the existing land register status and the attached documents,[349] the land registry court approves of the entry by ruling on it.[350] On the basis of its ruling, an entry in the land register is made.[351] In order for an entry to have legal effects, it is necessary for the ruling on entry to become final.[352]

B. Subject of Entries

99. Through land register entries, the competent land registry court, in separate land register procedures, enters and records in the main land register any data on immovables and their legal status that are important for legal transactions. The legal effects of entries depend on their subjects, types and whether all the necessary preconditions have been fulfilled. The subject of an entry into the land register is immovables,[353] property rights[354] and some personal rights concerning immovables[355] (land registry rights; *knjižna prava*), the personal relationship of the holders of such rights, as well as any legal data whose entry in the land register is prescribed by the LRA or any other act. The rights entered in the land register must be related to immovables.

100. The land registers also show all other legally relevant facts important for the legal status of immovables. In addition, the data on limitations imposed on the holders of land register rights to dispose of these rights are particularly important in legal transactions. Therefore, the personal data of the holders of land register rights that are important for their positions in the disposition of immovables are also

347. Articles 103,104 LRA. Any person who, through an entry, acquires, modifies or loses a registrable right, or a person who has a legal interest in a fact to be entered in the land register, is authorized to submit a proposal for it to be made (Art. 103 LRA).
348. Articles 105-108 LRA.
349. Article 117 LRA.
350. Article 118 LRA.
351. Article 127 LRA.
352. For more on the ruling on proposals for entries, *see* Part I, Ch. 2, §5. Land Register Procedure.
353. Immovables not capable of being an object of property rights (common goods) are not entered in the land register. Common goods are entered in the land register only at the request of a person possessing legal interest in them (e.g., at the request of a person having a concession of some common good in order for that concession to be entered in the land register).
354. Property rights entered in the land register are the following: (a) ownership/co-ownership/joint ownership/condominium ownership entered in the part B – Ownership Right (Art. 36 LRA); (b) easements, real burdens, right to build, mortgage entered in the part C-Charges Register (Arts 24, 37, 38, 39 LRA).
355. As personal rights, the right to buy back, pre-empt, lease and let and concession are entered. They are entered in the Part C-Charges Register (Art. 24 LRA).

entered in the land register, particularly personal relations, which constitute restrictions in the disposition of immovables and rights on such immovables.[356] These are personal relations essential for the establishment of the identity or status of the holder of real property rights in terms of his capacity to dispose of a property right. Specific provisions on personal relations which may be entered, and the preconditions for their entry and removal, are contained in the existing regulations providing for the personal status of natural and legal persons.[357]

101. Any legal facts by which some legal effects are established or constituted, applicable for the legal status of immovables and for the disposition of land register rights,[358] are also entered in the land register. Besides the LRA, the registration of some legal facts in the land register is laid down in other regulations[359] such as the PA,[360] the EA,[361] the ExA[362] and other acts. The legal effects of entering a legal fact are set forth in the rules providing for the possibility of their being entered in the land register. These rules also provide for the preconditions for entry, the duration of legal effects resulting from their being entered in the land register, as well as the preconditions for their removal. The legal effects created by entering a legal fact depend on its content and nature.

C. Types of Land Register Entries

102. Land register entries differ depending on their subject, their legal effects and the preconditions that must be fulfilled in order for entries to be allowed and

356. Articles 34/4, 44 indent 1, 76 LRA.
357. The LRA does not provide a list of personal relations entered in the land register. It only gives some examples of personal relations such as the age of minority, guardianship, extension of parental rights, declaration of bankruptcy, and so on (Art. 44 indent 1 LRA). In addition, the change of the holder's name, the change of temporary residence and other facts important for the establishment of the identity, or position of the holder of a land register right regarding his subjective capacities and restrictions regarding the disposition of the land register right are also entered in the land register.
358. Articles 34/4, 44 indent 2, 77-96LRA. The LRA also provides that the following legal facts are entered in the land register: the establishment of the order of priority for the alienation of immovable or the establishment of a mortgage (Arts 77-82), a mortgage securing a claim (Arts 83-85), a dispute over a land register right (Arts 86-89), institution of the proceedings in which entry in the land register may be ordered (Art. 90), an action to contest any creditor's legal actions (Arts 91, 92), an extraordinary legal remedy (Art. 93), the appointment or dismissal of a trustee of immovable (Art. 94), the rejection of enforcement (Art. 95), award ruling (Art. 96), as well as many other facts emerging in the course of the land register procedure.
359. Article 75/1 LRA.
360. The PA stipulates that the prohibition of alienation or encumbrance (Art. 34/2), the limitation of ownership in the form of a condition or a time limit (Art. 34/3), the obligation to obtain the deletion of a mortgage (Art. 347/3), the retention of the order of priority (Art. 348) as well as some other facts are also entered in the land register.
361. The EA stipulates that a writ of enforcement relating to real property (Art. 84 of EA), a claim secured by a mortgage has become enforceable (Art. 297/3 of EA), prohibition of alienation or encumbrance of real property (Arts 345/1/3, 347/1/4) must also be entered in the land register.
362. According to the Expropriation Act, the fact that expropriation proceedings regarding some specific real property are pending must be entered in the land register (Art. 33).

carried out. There are three types of entries: registration, conditional registration and recordation.

103. Registration (*uknjižba*) includes entries whereby land register rights are acquired, transferred, restricted or terminated without any specific subsequent justification.[363] [364] Through registration, the property rights are entered (ownership, easement, real burden, right of build, mortgage) as well as personal rights on immovables (buyback, pre-empting, lease, rent) and concessions. Apart from the preconditions required for any land register entry,[365] the documents on the basis of which a registration is made must fulfil some additional requirements. They differ depending on whether the registration is requested on the basis of a private document on a transaction (e.g., a contract of sale, a contract of gift, a mortgage contract, a contract for easement, a life-maintenance contract, etc.)[366] or on the basis of public documents (a court ruling, decisions by administrative bodies, etc.) drawn up by a competent body, or a notary public.[367] The legal effects of registration include unconditional and final acquisition, transfer, restriction or termination of land register rights in accordance with the scope and content entered into the land register. Such legal effects of registration are not conditioned by anything or in any way and are not limited in time. Registration is of particular substantive law significance for the acquisition, modification or termination of the property rights on immovables by contract *inter vivos*. When it is stipulated in a separate law that an entry into the land register is a precondition for the acquisition, modification or termination of a right on real property, this precondition is fulfilled by entering such registration. This is the mode in which property rights on some immovables are acquired, modified or terminated, and they are considered as such only upon registration.[368]

104. Conditional registration (*predbilježba*) is an entry whereby registrable rights are acquired, transferred, restricted or terminated only on condition that the entry is subsequently justified and in the scope in which it is justified.[369,370] By conditional registration, just as by registration, the property rights on immovables are

363. Article 34/2 LRA.
364. Josipović in *Land Registration Law*, 191–196.
365. For more details, *see* Part I, Ch. 2, §4. I. Preconditions for Entries.
366. These documents must fulfil the following preconditions: they must contain a precise designation of the land or right whose registration is requested (Arts 59/1/a, 60/1/a LRA); a representation made by the person whose rights have been restricted, encumbered, terminated or conveyed and given to another person stating the agreement to registration – *clausula intabulandi* (Arts 59/1/b, 60/1/a LRA) and the signature of the person who lost his property right certified by a notary public (Art. 57/1,6 LRA); when a document is signed by an authorized representative, a power of attorney must have been issued precisely for that particular transaction (a specified power of attorney); if the authorized representative has only a general power of attorney, or a power of attorney issued for such a type of transaction (a generic power of attorney) at the time at the time of drawing up the document, it must not be older than one year (Art. 58/2 LRA).
367. Rulings passed by a court or another competent body are deemed appropriate for registration if, pursuant to the rules of enforcement proceedings they are considered as enforcement documents and if they contain a precise designation of the land or the right being entered (Art. 60/1/b LRA).
368. Articles 120, 119/2, 220/1,4, 263/1,4, 288/1,5, 309/1,4 PA.
369. Article 34/3 LRA.
370. Josipović in *Land Registration Law*, 196–206.

entered (ownership, easements, real burdens, right to build, mortgage) and personal rights (buyback, pre-empting, lease, rent), as well as concessions. Conditional registration is carried out on the basis of private documents fulfilling the general preconditions for entries but not fulfilling all the necessary preconditions for registration.[371] Conditional registration is also carried out on the basis of some public documents.[372] The legal effects of conditional registration are the acquisition, loss, restriction or transfer of land register rights under the condition of subsequent justification.[373] Such legal effects exist until the conditional registration is justified, i.e., until the fault, due to which registration was not allowed, is set aside or until the conditional registration is deleted from the land register as unjustified. With the justification of the conditional registration, or with the subsequent fulfilment of the precondition which was missing in order for the registration to be carried out, the conditional registration is turned into full registration. The legal effects of such justification ensue at the time of the submission of the request to the land register court to enter a conditional registration, i.e., from the moment it is entered in the land register.[374] Conditional registration can be justified in various ways.[375] If conditional

371. For example, conditional registration will be allowed if a private document does not contain the necessary clause (*intabulandi*), or a precise designation of the land or the right being entered, or when in such a private document the signature of the person whose right is restricted, encumbered, abolished or transferred by the entry is not certified (Arts 57 LRA). Conditional registration will be allowed instead of registration when a private document has been drawn up by an authorized representative and when the power of attorney has not been certified, or when it is older than one year (Art. 58 LRA). Conditional registration will be allowed when the land registry clause (clausula *intabulandi)* is given, subject to a condition or a time limit (Art. 61/2 LRA). For example, when the seller agrees in the sale contract that the buyer be entered as the owner but only after he has paid the purchase price in full.
372. Conditional registration will be allowed on the basis of the following public documents: (a) unenforceable domestic court decision by which a proprietary right is unconditionally determined, awarded, or unconditionally dismissed (Art. 64/a LRA); (b) domestic court rulings or decisions by other authorities having equivalent effect whereby conditional registration is ordered as a security measure (Art. 64/b LRA); (c) other public documents specified by a separate law.
373. Due to the fact that upon justification, conditional registration can be turned into full registration, conditional registration is of particular substantive law significance for acquisition, modification or termination of proprietary rights on real property based on a legal transaction. It also constitutes a particular mode of acquisition, modification or termination of property rights on immovables by contract *inter vivos*. Under the condition of subsequent justification, it results in the acquisition, modification or termination of property rights on immovable by contract whose registration was not possible at the moment of the submission of the proposal for entry because not all the necessary preconditions had been fulfilled (Arts 121/1,2,3, 220/2, 263/2, 309/2 of the PA). If conditional registration is subsequently justified, the property right is considered as acquired, modified or terminated from the moment the proposal on entry by conditional registration has been submitted to the court (Arts 121/4, 220/2, 263/2, 309/2 PA).
374. Article. 65 LRA. Therefore, one of the most important functions of conditional registration is to reserve the order of priority for a right for which, at the moment of entering it in the land register, not all the preconditions for full registration have been fulfilled.
375. Conditional registration is justified: on the basis of a document appropriate for registration by which the fault, due to which registration was not allowed, is eliminated (Art. 66/a LRA); on the basis of a certificate on enforceability of a ruling rendered by a court or another competent authority (Art. 66/b of LRA); on the basis of a final ruling whereby conditional registration is justified (Art. 66/c LRA); on the basis of a public document, or a notarized document proving that the condition for the issuance of consent for registration has been met, or that the specified time limit has expired (Art. 66/d LRA).

registration is not justified, the court will, at the request of the authorized person, delete conditional registration.[376] The deletion of conditional registration creates the legal status as though such a conditional registration had never been entered and as though the conditionally entered registration of modification, transfer, restriction or termination of the land register right had never occurred.

105. Recordation (*zabilježba*) is an entry by which all relevant circumstances, according to law, may be recorded in land registers or by which certain legal effects are provided if stipulated by law.[377,378] The subject of recordation is the particular personal relations of the holders of land register rights or restrictions that are important for the legal transactions of immovables and for the management and disposition of immovables and land register rights. The subject of recordation is also various other legal facts indicating the special legal status of some immovables or legal facts that create particular legal effects of importance for the disposition of land register rights, their realization or protection.[379] The basic legal effects of every recordation are reflected in the publication of particular relations and legal facts relevant to the legal status of immovables, the possibility of disposition of land register rights and their order of priority. By recordation, it becomes transparent that in relation to a holder of a land register right or to a particular land register right itself, there are some particular relations or facts which may have an impact on the validity, possibility and model of disposition over a land register right, its acquisition, order of priority, and the like. An entry of recordation, regardless of its subject, in principle does not prevent nor eliminate the possibility of further disposition of a particular land register right unless it is otherwise specified by a regulation providing for the entry of particular recordation. In order for recordation to be entered, all material and procedural preconditions must be met, which are also prescribed for other land register entries. A recordation will be allowed only against a person who is entered in the land register as the holder of the right for which recordation is made.[380] In order to enter a recordation in the land register, it is necessary to provide a document fulfilling all the general preconditions for its validity.[381] As a rule, any recordation is entered upon the proposal of an authorized person,[382] i.e., a person who has a legal interest in the entry of a recordation or is authorized to do so pursuant to a separate regulation.[383] A recordation will also be entered on a proposal given by a court or any other competent body. In some cases, it can also be

376. A deletion of unjustified conditional registration may be requested by the person against whom such conditional registration was allowed (Art. 68LRA).
377. Article. 34/4 LRA.
378. Josipović in *Land Registration Law*, 206–233.
379. A recordation does not entail any land register rights and no acquisition, modification or termination of such rights can take place by recordation. Any recordation of land register rights (e.g., entry of condominium ownership) prior to the entry into force of the LRA and PA are considered after the entry into force of these Acts as registration of land register rights carried out pursuant to the provisions of the LRA and the PA (Art. 370/6 PA).
380. Articles 45-47 LRA.
381. Articles 48, 49 LRA.
382. Articles 103, 104 LRA.
383. Article 103/2 LRA.

entered ex officio by the land register court. With regard to the subject matter, Croatian land register law distinguishes a recordation of personal relations (*zabilježba osobnih odnosa*) and a recordation of legal facts (*zabilježba pravnih činjenica*). A recordation of personal relations in the land register clearly indicates the holder's personal relations, particularly those that are relevant for the determination of positions, capacities, scope of powers and subjective restrictions in respect of property management and disposition of land register rights.[384] The legal effects ensuing from recordation constitute the publication and transparency of the holder's personal relations with third parties. Such personal relations in legal transactions involving immovables have an absolute effect on any third parties so that no one can claim not knowing or not having known about the entered restrictions with respect to the management or disposition of immovables.[385] A recordation of legal facts results in various legal effects as stipulated in the provisions of the LRA and some other laws.[386]

§5. Land Register Procedure

106. Land registers are kept by the courts.[387] The maintenance of land registers and the adjudication of land register cases fall within the competence of courts, specifically under the competence of the land registry department within the municipal court responsible for immovables located within the court's territorial jurisdiction.[388] The first-instance court is competent for the maintenance of the land register, and it is called the land registry court. The land registry procedure is a non-contentious procedure conducted in accordance with the procedural rules established in the LRA. The legal rules of a non-contentious procedure and the CPA are applied in a subsidiary manner.[389] The land registry procedure is initiated by a proposal for entry.[390] Any natural or legal person having acquired, modified or lost a land register right is entitled to request registration or conditional registration.[391,392] Such a proposal may be submitted by a person having a legal interest in such an entry or being authorized for it by a special regulation.[393] A proposal for

384. Articles 34/4, 44 indent 1, 76 LRA.
385. The LRA only provides some examples of personal relations that are entered in the land register (minority, guardianship, extension of parental rights, declaration of bankruptcy, etc., Art. 44/al.1 LRA).
386. Article 44/al.2 LRA. The LRA provides for a large number of cases of recordation of legal facts (Arts 77-96 LRA) such as the recordation of the order of priority (Arts 77-82), recordation of a mortgage surrender and mortgage action (Arts 83-85), recordation of dispute (Arts 86-891–84), recordation of the institution of the proceedings (Art. 90 LRA), recordation of *actio Pauliana* (Arts 91, 92 recordation of an extraordinary legal remedy (Art. 93 LRA), recordation of appointment or recall of a trustee (Art. 94), recordation of the rejection of enforcement (Art. 95), recordation of an award in the enforcement procedure (Art. 96).
387. Josipović in *Land Registration Law*, 282–283.
388. Article 5 LRA.
389. Article 99 LRA.
390. Josipović in *Land Registration Law*, 288–292.
391. Article 105/1 LRA.
392. Josipović in *Land Registration Law*, 283–287.
393. Article 103/2 LRA.

entry is submitted electronically by a notary public or an attorney, as authorised users of the information system, through the e-Citizens system or in writing (directly or via post service providers).[394] On the basis of a proposal submitted by an authorized person, a decision on the entry is passed.[395] Such a decision may be passed by an authorized land registry officer, court advisor or judge.[396] The court decides whether the proposal for an entry is well-founded on the basis of the state of affairs in the land register and on the basis of the proposal and the attached documents at the time when the proposal for entry was received by the land registry court.[397] A complaint or an appeal against a ruling rendered in a land registry procedure is permitted as a regular legal remedy.[398,399] The time limit for appeals is fifteen days.[400] The time limit for an appeal may not be extended, nor is a return to the previous state of affairs allowed.[401] The jurisdiction for deciding upon the appeal depends on the organ which has rendered the first-instance decision following the proposal on entry.[402]

394. Article 105/1 LRA
395. Josipović in *Land Registration Law*, 295–299.
396. Article 122 LRA.
397. Article 116LRA. Proposals on entry are decided upon in the order of their submission to the court, or of their being received by the court. A proposal received first will be decided upon and entered in the land register before all other subsequently received proposals.
398. Article 143/1, 144 LRA.
399. Josipović in *Land Registration Law*, 305–308.
400. Article 143/5 LRA. An appeal against a ruling on entry does not postpone the execution of an entry because it is made prior to the delivery of the ruling on an entry to the parties (Arts 137/2 LRA).
401. Article 102 LRA.
402. A complaint against a ruling rendered by an authorized land registry officer will be decided upon by a land registry judge, i.e., the first-instance judge (Art. 144/2 LRA). The second-instance court (County Court) decides on an appeal against a first-instance ruling rendered by a land registry judge (Art. 146/1 LRA), as well as against a ruling by which a judge has decided on an appeal against a first-instance ruling by an authorized land registry officer (Art. 146/1 LRA).

Chapter 3. Ownership of Immovable Property

§1. CONCEPT

107. The right of ownership (*pravo vlasništva*) is a property right over a particular immovable authorizing its holder to do whatever he sees fit and to exclude any other person from it unless this is contrary to such other person's rights or limitations imposed by law.[403,404] The owner of an immovable has the same rights as the owner of any other thing (the right to possession, use, utilization and disposal of an immovable).[405] When exercising his ownership rights, the owner of an immovable is, like any other owner, limited by all general and particular statutory limitations to ownership.[406] The owner may voluntarily limit his owner's entitlements on the basis of a contract *inter vivos*. He may impose limitations on his ownership right by establishing limited property rights[407] or leasehold interests in favour of other persons.[408] The owner may also impose the prohibition to alienate or encumber his immovable[409] and lay down as a precondition for the cessation of ownership, the fulfilment of specific conditions or the expiry of a time limit.[410] He may transfer or retain his right of ownership on an immovable for the purpose of securing a claim.[411] All such limitations have an effect on third parties only if they are entered into the land register.[412]

108. The owner of immovable property may be any natural or legal, domestic or foreign person.[413] An immovable may be owned by two or more persons who, as co-owners or joint owners, possess, use or dispose of such immovable property.[414] The Republic of Croatia and other legal persons of public law who are holders of ownership rights have the same position in legal transactions as any private owners unless provided otherwise by law.[415] Foreign natural and legal persons, as holders of ownership, are generally equated with domestic persons. When acquiring ownership over immovable property, the position of foreign persons differs depending on whether a foreign person is a national or a legal person from an EU Member State. Foreign persons from the EU acquire ownership over immovable property under the same conditions as domestic persons. However, specific conditions are required when foreign natural or legal persons from outside the EU acquire immovable property.[416] In such cases, apart from the general conditions for acquisition

403. Article 30/1 PA.
404. Gavella in *Property Law I*, 373; Klarić / Vedriš in *Civil Law*, 226–230.
405. Article 30/2 PA.
406. For more details, *see* General Introduction, §2. VI. B. 3.b. Limitation of Ownership.
407. For more details, *see* Part I, Ch. 5. Limited Property Rights on Immovables.
408. For more details, *see* Part I, Ch. 6. Leasehold Interests.
409. Article 34/2 PA.
410. Article 34/3 PA.
411. Articles 34/4,5 PA. For more details, *see* Part VI. Security Rights.
412. Articles 34/3,6 PA.
413. Gavella in *Property Law I*, 388–401; Klarić / Vedriš in *Civil Law*, 245–246.
414. For more details *see* Part I, Ch. 3, §2. Ownership by More Persons.
415. Article 35 PA.
416. Articles 354–358 PA.

which must be fulfilled when domestic persons acquire immovable property, additional conditions must be met, which differ depending on the legal basis for acquisition. Besides, it is provided in separate acts that foreign natural and legal persons may not own some specific immovable property in the Republic of Croatia, and they cannot acquire it on any legal basis whatsoever.[417]

§2. Ownership by More Persons

I. Co-ownership

A. Concept

109. Co-ownership (*suvlasništvo*) is the ownership of a part (co-ownership shares, *suvlasnički dio*) of a physically undivided immovable calculated pro rata to the whole immovable owned.[418,419] Co-owners own a physically undivided immovable, and they each own a part of it arithmetically calculated pro rata to the entire right of ownership. This part of ownership is called co-owned, proportional or aliquot shares (*idealni dijelovi*).[420] Co-ownership shares are determined as fractions. If there is doubt about the size of co-ownership shares, they are considered to be equal. Co-ownership of immovable property is entered in the land register in favour and in the name of all co-owners as shares expressed in fractional numbers.[421]

110. In the case of co-ownership, ownership is divided on the basis of volume – each co-owner simultaneously possesses all ownership rights but only with respect to his proportional share. Each co-owner is the owner of a proportional share of the immovable that corresponds to his co-ownership share, and, with respect to such a share, he has the entitlements which normally belong to owners.[422] In legal transactions, the proportional share of an immovable, which is inseparable from the co-ownership share, is considered an independent thing which the owner independently disposes of.[423] A co-owner may alienate (sell, donate, exchange) his proportional share or pledge it. When a co-owner sells his co-ownership share, other co-owners do not have the right of pre-emption unless they are entitled to such right on the basis of a specific agreement between co-owners or a legal act.[424] In order to legally dispose of his proportional share, a co-owner does not need the consent or permission of other co-owners.[425,426] Each co-owner may protect his co-ownership

417. For more details, *see* Part I, Ch. 8.
418. Article 36/1 PA.
419. Gavella in *Property Law I*, 683; Klarić / Vedriš in *Civil Law*, 247–250.
420. Article 36/1 PA.
421. Article 36/1 LRA.
422. Article 37/4 PA.
423. Article 37/3 PA.
424. Article 37/5 PA.
425. A co-owner may legally dispose of his proportional share only if in such a way he does not infringe the rights of other co-owners and if by such disposal of a proportional share his rights are established that can be exercised only with respect to this proportional share and not necessarily with

and impose any requirements regarding his co-ownership share on any third party and on other co-owners.[427] All co-owners are also entitled to the right to co-possess an immovable.[428]

B. Management of Co-owned Immovable Property

111. Each co-owner is entitled to participate, together with other co-owners, in the management of co-owned immovable property.[429] They each have the right to participate in the decision-making process regarding everything that concerns the immovable property under their co-ownership with other co-owners.[430] When speaking of the management of co-owned immovables, we distinguish between the operations of ordinary management and the operations of extraordinary management:

- operations of ordinary management (e.g., minor repairs, regular maintenance, necessary maintenance, letting immovable property or leasing it for a period shorter than one year and the like) where co-owners decide by a majority vote.[431] The majority vote is calculated on the basis of co-ownership shares and not on the basis of the number of co-owners. In order to undertake operations of regular maintenance, it is necessary to reach an agreement with the co-owners whose proportional parts constitute more than half of the co-owned immovable. If such a majority vote cannot be reached, and the operation is really necessary to maintain the thing, the court will render a decision at the request of any of the co-owners;[432] and
- operations of extraordinary maintenance exceeding the framework of regular management (e.g., changing the purpose of the co-owned immovable, major repairs, additional construction works, construction of annexes, additions, adaptations, alienation of the entire immovable, leasing it for a period of more than one year, a mortgage against the entire immovable or establishment of limited

respect to the entire immovable (Art. 37/5 PA). Thus, a co-owner may establish a lien or easement of usufruct on his proportional share but he may not let or lease only his proportional share because such rights may be exercised only on the entire immovable and therefore liens or easements may be established only on the entire immovable.

426. However, co-owners may legally dispose of the entire immovable only on the basis of an agreement or in accordance with the rules on management, i.e., on decisions regarding extraordinary management (Art. 41 PA).

427. Article 46/1 PA. Each co-owner also has the right to impose requirements on other co-owners which follow from his co-ownership with respect to the entire immovable. He may also impose any requirements against third persons which may be imposed by the owners of immovables (Art. 46/2 PA).

428. Possession of an immovable may be exercised by co-owners successively (i.e., each of them at a particular time), or one co-owner may exercise possession for all other co-owners, or possession may be exercised via a third person (i.e., they may give a thing into a third person's possession).

429. Gavella in *Property Law I*, 692; Klarić / Vedriš in *Civil Law*, 251.

430. Article 39/1 PA.

431. Article 40/1 PA.

432. Articles 40/2-4 PA.

property rights on the entire immovable, appointment of a manager)[433] require an agreement reached by all co-owners.[434] If no agreement is reached among the co-owners on an operation of extraordinary management, a court cannot render a decision at the request of a co-owner who has proposed a particular operation. This co-owner may then only request a dissolution of co-ownership.[435]

C. Dissolution of Co-ownership

112. Each co-owner has the right to dissolve co-ownership (*razvgrnuće suvlasničke zajednice*),[436] i.e., he may request its partition. The dissolution of co-ownership results in its expiry, and each co-owner acquires the right of ownership over a particular physical part of the divided immovable property previously co-owned or may acquire some other right ensuing from the co-ownership share with which he participated in the dissolution (i.e., the right to be paid out in accordance with his co-ownership share after the immovable is sold). A co-owner may not validly waive his right to dissolution in advance, and it is only possible to stipulate limitations to the right to dissolution.[437] A co-owner may request dissolution at any time unless this would be to the detriment of other co-owners.[438] The right to dissolution can be exercised:

> in agreement with other co-owners (voluntary dissolution, dobrovoljno razvrgnuće), whereby all co-owners agree on the method of dissolution which is possible and permitted.[439] If the partition of a thing is prohibited by a statutory provision, this does not relate to dissolution by payment or civil dissolution;[440]
>
> through the court (court dissolution, sudsko razvrgnuće). In this case, the method of dissolution is decided by the court, which is bound by strict statutory provisions and by the agreement of the parties if it exists and by the

433. Co-owners may agree on entrusting management of their co-owned immovable to a person acting as manager (Art. 44 PA). They may choose one or more persons among themselves, but they can also entrust management to any other person. A manager receives orders from the co-owners and when it comes to his rights, duties and termination of duty, the rules on orders apply accordingly, unless it is otherwise determined in the management agreement. The appointment of a manager is entered in the land register on the motion of any of the co-owners (Art. 87/1 PA).
434. Article 41/1 PA.
435. Article 41/3 PA.
436. Articles 47–56 PA.
437. For example, a co-owner may oblige himself not to request dissolution for a certain period of time, but he may not waive his right to request it. The limitation of the right to dissolution is entered in the land register on the proposal of an interested person based on a contract on the limitation of the right to dissolution. This limitation then obliges any successors of the co-owner who has limited his right to dissolution. For more details on the recordation of the limitation of the right to dissolution, *see* Arts 247–248 PA.
438. However, even then it is possible to request dissolution if, concerning the circumstances, it is not reasonable to expect them to change so that dissolution is not detrimental to other co-owners (Art. 47/2 PA).
439. Article 49/1 PA.
440. Article 49/2 PA.

right of any of the co-owners to civil partition by payment.[441] If the court is not bound by strict statutory provisions or by a valid, possible and permissible agreement by the parties regarding the method of dissolution, the court will order the following:

geometrical partition of immovable property (geometrijska dioba).[442] The court orders geometrical partition only when this is possible without significantly diminishing the value of the particular immovable property.[443] On the basis of a court decision on geometrical partition, each co-owner acquires ownership of a particular plot (cadastral unit) created by partition, but only after it has been entered in the land register;[444]

civil partition (civilna dioba), if geometrical partition, would significantly diminish the value of the particular immovable property.[445] The immovable is then sold at an auction or in any other appropriate way, and the received amount is divided in proportion to the co-ownership shares. The special form of civil partition is civil partition by payment (dioba isplatom). With such a partition, the immovable in question comes under the ownership of one of the co-owners, who must then pay the other owners the equivalent of the value of their shares within the time limit prescribed by the court, depending on the existing circumstances.[446] The civil partition by payment is possible if it is stipulated by law, or determined by a legal transaction, or if on the side of one co-owner, a particularly serious reason exists for such partition;[447]

equivalent dissolution of co-ownership (dioba po ekvivalentu).[448] This applies when the same persons own as co-owners several pieces of immovable property. Dissolution is carried on the request of any of the co-owners if such a request is justified. Instead of dividing every single immovable, each co-owner receives one or more pieces of immovable property in

441. Article 50/1 PA.
442. Article 50/2 PA.
443. In the case of geometrical partition, the court may establish servitudes, real burdens and the right to build on other parts if it is deemed necessary for the use or utilization of the part being separated by such partition (Arts 50/3, 226, 265, 289 PA).
444. Article 55/2 PA. Enforcement of the decision on dissolution, as well as an entry in the land register, may be requested by any of the co-owners participating in the dissolution, regardless of the fact upon whose motion the court has adjudicated (Art. 55/3 PA). When dissolution is carried out by geometrical partition, it is necessary first to carry out the procedure of writing off plots from a former land register unit and then enter the ownership of the individual plots resulting from the partition in favour of all co-owners in conformity with the court decision on dissolution in new established land register unit for new plots. If the immovable on which geometrical partition was carried out had been encumbered by a lien and the lienor did not agree to unencumbered write off, the lien would continue burdening, in an undivided manner, all plots which came into being by geometrical partition (Art. 56/2 PA).
445. Article 50/4 PA.
446. In order to carry out partition by payment, a co-owner who seeks to own an immovable must prove that there is an extremely serious reason for such partition. This is not necessary if the co-owner seeking partition by payment owns at least 9/10 of the entire immovable (Art. 51/3 PA).
447. Article 51 PA.
448. Article 52 PA.

proportion to the size of their co-ownership shares, taking into account their needs; and

dissolution by the establishment of condominium[449] will be ordered by the court only if all co-owners have agreed to establish condominium on their immovable. The court is not bound to order such dissolution at the request of an individual co-owner despite the fact that he has enough big co-ownership share and justified interest in such dissolution unless there is an agreement reached by all co-owners to establish the condominium on the whole immovable.[450]

II. Joint Ownership

A. Concept

113. Joint ownership (*zajedničko vlasništvo*) is the ownership of more persons on a physically undivided immovable whereby all of them have shares in it whose size is not determined, although it is determinable.[451,452] An immovable may be jointly owned only on the basis of the law.[453] Joint ownership of immovable property is entered in the land register in favour and in the name of all joint owners, with the indication that such entry refers to joint ownership.[454] The rules on ownership apply subordinately to joint ownership unless this is regulated by some other act or different circumstances arise from the nature of such ownership.[455]

B. Management of Jointly Owned Immovable Property

114. Joint owners are authorized to enforce together their entitlements regarding jointly owned immovable property.[456,457] Fruits and other benefits deriving from a jointly owned immovable belong to all joint owners. They are held jointly and severally liable for any costs and burdens relating to the jointly owned immovable. Any joint owner is entitled to participate in the decision-making process concerning a

449. Article 53 PA.
450. For more details on the dissolution of co-ownership, *see* Gavella in *Property Law I*, 704–718; Klarić / Vedriš in *Civil Law*, 254–256.
451. Article 57/1 PA.
452. Gavella in *Property Law I*, 721–723; Klarić / Vedriš in *Civil Law*, 256.
453. For example, at the time of death of a testator, a successor acquires joint ownership of things constituting the legacy until their shares are established (the so-called community of successors, Arts 141–145 of Inheritance Act/IA NN RC 48/03, 163/03, 35/05). The property of a partnership is the property of all partners (Art. 638/3 of OA). Joint reserve funds paid by all co-owners based on their ownership on flats/condominium (Art. 89 PA) are the joint property of all co-owners (Art. 90/1 PA).
454. Article 36/3 of LRA.
455. Article 65 PA.
456. Article 59/1 PA.
457. Gavella in *Property Law I*, 727–730; Klarić / Vedriš in *Civil Law*, 257.

jointly owned immovable with other joint owners. The decisions on the management of a jointly owned immovable are made by all joint owners together and by mutual agreement.[458] All joint owners dispose together of such a jointly owned immovable. An individual joint owner may independently dispose of an immovable only if authorized by all other joint owners.[459] A third person may not acquire the rights on an immovable on the basis of a legal transaction not entered into by all joint owners.[460] However, a third person may exceptionally acquire ownership of the entire jointly owned immovable even when the third person has entered into a legal transaction with only one joint owner in whose favour the ownership of the entire immovable is entered in the land register under all the preconditions providing for the protection of trust in the completeness of the land register when entering into legal transactions.[461]

C. Partition of Joint Ownership

115. Partition of joint ownership is performed on request of any joint owner. It is performed by determining the size of his share in the jointly owned immovable property.[462] The size of a share is determined in an agreement made by all joint owners. If such an agreement does not exist, the court decides on the size of a share on the request of any joint owner under the criteria for a particular case provided for in the statutory act regulating the joint ownership of things. The partition of joint ownership of immovable property results in co-ownership in favour of the previous joint owners. Any legal relations are then regulated by the provisions of the PA providing for co-ownership.[463]

III. Ownership of Individual Parts of Immovable Property (Condominium)

A. Concept

116. In Croatian law, ownership of an individual part of immovable property/condominium (*vlasništvo posebnog dijela nekretnine, etažno vlasništvo*) such as a flat, business premises or some other independent space in a building is regulated as

---

458. Article 60/2 PA.
459. Article 61/1 PA.
460. A joint owner may transfer his share of joint ownership in legal transactions *inter vivos* either fully or partially only to another joint owner, and the joint owner's share in such joint ownership, upon his death, will pass onto his heirs (Art. 58/1,2 PA).
461. Article 61/2/al.2 PA. Due to the fact that in the land register ownership of immovable property is entered only in favour of one joint owner, the land register *status quo* will be considered as incomplete because not all other joint owners have been entered. A decent acquirer who has acted bona fide will then, under the rules on the protection of trust, acquire full ownership of immovable property. The same rules apply when a decent acquirer requires limited real rights on immovable property from the registered owner (e.g., a lien). For more details, *see* Part I, Ch. 2, §2. III. The Protection of Trust.
462. Article 63/2 PA.
463. Gavella in *Property Law I*, 730-731; Klarić / Vedriš in *Civil Law*, 258.

a special form of ownership based on the co-ownership of the entire immovable property (land with a building). The ownership of a specific, individual part of immovable property is based on the co-ownership of the entire immovable property, i.e., the land with a building.[464] Ownership of such an individual part of immovable property follows, and it is inseparably connected to the corresponding co-owned share (proportional share) of the immovable on which it is established.[465,466] The owner of an individual part of immovable property is actually the co-owner of the entire immovable property consisting of the land with the building, but the enforcement of his co-owner's rights is limited only to the individual part of the immovable property constituting an independent whole for specific use, such as a flat, business premises or any other kind of independent space. Only a person who is a co-owner of an immovable may be the owner of its individual part, i.e., he may limit his co-ownership rights to be enforced only on a particular individual part of immovable property.[467] A particular co-owner's right to use and dispose of an individual part is inseparably connected to his co-ownership share. Co-ownership and the use of an individual part of immovable property constitute a legal unity: ownership of an individual part follows from and is inseparably connected to the co-ownership share of the entire immovable.[468] Such ownership is entered in the land register and is added to the co-ownership share of the co-owner with whose co-owned share the ownership of an individual part is connected. An individual part of immovable property (a flat, business premises and the like), with an indication of all accessory particles to which it extends (balconies, terraces, cellar or loft rooms, gardens and the like), is entered into the land register and inscribed on the co-ownership share of the co-owner with whose share the ownership of an individual part is connected.[469]

B. An Individual Part of Immovables

117. Ownership of an individual part of immovable property may be established only on an individual part of immovable property (*samostalna uporabna cjelina*) – a part of an immovable considered as an independent unit which is suitable for use in the independent exercise of the owner's rights, such as a flat, business premises, independent garages or other clearly demarcated places in a building where motor vehicles are kept.[470,471] An individual part of an immovable is a unit which can be

464. Ownership of an individual part of immovable property, apart from the fact that it may be established on land with a building on it, may also be established on the right to build with a building. All the rules which apply to the ownership of an individual part established on the land with a building apply accordingly to the ownership of an individual part of a building built on land with the right to build with a building (Arts 66/3, 75/1 PA).
465. Article 66/1 PA.
466. Belaj in *Property Law I*, 735–742; Klarić / Vedriš in *Civil Law*, 264–265.
467. Therefore, the rules on co-ownership apply to the ownership of an individual part of immovable property, unless separate rules on the ownership of individual parts of immovable stipulate otherwise (Art. 66/4 PA).
468. Article 66/1 PA.
469. Article 36/2 LRA.
470. Articles 67/1,2 PA.

used independently and where the owner can exercise his rights independently, without limiting, disturbing or bothering other co-owners in the exercise of their rights in other independent parts of the same immovable.[472]

C. Accessory and Common Parts of Immovables

118. Ownership of an individual part may not be established on so-called accessory parts of the immovable (open balconies, terraces, cellars, attics, gardens, etc.). If any such parts serve for exclusive use in favour of only one individual part, the ownership of that individual part may also extend to such an accessory part (*sporedni dijelovi*).[473] [474] Ownership of an individual part may not exist on the common parts of immovable property, i.e., the parts which all co-owners use while exercising their rights in individual parts of the immovable.[475] It also may not exist on the part whose purpose prevents the exclusive use in favour of a specific individual part.[476]

119. Accessories and common parts (*zajednički dijelovi*) may not be independent objects at the owners' disposal in legal transactions. They are disposed of together with individual parts of immovable property. When ownership of an individual part of an immovable is alienated, the alienator's rights on accessory and common parts of an immovable are also transferred on to the new owner. The purpose of some accessory or common parts of an immovable may be changed into an individual part of the immovable but only with the consent of all co-owners.

D. Rights and Duties of Owners in Relation to Individual Parts of Immovables

120. Ownership of individual parts of immovables differs from 'ordinary' co-ownership in the way the co-ownership rights and duties are exercised. The owner of an individual part of an immovable has his co-ownership rights on the

471. Gavella in *Property Law I*, 744; Klarić / Vedriš in *Civil Law*, 265–266.
472. An administrative body competent for construction must confirm whether a specific part of an immovable constitutes an independent-use unit (Art. 73/3 PA). Such confirmation is one of the preconditions for entering the ownership of an individual part of immovable in the land register.
473. Ownership of an individual part may extend to an accessory part only if these accessory parts are clearly bordered off from other parts of an immovable and accessible from the boundary of the immovable or its common parts, or from a flat or an independent space whose accessory part they constitute, such as clearly demarcated spaces in cellars, attics or the like (Art. 67/4 PA). The rules which apply to appurtenances apply accordingly to accessory parts (Art. 67/5 PA).
474. Belaj in *Property Law I*, 743; Klarić / Vedriš in *Civil Law*, 266.
475. Common parts of a building are determined in the Ordinance on Building Maintenance (OG No. 64/97). Common parts of a building are as follows: the bearing construction of a building (foundations, bearing walls, pillars, constructions between floors, roof constructions, and the like), roofing tiles, passable and impassable terraces, façades including windows and doors, fire prevention systems, common stairways, elevators, etc.
476. Article 67/6 PA. When there is doubt about whether a part of an immovable is accessory or common, it will be considered as common and its purpose may not be the exclusive use in favour of a specific individual part (Art. 67/6 PA).

entire immovable, but he actually does not exercise them with respect to the entire immovable. The exercise of his co-ownership rights and duties focuses on a specific individual part of the immovable which he may legally and factually dispose of, manage it in place of all other co-owners, as well as exercise all his rights and duties, as if this particular individual part were his own.[477] Other co-owners of the same immovable are excluded from exercising their owner's entitlements on this particular co-ownership share.

121. The co-owner, i.e., the owner of an individual part of an immovable, manages his individual part alone, without other co-owners. He exercises all his rights and duties on this individual part as if it were his own property. All fruits and other benefits coming from this individual part belong to him.[478] The owner is obliged to look after it and maintain it, and in such a way, avoid any damages caused to other co-owners.[479] He maintains this individual part at his own expense, and he alone fulfils all his public obligations and burdens. A co-owner on whose co-ownership share ownership of an individual part is established must pay the fees for electricity, gas, heating, waste collection, and the like. He may do repairs and change the purpose of his individual part, but such changes may not cause any damage to the building or to other parts of the immovable, and they must not infringe on other co-owners' rights.[480]

E. Disposing of an Individual Part of an Immovable

122. The owner of an individual part of an immovable may independently dispose of his individual part in legal transactions, as is the case with any other owned thing. In order to dispose legally of the ownership of an individual part of immovable property, it is not necessary to obtain the consent of the owners of other individual parts of the immovable.[481] However, in order for an individual part of an immovable to be legally disposed of in legal transactions, a special procedure of establishing ownership on individual parts of an immovable must be carried out. Ownership of an individual part of immovable property must be entered in the land register.[482,483]

123. The owner may sell, donate, exchange or alienate his individual part in any legal transaction *inter vivos* and in the case of death. Easements may be established on individual parts, including personal servitudes, which otherwise could not be

477. Articles 66/2, 79 PA.
478. Article 79 PA.
479. Article 80 PA.
480. Article 84 PA.
481. Belaj in *Property Law I*, 766–779; Klarić / Vedriš in *Civil Law*, 269.
482. Article 69/2 PA. Prior to the establishment of ownership on an individual part of an immovable, a co-owner may dispose only of his co-ownership share in accordance with the general provisions on disposing of co-ownership.
483. For more on the establishment of ownership on individual parts of immovables, *see* Part I, Ch. 3, §2. III. G. Establishment of Ownership on an Individual Part of Immovable Property.

established on a proportional (ideal) share of an immovable.[484] Namely, due to its content and nature, the right of use[485] and the right of habitation[486] may not be exercised on a proportional part of immovable property. The owner of an individual part may establish any security right on his individual part. He may mortgage his co-ownership share connected to the ownership of an individual part of immovable property, or he may fiduciary transfer ownership of an individual part as a form of security.[487] Every new owner of an individual part of immovable property or an acquirer of a limited property right on an individual part enters into a legal relationship which arises from the establishment of ownership of an individual part. The legal position of each acquirer, regardless of the right acquired on the individual part of an immovable, is determined by the legal relations created between the co-owners upon the establishment of ownership on individual part of immovable property, by the limitations following the ownership of an individual part, as well as by the limitations entered in the land register with regard to a co-ownership share.

124. In legal transactions involving individual parts of immovable property, the object of legal disposal is always a co-ownership share of an immovable to which the ownership of an individual part of an immovable is inseparably connected.[488] Any disposal of an individual part of an immovable is actually a disposal of the co-ownership share of the entire immovable (land with a building).[489] Such disposal relates to the individual part to which it is connected, the accessory part to which the ownership of an individual part extends, the co-ownership share of the land (cadastre unit) on which the building is erected, and the co-ownership share of common parts and installations in and on the building because they together constitute a particular immovable.

125. All provisions of the PA and other regulations on acquisition, disposal and termination of property rights on immovable property apply accordingly to the legal disposal of individual parts of immovables, their disposal and termination. When property rights on an individual part of immovable property are acquired, transferred, limited or terminated on the basis of a legal transaction, entry in the land register is a way and a model for the acquisition, transfer or termination of property

484. Article 200/2 PA.
485. Articles 212–216 PA.
486. Article 217 PA.
487. When enforcement is carried out to cover a secured claim, it is carried out on a proportional share connected with an individual part. In the case of a forced auction, all limitations resulting from the ownership of an individual part of an immovable are transferred on the purchaser, regardless of the rank in the land register and without calculating it into the highest bid (Art. 69/3 PA).
488. Article 66/1 PA.
489. Legal transactions in which the object of disposal is only an individual part, without the co-ownership share to which it is connected, or only some accessory and common parts of the immovable, a physical part of land or the like, are contrary to the principle of the legal unity of immovable property, and they do not produce any legal effects (Art. 366/3 PA).

rights on an individual part of immovable property.[490] In all other cases, when property rights on individual parts of immovable property are acquired, transferred, limited or terminated based on law, succession, a court decision, or when a decision is rendered by another competent body, the change entered in the land register is only declaratory, i.e., of a public nature.

F. Rights and Duties of Owners with Regard to the Entire Immovable

126. Co-owners, on whose co-ownership shares the ownership of individual parts is established, manage the entire immovable, i.e., the whole land with a building, according to the general rules on the management of a co-owned immovable.[491] The co-owners are obliged to participate in the management of immovable property, appoint a person as their joint manager and establish their joint reserve funds. Their mutual relations regarding the management of immovable property may be decided upon in an agreement.[492] All decisions regarding individual operations are made in writing. We distinguish between regular and extraordinary management.[493] Co-owners are obliged to cover the expenses for the maintenance and improvement of their immovable property in proportion to their co-ownership shares. In order to cover their expenses for the maintenance and improvement of their immovable property and to pay back the loans for such expenses, co-owners are obliged to establish their joint reserve funds and pay regular contributions to cover such expenses in proportion to their co-ownership shares.[494] They must also choose a person to carry out the tasks of a joint manager.[495] A joint manager may be appointed by the co-owners, and decisions on his appointment and dismissal must be made by a majority vote of the co-owners according to their co-ownership shares.[496]

490. Articles 119/1, 120/1, 220/1, 263/1, 288, 309/1,2 PA.
491. Article 85/1 PA.
492. Articles 85/2,3 PA.
493. The operations of regular management requiring an agreement reached by the co-owners who together own more than half the immovable property include the following: regular maintenance of common parts and equipment in and on their immovable, a plan how to use their joint reserve funds, taking loans to cover the costs of maintenance which are not covered by the reserve funds, the appointment and dismissal of a joint manager, determining and changing the house rules, and the like (Art. 86 PA). For any extraordinary operations and to make decisions on various improvements of the common areas and equipment in and on the immovable (e.g., reconstruction of roofs, new elevators, etc.), it is necessary to have the approval of all co-owners of the immovable (Art. 87/1 PA).
494. The amount paid into the joint reserve funds is decided upon by a majority vote of all co-owners because such a decision is considered to belong to regular management. The funds kept as joint reserves are managed by all co-owners or by a manager appointed by them (Art. 90 PA).
495. Article 85/2 of /A.
496. Gavella in *Property Law I*, 772-773; Klarić / Vedriš in *Civil Law*, 270–271.

G. Establishment of Ownership on an Individual Part of Immovable Property

1. Concept

127. The establishment of ownership on an individual part of an immovable (land with building) means connecting a corresponding co-ownership share of the immovable to a particular individual part of the same immovable.[497] In the procedure of establishment of ownership on an individual part, the co-owners agree on their legal relations in terms of exercising their co-ownership rights on land with a building, i.e., on particular parts of the immovable (individual, common and accessory parts of immovable property).

128. In order to establish ownership of an individual part of immovable property, the following general and specific preconditions set forth in Articles 71–75 of the PA must be fulfilled. The first precondition for the establishment of ownership on an individual part is that a building is already finished, which, together with the land, makes up a legal unity.[498] Ownership may be established only on an individual part of immovable property, which is considered an independent-use unit (a flat, business premises, etc.). A co-owner who requests the establishment of ownership must possess a corresponding co-ownership share unless it is otherwise determined by law. In order to establish ownership of an individual part, it is also necessary to have a valid legal basis and an appropriate mode of establishment. Ownership of an individual part of immovable property is established by its entry in the land register.[499]

2. Establishment of Ownership on Co-ownership Shares of All Co-owners of Immovable Property

129. The establishment of ownership of an individual part on the co-ownership shares of all co-owners is based on an agreement reached by all co-owners, i.e., when all co-owners of the immovable agree and decide that they will all connect ownership of particular individual parts of immovable property to their co-ownership shares.[500] Ownership of an individual part is then established on the entire immovable, i.e., on all individual parts of the building. It is established on the basis of a written co-owners' agreement where each co-owner clearly and unambiguously expresses his will and approval that each co-owner will connect a specific individual part to his co-ownership share. Due to the fact that all co-owners have agreed on which individual part will be connected to the proportional share of

---

497. Articles 66/1, 68 PA.
498. A building whose individual parts are connected to the corresponding co-ownership shares must be built and must be entered in the land register. A building is entered in the land register according to the rules governing an entry of a change of a built-up land (Art. 10/4 LRA).
499. Article 721 PA. All these preconditions must be fulfilled even when ownership of an individual part is established on the right to build with a building.
500. Articles 43/4, 68/3 PA.

each co-owner, it is not crucial that their parts correspond to the size of their co-ownership shares. Ownership of an individual part may be established regardless of the size of co-ownership shares, even when a particular co-ownership share is not of a corresponding size.[501] The legal foundation for the establishment of ownership on an individual part of immovable property is the written agreement of all co-owners to connect ownership of a specific individual part of immovable property to their co-ownership shares.[502] Ownership of an individual part will be established only after it has been entered in the land register,[503] i.e., only after registration has been made in the land register. An entry in the land register is of a constitutive nature for the establishment of ownership on an individual part of immovable property.[504] In order to register, apart from this document, a competent administrative authority must confirm that individual parts are independent-use units.[505,506]

3. Establishment of Ownership on a Co-ownership Share of a Single Co-owner

130. Ownership of an individual part may be established on a co-ownership part of only one co-owner in such a way that the ownership of a particular individual part is connected only to his co-ownership share. This is possible only if the co-owner who requests it has at least a corresponding co-ownership share in immovable property.[507] A co-ownership share must at least be big enough so that it corresponds to the relationship of the use value of an individual part against the use value of all the flats and other premises of the same immovable.[508]

131. In order to connect the ownership of an individual part of immovable property to the co-ownership share of a co-owner, it is necessary to have the consent of all the co-owners of a particular immovable.[509] A document in which all the co-owners give consent for a particular co-owner to connect the ownership of an individual part to his co-ownership share is the legal basis for the establishment of

501. Article 68/3 PA. Therefore, no court decision on the corresponding co-ownership share is necessary for the establishment of ownership of individual parts. It is replaced by a co-owner's document where all co-owners express their will concerning which co-owner will become the owner of which individual part (Art. 73/4 PA).
502. A document containing such an agreement must expressly specify which individual part is connected to whose co-ownership share and to which accessory parts the ownership of an individual part is connected.
503. Article 72 PA.
504. Ownership does not exist before it is entered in the land register and it is, therefore, impossible to dispose of the ownership of an individual part of immovable property. A co-owners' agreement on the establishment of ownership on an individual part prior to registration is only an agreement on the execution of co-ownership powers on immovable property (Art. 43/5 PA).
505. Article 73/3 PA.
506. Belaj in *Property Law I*, 738–759; Klarić / Vedriš in *Civil Law*, 256.
507. Article 71/1 PA.
508. Article 68/1 PA. This is decided by the court in contentious proceedings initiated on the proposal of co-owners in accordance with the rules referred to in Art. 74 PA. The establishment of ownership on an individual part is possible only on the basis of a final court decision on the establishment of the use value of a flat (Art. 73/4 PA).
509. Article 73/1 PA.

flat ownership. If a co-owner does not want to give consent, he cannot in any way be forced to do so, and no court decision may be a substitute for his consent.[510] An exception to this rule exists only in the case of a co-owner to whose co-ownership share the ownership of an individual part had already previously been connected. This co-owner, as a rule, cannot deny consent to another co-owner for the establishment of ownership on an individual part.[511] At the request of a co-owner who has a corresponding co-ownership share, the ownership of an individual part of immovable property will also be established only upon registration in the land register.[512]

4. Establishment of Ownership on the Basis of a Declaration by the Owner of Immovable Property

132. Ownership of an individual part of immovable property may also be established on an immovable (land with a building) owned by a single person. In order to establish ownership of an individual part of immovable property owned by a single person, the owner must first divide his ownership into co-ownership shares.[513] In a document suitable for registration in the land register, the owner must declare that he is dividing his ownership into co-ownership shares. Only after having divided his ownership into co-ownership shares may the owner, in a document suitable for registration, declare that he is connecting ownership of particular individual parts of immovable property to a particular co-ownership share. The ownership of an individual part will be established when, on the basis of such documents, registration or conditional registration in the land register is carried out.[514]

5. Establishment of Ownership of an Individual Part by Additions, Annexes or Conversions

133. It is possible to acquire ownership of an individual part by additions, annexes or adaptations of someone else's building or business premises through alterations, building in, or investing only if the owner of the building, or all co-owners, have agreed to this, and if all the preconditions required for the establishment of ownership of an individual part of immovable property have been fulfilled. When annexes, additions or any other alterations are carried out without the

510. If there is no co-owners' agreement on the establishment of ownership on an individual part, each of them may request dissolution of co-ownership pursuant to the corresponding provisions PA.
511. Article 73/2 PA. A co-owner with whose co-ownership share the ownership of an individual part is already established may deny his consent only if, by such establishment, the rights which already belong to him on the basis of his previously established ownership of an individual part would thus be revoked or limited (Art. 73/2 PA).
512. Article 72 PA.
513. Article 75/1 PA.
514. Article 72/1 PA. In the case of the establishment of ownership on an individual part of immovable property owned by one person, it is not necessary for the court to render a decision on the establishment of use values (Art. 75/2 PA).

owner's or the co-owners' consent, whatever is added, annexed, or built-in belongs to the owner or co-owners of immovable property pursuant to the rules on its legal unity.[515]

134. A decision by which someone is allowed to add, annex or reconstruct a building or a part of the building in such a way that it becomes an individual part of the immovable owned by the person who has built it is an operation of extraordinary management, and all co-owners must agree to it. Such consent must be given in the form of a document appropriate for registration in the land register. A court decision may not be a substitute for the denied consent of a co-owner, regardless of the size of his co-owned part and regardless of the reasons for which such consent is denied.

135. Ownership of an individual part created by additions, annexes and adaptations is entered in the land register according to the general rules on registering the ownership of individual parts. The person responsible for building it will be entered in the land register as a co-owner of immovable property to whose co-ownership share the ownership of an individual part (e.g., an annexed flat) is connected. A land register entry will be made on the basis of the written consent of all co-owners and other documents necessary for the ownership of an individual part to be entered into the land register. The application for ownership to be entered in the land register must contain a document in which the co-owners have agreed in establishing the new sizes of their co-ownership shares of immovable property and have re-determined their legal relations resulting from the changed use values of individual parts of the immovable.[516] The construction of a new individual part of immovable property changes the use values of particular individual parts and their relations towards the entire use value of all flats and other premises of the entire immovable, as well as their proportional shares and the shares in co-ownership of all co-owners of the relevant immovable property.[517]

136. Ownership of an individual part of immovable property acquired by a change of purpose or by additions, annexes or adaptations on a socially owned building before the PA came into force is governed by separate rules referred to in Articles 372 and 373 of the PA. In that case, ownership of an individual part of immovable property is established *ex lege* at the time when the PA became effective (1 January 1997) under the preconditions specified in Articles 372 and 373 of the PA. Ownership of an individual part is acquired if the construction works are carried out at a person's own expense and on the basis of an approval obtained from

515. The provisions of the Obligations Act determine whether those who add, annex, reconstruct or invest in the building are entitled to compensation (Art. 156/2 PA).
516. Articles 76–78 PA.
517. The new co-ownership shares may be established with the agreement of all co-owners in a special agreement without a court decision. The change of use values may be established by the court on the proposal of a person who wishes to acquire ownership of an individual part after the construction (Art. 77/1 PA) with the preconditions set forth in Art. 77 PA. When the court has established the new use values, the co-owners are obliged to take over or to transfer their co-ownership shares in order for each co-owner to have a corresponding co-ownership share (Art. 77/2 PA).

the competent authority given within the limits of its powers for such proprietary disposition.[518] With the entry into force of the PA, the persons who changed the purpose, built on, added or annexed an individual part became *ex lege* co-owners of the immovable to whose co-ownership share the ownership of a flat or another independent room was inseparably connected.

§3. Acquisition of Ownership

I. Legal Titles for Acquisition

137. Ownership of immovable property may be acquired by contract *inter vivos*, on the basis of a court decision or a decision by some other competent authority, upon death (by inheritance) or on the basis of law.[519] In each of these legal titles for acquisition, ownership is acquired only when all the preconditions stipulated by law have been fulfilled.[520] The PA specifies the conditions for each of these legal titles for acquisition.[521]

II. Acquisition by Contract *Inter Vivos*

138. Ownership of immovable property may be acquired by contract *inter vivos* if three conditions are fulfilled: ownership of the predecessor – a person who is registered as such in the land register, a valid contract whose aim is the transfer of ownership concluded in writing[522] and an entry in the land register as a modus, i.e., registration, or conditional registration in favour of the acquirer.[523,524] The ownership of property not entered in the land register is acquired by depositing a legalized document with the court, which is competent for the registration of the right in the land register.[525,526]

III. Acquisition on the Basis of a Court Decision or the Decision of Another Competent Authority

139. When ownership is acquired on the basis of a court decision or the decision of another competent authority, it is acquired at the moment a court decision,

518. Articles 372/1,2 PA.
519. Article 114/1 PA.
520. Article 114/2 PA.
521. Gavella in *Property Law I*, 429-432; Klarić / Vedriš in *Civil Law*, 273–274.
522. Article 115/3 PA.
523. Articles 119/1, 120, 121 PA.
524. Gavella in *Property Law I*, 433-471; Klarić / Vedriš in *Civil Law*, 285–294.
525. Articles 120/4, 121/5 PA.
526. For more details, *see* Part III, Ch. 2, §4. Acquisition of Ownership on the Basis of Contract *Inter Vivos*.

or the decision of another competent authority becomes enforceable unless it is otherwise stipulated in a separate act.[527] Entry in the land register is not then a condition for the acquisition of ownership on the basis of a court decision or the decision of another authority. Ownership can be entered in the land register on the acquirer‘s request.[528] An entry in the land register is necessary for the protection of ownership against all third persons and for the subsequent free disposal of the immovable, as well as to exclude the bona fide acquisition of ownership.[529,530]

IV. Acquisition upon Death (by Inheritance)

140. Ownership is acquired by inheritance at the moment of initiation of inheritance proceedings, e.g., upon the testator’s death.[531] Entry in the land register is not a precondition for the acquisition of ownership by inheritance, but an heir has the right to request to be entered in the land register as the owner.[532] The legal title for registration is a court or a notary public decision on inheritance.[533,534]

V. Acquisition on the Basis of Law

141. Ownership of immovables is acquired on the basis of law upon the fulfilment of the stipulated conditions.[535] The ownership is acquired at the moment the statutory conditions have been fulfilled.[536] The ownership of an immovable on the basis of law is acquired even without it being entered into the land register. However, a person who has acquired ownership of an immovable by operation of law is entitled to request its registration in the land register. The registration of ownership acquired by operation of law is important so that it can be proven and protected in relation to any third persons and to preclude the bona fide acquisition of ownership by third persons.[537] The ownership of an immovable can be acquired on the basis of law in several cases, such as building on the land of another,[538] additions, adaptations, reconstructions or investments in another’s building,[539] acquisitive prescription,[540] etc.[541]

---

527. Articles 126/1,2 PA.
528. Article 127/1 PA.
529. For more details *see* Part III, Ch. 3, §2. Acquisition of Ownership on the Basis of a Court Decision or the Decision of Another Competent Authority.
530. Gavella in *Property Law I*, 471–492.
531. Article 128/1 PA.
532. Article 128/2 PA.
533. For more details *see* Part III, Ch. 4. Acquisition of Property Rights Upon Death (by Inheritance).
534. Gavella in *Property Law I*, 492–497; Klarić / Vedriš in *Civil Law*; 708, Gavella/ Belaj in *Inheritance Law*, 20.
535. Gavella in *Property Law I*, 497–579; Klarić / Vedriš in *Civil Law*, 274–285.
536. Article 129/1 PA.
537. Article 130 PA.
538. Article 135 PA.
539. Article 156 PA.
540. Articles 159,160. PA.

§4. Protection of Ownership

142. Ownership of immovables is protected in court proceedings before municipal courts. Territorial jurisdiction to conduct proceedings for the protection of ownership of immovable property is vested in the municipal court on whose territory the relevant immovable is located.[542] The PA stipulates various actions for the protection of ownership depending on whether an immovable has been taken from the owner's possession or if he is in some other way, except by seizure, prevented without any foundation in exercising his owner's rights. The right to the protection of ownership is not barred by the statute of limitations.[543,544]

143. When immovable property is taken from the owner's possession, the owner is entitled to take action for the return of the immovable (a true owner's action; *rei vindicatio*; *prava vlasnička tužba*).[545] This is an action by which the owner requests that the defendant (the person who possesses his immovable) surrenders it to his possession.[546] In order to succeed in the proceedings instituted by the owner's action, the owner must prove his ownership[547] and the fact that the immovable is currently in the defendant's possession. He must also individualize the immovable whose return is requested.[548,549] After the immovable is surrendered to the owner's possession, the legal relations between the owner and the possessor of the immovable are regulated depending on whether the defendant possessed the relevant immovable as a fair or an unfair possessor. This will determine the conditions for the return of the immovable, namely whether the owner is entitled to seek compensation for the use of the immovable and whether a fair possessor is entitled to be compensated for the costs incurred while using the immovable or having invested in it.[550]

541. For more details *see* Part III, Ch. 5, §2. Acquisition of Ownership on the Basis of Law.
542. Article 56 CPA.
543. Article 161/2 PA.
544. Gavella in *Property Law I*, 579–641; Klarić / Vedriš in *Civil Law*, 294–302.
545. Gavella in *Property Law I*, 592–620; Klarić / Vedriš in *Civil Law*, 294–300.
546. Article 162 PA. All co-owners or joint owners of immovables are also entitled to take action together. A court action may be taken by individual co-owners, or by a joint owner, but in that case, they may only request the return of the immovable to all co-owners or to joint owners. For more, *see* Gavella in *Property Law I*, 593.
547. Ownership of immovable property is proven exclusively by an excerpt from the land register showing that the claimant is registered as the owner of the relevant immovable.
548. Immovable property is individualized by the number of the cadastre unit and the name of the cadastral municipality. These data are given in the land register.
549. When the proceedings are initiated by an action and their outcome may have an impact on the change of registration in the land register, recordation of the dispute may be sought from the land register court or other competent court before which the proceedings are conducted (Arts 81–84 LRA).
550. Articles 164–165 PA. The position of a fair possessor is, as a rule, more favourable than that of an unfair possessor. A fair possessor does not need to pay compensation for the use of immovable property, and he is entitled to request compensation for the necessary and beneficial costs (Art. 164 PA). An unfair possessor must compensate for any damages incurred on the immovable, and he is entitled to compensation of only the necessary costs that the owner himself would have had (Art. 165 PA).

144. A person who cannot prove his ownership of immovable property may request re-possession by a specific action (an action by a presumed owner; *actio Publiciana*; *vlasnička tužba predmnjevanog vlasnika*).[551] Such an action is made by a person who is not yet the owner of a thing but is a fair possessor and has a valid legal title for the acquisition of ownership (e.g., a valid contract of sale) and has acquired possession of the alienated immovable in a truthful manner.[552] This person will be considered the owner of the immovable as opposed to a person who possesses the relevant immovable without any legal title or on a weaker legal title. In the action, the surrender of the immovable to the possession of the presumed owner is sought.[553]

145. If the immovable has not been taken from the owner's possession, but a third person unjustifiably harasses the owner in exercising his owner's entitlements, the owner is protected by a special action for harassment (*actio negatoria*; *negatorijska tužba*).[554] [555] In the proceedings, the owner must prove that he is the owner of the immovable and that the defendant is unjustifiably harassing him in exercising his owner's entitlements. The owner is then entitled to request compensation for the damage caused by harassment.[556]

146. If the violation of ownership rights is caused by an invalid entry in the land register (e.g., unjustifiable cancellation of ownership, wrong registration of a lien, etc.), the owner of immovable property is protected by a cancellation action (*brisovna tužba*).[557,558] With such an action, the owner seeks the cancellation of an invalid registration.[559] A cancellation action, as a rule, is not subject to the statute of limitations. However, if, on the basis of an invalid registration, acquisition of a property right on an immovable has occurred in favour of a bona fide acquirer, a cancellation action can no longer be filed. A cancellation action against a bona fide acquirer may be filed only within the time limits referred to in Article 129/2 of the LRA.[560]

551. Gavella in *Property Law I*, 620–624; Klarić / Vedriš in *Civil Law*, 301–302.
552. Article 166 PA.
553. All the rules on the legal position of a fair/unfair possessor, compensation for the use of immovable property, costs, exemptions from the statute of limitations et al. which are valid for *rei vindicatio* (Art. 166/4 PA).
554. Article 167 PA.
555. Gavella in *Property Law I*, 625–630; Klarić / Vedriš in *Civil Law*, 300–301.
556. Articles 167/2,3 PA.
557. Article 168 PA, Art. 150 LRA.
558. Gavella in *Property Law I*, 632–633; Klarić / Vedriš in *Civil Law*, 311–312.
559. When the owner files a cancellation action, he is authorized to seek its recordation in the land register (Art. 150 LRA).
560. For more details on the time limits for filing a cancellation action against a bona fide acquirer and on the protection of trust in the truthfulness of the land register, *see* Part I, Ch. 2, III. The Protection of Trust.

§5. TERMINATION OF OWNERSHIP

147. Ownership of immovable property may terminate in several ways as specified in Articles 163–173 of the PA.[561] Ownership ceases to exist for the prior owner when another person assumes ownership.[562] Ownership is terminated when immovable property can no longer be subject to legal transactions, i.e., when it is stipulated accordingly in the law, and it is proclaimed to be a common good.[563] Ownership of immovable property can be terminated by an owner's express statement waiving his ownership right.[564,565] Finally, ownership terminates on the basis of a separate act under the preconditions and in the way stipulated in such an act.[566]

561. Gavella in *Property Law I*, 673–683; Klarić / Vedriš in *Civil Law*, 303.
562. Article 171 PA. For example, when another person acquires immovable property by acquisitive prescription, by building on another's land, by a court decision or a decision of another competent authority, or when on the basis of a legal transaction, ownership is transferred from the previous owner on another person (Art. 171 PA).
563. Article 170 PA. The owner is then entitled to compensation according to the rules on compensation for expropriation.
564. When the owner of immovable property has waived ownership, his ownership is cancelled in the land register. At that moment, the Republic of Croatia *ex lege* becomes the owner of the particular immovable (Art. 172/2 PA).
565. In all these cases, ownership of immovable property terminates only by cancellation from the land register.
566. Article 173 PA. When ownership of immovable property terminates on the basis of an act, it ceases to exist without cancellation from the land register. Even then, bona fide acquirers are protected if they have acted by trusting the completeness of the land register. The termination of ownership of immovable property on the basis of law cannot be carried out to the detriment of those who did not know or had no reason to know about its existence (Art. 173/2 PA).

Chapter 4. Neighbourhood Law

§1. Concept

148. In Croatian property law, there are express rules which provide for the relations between owners of neighbouring immovables.[567] These rules ensure mutual respectful exercise of ownership of the neighbouring immovables. Neighbourship rights (*susjedska prava*) authorize the owner of an immovable, for the purpose of exercising his right of ownership, to request the owner of a neighbouring immovable to suffer, omit or perform something on his immovable.[568,569] The owner of an immovable is entitled to seek through the court that the owner of a neighbouring immovable suffers or omits particular activities on his immovables pursuant to the rules on neighbourship rights.[570] Neighbourship rights must be exercised in a way to restrict or burden to the minimum the owners of the neighbouring immovables. Besides the general provisions on neighbourship rights, the PA also provides for a series of specific neighbourship rights.

§2. Fences Between Neighbouring Immovables

I. A Boundary Fence (a Common Fence)

149. Fences between neighbouring immovables and other things serving as boundary markers are considered common fences co-owned by the owners of both the neighbouring immovables.[571] Such co-ownership is undividable until the fences lose their purpose. The common fence (*zajednička ograda*) may be used by each owner of the neighbouring immovables up to half of its width.[572] While exercising this right, the owners must neither bring the fence into any kind of danger nor prevent their neighbour from using it. The costs of the maintenance of the boundary fence are borne by the owners of the neighbouring immovables in equal shares.[573,574]

567. Articles 100–113 PA.
568. Article 100/1 PA.
569. Gliha in *Property Law I*, 646–673; Klarić / Vedriš in *Civil Law*, 236–243.
570. Article 100/2 PA. The same entitlement belongs to persons who are permitted by the owner, on the basis of a legal transaction, to possess and use his immovable (e.g., a lessee, a usufructuary and the like). However, a request for the respect of neighbourship rights may also be submitted not only with regard to the owners of neighbouring immovables, but also persons whom the owner, on the basis of a legal transaction, authorizes to possess and use his immovable (Art. 100/2,4 PA).
571. Article 100/1 PA.
572. Article 101/3 PA.
573. Article 101/4 PA. Any damages incurred to third parties because the fence has not been maintained are borne jointly and severally by the co-owners of the neighbouring immovables.
574. Gliha in *Property Law I*, 653.

II. Fences under Sole Ownership

150. A fence located exclusively on the property of one owner is under his sole ownership.[575] Regarding the construction and maintenance of such fences, the PA lays down the owner's obligation to fence off his own space on the right of the main entrance (looking from the path) and to separate it from the neighbour's space and the neighbouring immovable.[576] The owner of the fence is responsible for maintaining it in order to prevent any damages caused to the owner of the neighbouring immovable.

§3. Regulation of Boundaries

151. In the procedure of regulating boundaries (*postupak uređenja međe*), a boundary between the neighbouring immovables is renewed or corrected in cases where it is no longer identifiable (e.g., the boundary markers are damaged) or where the boundary is disputable.[577,578] The procedure of regulating boundaries is conducted by the municipal court on whose territory the relevant neighbouring immovables are located.[579] The PA expressly provides for the criteria under which a boundary is regulated.

152. The court will reconstruct or correct the boundary on the basis of a cadastral plan[580] if possible and if the parties have given their consent.[581] If this is not possible, the court will reconstruct the boundary on the basis of a neighbour's agreement. If the owners of the neighbouring immovables cannot reach an agreement, the boundary is determined in accordance with the last peaceful enjoyment of possession, and if that is not possible either, the court determines the boundary according to a fair assessment.[582]

153. Ownership of neighbouring immovables up to the boundary between them exists from the moment the court has rendered a decision on the regulation of the boundary.[583] However, each party to the boundary regulation proceedings, as well as any third party not having taken part in the proceedings, may challenge the regulation of the boundary in litigious proceedings. The parties participating in the

575. Article 102 PA.
576. Article 102/2 PA.
577. Article 103/1 PA.
578. Gavella in *Property Law I*, 641.
579. The regulation of boundaries is carried out in a non-litigious civil procedure instituted by any of the owners of the neighbouring immovables (Art. 103/1 PA).
580. Cadastral plans are developed in cadastral survey procedures. In this procedure, among other things, the boundaries of plots that are shown in cadastral plans are determined. Cadastral surveys are carried out for the entire territory of the Republic of Croatia pursuant to the same methodology specified in the Cadastre Act.
581. Article 103/2 PA.
582. Article 103/3 PA. In parallel with the adoption of the decision, the court marks the boundary by placing new boundary markers.
583. Article 103/5 PA.

boundary regulation proceedings may institute litigious proceedings within six months of the finality of the decision rendered in the boundary regulation proceedings. There is no time limit for the initiation of litigious proceedings for a person who has not taken part in the proceedings for the regulation of the boundary but claims to be the owner of one of the neighbouring immovables.[584]

§4. A Tree, Branches or Roots on a Boundary

154. A tree that grows on a boundary belongs to the person on whose land it is growing.[585] A tree which is growing on the boundary between two neighbouring immovables is co-owned by the owners of these immovables.[586,587]

155. The owner of an immovable is entitled to pull out the shoots and the roots of a neighbour's tree growing on his land, cut off the branches extending into the air space above his land and appropriate them.[588] The owner of the land where such trees and other vegetation are growing must act carefully and maintain them properly so as not to cause damage to the owner of the neighbouring immovable.[589]

§5. Use of the Neighbouring Immovable

I. Access to Another's Property

156. When an animal or any other thing enters another's property, the owner is entitled to enter such property within a reasonable time in order to take it back. The owner of such property may forbid access only if he, without delay, hands over the thing to its owner. The owner of the accessed property is entitled to compensation for any damage or for the necessary costs he may have suffered on his immovable because of such a thing. The owner of such property may keep another person's thing until the damage and the incurred costs have been compensated.[590,591]

II. Use of Another's Immovable to Carry Out Works

157. The owner of an immovable on which works must be carried out to enable its use may temporarily use the land of another to do the works, to erect scaffolding or similar equipment if such works cannot be carried out in any other way. As soon

584. Article 103/6 PA. Such a person brings an action for the establishment of ownership, and in Croatian law, such an action is not subject to the statute of limitations (Art. 161/2 PA).
585. Article 104/1 PA.
586. Article 104/2 PA.
587. Gliha in *Property Law I*, 654.
588. Article 105/1 PA.
589. Article 105/2 PA.
590. Article 106 PA.
591. Gliha in *Property Law I*, 658.

as the need for such works ceases to exist, the owner who uses another's land must restore it to the previous condition and compensate for the damage caused to the owner of such land. The owner of the used land is also entitled to compensation for the temporary use of his immovable.[592]

III. Way of Necessity

158. A way of necessity (*nužni prolaz*) is established by the court in non-litigious proceedings at the request of the owner of an immovable which has no connection, or does not have any convenient connection, with a public road, and if the benefit of making a way of necessity for the use of the immovable is greater than the damage incurred on the used immovable.[593] A way of necessity is established as easement. In its decision on the establishment of a way of necessity, the court determines how the neighbouring immovable will be used so that the burden on this immovable is minimized. The court also determines the compensation to be paid by the owner of the dominant immovable to the owner of the servient tenement[594] since a condition for the establishment of the way of necessity is the full payment of such compensation.[595]

IV. The Right to Have Part of a Building or Equipment on Another's Immovable

159. The right to have part of a building or equipment on another's property is real easement[596] established on the basis of a contract between the owners of two neighbouring immovables in pursuance of the decision of a court or another competent body[597] pursuant to the law.[598,599]

160. On the basis of easement, the owner of the dominant immovable is entitled to have part of his building, other equipment, devices or conduits serving his immovable on the neighbouring immovable, on its surface, underneath it, or in its air space.[600] He is bound to maintain such a part of his building or equipment and pay the owner of the servient immovable compensation for the use of his immovable property in the appropriate amount of rent.[601]

---

592. Article 107 PA.
593. Article 224 PA.
594. The compensation may not be less than would be paid if the immovable were expropriated (Art. 224/4 PA).
595. Gavella in *Property Law II*, 20.
596. Article 196 PA. For more details *see* Part I, Ch. 5, §1. Easements.
597. Article 108 PA.
598. Article 155/2 PA.
599. Gavella in *Property Law II*, 36.
600. Articles 196/1,2 PA.
601. Article 196/1 PA.

V. Installation of Conduits or Other Devices

161. It is permitted to instal conduits and other devices (for electricity, sewage, gas, water supply, telecommunication, etc.) on another's immovable. This is possible when the installation of conduits is in the interest of the Republic of Croatia or in someone's private interest.[602,603]

162. When the installation of conduits or other devices is in the interest of the Republic of Croatia, the provisions of the ExA on the expropriation of immovables apply accordingly.[604] In expropriation proceedings, the rules on the establishment of real easement apply accordingly.[605] Easement is established on the basis of a decision on expropriation rendered in expropriation proceedings.[606,607] The owner of the immovable charged by easement is thus entitled to full compensation,[608] which may not be less than the compensation paid in expropriation proceedings as the result of the diminished market value of the immovable.[609]

163. When the installation of conduits and other equipment is in some private interest, the provisions on the establishment of easement of conduits and other equipment are applied on the basis of a court decision.[610] Easement is established at the request of the owner of an immovable having no connection, or lacking an appropriate connection, with the supplier of the substance or energy supplied via conduits when the advantage of installing conduits is greater than the damage to the servient immovable. The owner of the immovable to whose benefit the easement of conduits and other equipment is established is bound to pay the owner of the servient immovable compensation for the use of his immovable[611] and to maintain these conduits and equipment at his own cost.[612]

VI. Crossing the Boundary by Construction Works

164. If a boundary is crossed as the result of construction works and a part of a building is erected on the neighbouring land, the owner of the neighbouring land is

602. Article 108 PA.
603. Gliha in *Property Law I*, 660.
604. The Expropriation Act, OG 74/14, 69/17, 98/19.
605. Article 6 of ExA.
606. A decision on expropriation may be rendered in favour of any natural or legal person (Art. 3 of ExA).
607. The provisions on the acquisition of ownership by expropriation apply accordingly to the proceedings of expropriation for the establishment of easement in order to install conduits or other equipment. For more on the acquisition of ownership by expropriation, *see* Part III, Ch. 3, §2. II. Acquisition of Ownership by Expropriation.
608. Article 225/1 PA.
609. Articles 11, 46/1 of ExA.
610. Article 225 PA.
611. The provisions on the establishment of a way of necessity apply accordingly to the easement of conduits and other equipment (Art. 225/2 PA).
612. Article 196/1 PA.

entitled to request the removal of such a building and restoration to the previous condition.[613] However, until restoration to the previous condition is performed, the owner of the building has easement on the neighbouring land.[614] The owner of the land where a part of another's building is located is entitled to compensation for damage and compensation in the form of pecuniary rent.[615] The compensation is paid in the amount of rent which would be due for the land on which the part of another's building is erected. The owner of the building is bound to maintain the part of the building erected on somebody else's land at his own cost.[616]

165. The owner of the land where a part of another's building is located is entitled to request from the owner of the building to buy off his entire land at the market price. The buy-off of the land may also be sought by the owner of the building if, during construction, he behaved in a fair manner,[617] or if restoration to the previous condition (i.e., knocking down a part of the building) is not possible without significant damage to the remaining part of the building, or without disproportionately high costs.[618]

§6. Digging Underneath the Property of Another and the Danger of Collapse

166. The owner of an immovable is not allowed to dig on his land or do other works that can endanger the stability of another's immovable property.[619] The owner of an immovable whose stability is endangered may request all measures to be taken (e.g., construction of support installations to eliminate danger to the stability of his immovable, including the termination of the works which endanger its stability.[620,621]

167. If there is a serious danger of collapse of the building erected on the neighbouring land, the owner of the endangered immovable may request the owner of the building to take all necessary measures to prevent possible damage, as well as compensation for any future damage.[622]

---

613. Article 155/1 PA.
614. Article 196 in connection with Art. 155/2 PA.
615. Article 155/3 PA.
616. Gliha in *Property Law I*, 659.
617. The builder will be considered as being fair if he did not know or had no reason to know that he was building a part of his building on somebody else's land.
618. Article 155/4 PA.
619. Article 109/1 PA.
620. Articles 109/2,3 PA. The owner of the land on which construction works are carried out will be held liable for the damage suffered by the owner of the neighbouring immovable and is responsible for the maintenance of the constructions which are built in order to eliminate danger to the stability of the immovable (Art. 109/4 PA).
621. Gliha in *Property Law I*, 661.
622. Article 111 PA.

§7. Protection Against Emissions

168. If an owner of an immovable unlawfully disturbs the owner of the neighbouring immovable by emitting smoke, unpleasant odours, soot, wastewater, noise, etc. (*dirketne imisije*), resulting from the operation of various machines, or in some other way, the owner of the neighbouring immovable is authorized to request the end of such harassment and the payment of compensation for damage.[623,624]

169. The owner of an immovable is not allowed to use it so that smoke, unpleasant odours, soot, wastewater, earth tremor, noise, and the like (excessive indirect emissions, *indirektne imisije*) reach another person's immovable property by accident or by force of nature. Such emissions are prohibited if their impact on the neighbouring immovable is excessive with regard to their purpose or if they cause considerable damage.[625] The owner of the immovable exposed to harmful emissions may request the owner causing such emissions to eliminate their source, to pay adequate compensation and to stop the activities causing the emissions. If, however, excessive indirect emissions resulting from the activities carried out on the neighbouring immovable for whose execution permission has been granted by the competent authorities, the owner of the property exposed to such emissions may not seek their termination. He may only seek compensation and adequate measures to be taken to prevent or reduce future harmful emissions.[626]

623. Article 110/4 PA.
624. Gliha in *Property Law I*, 662–666.
625. Article 110/1 PA.
626. Article 110/2 PA.

Chapter 5. Limited Property Rights on Immovables

§1. Easements

I. Concept

170. Easements (servitudes; *služnosti*) are limited property rights on someone's immovable, authorizing the holder of such a right to use the immovable in a specific way, regardless of who the owner might be, whereby the everyday owner is bound to sufferance or omission as a result.[627,628] Easements are property rights on another's immovable property, authorizing the person to whose benefit they exist to use it in a specific way (servient immovable; *poslužna nekretnina*). Easements may not be arbitrarily separated from the servient immovable or transferred to another holder or immovable. They are transferable only with the servient immovable.[629] Easements are entered in the land register in the land register file where the immovable that is encumbered with an easement is registered, with an indication of its content and scope.[630]

171. The content of an easement is determined when the easement is established. When an easement is established by contract *inter vivos*, the parties determine its content. When an easement is established on the basis of a court decision or by law, its content is determined by the decision or by law.[631] In any case, the holder of an easement, when enforcing his rights, must act with consideration to make the least burden on the servient immovable.[632] The holder of the easement may significantly change the manner of enforcement of his entitlements only in agreement with the owner of the servient immovable.[633] The owner of the servient immovable may not do anything to prevent or significantly aggravate the enforcement of an easement.[634]

627. Article 174/1 PA. Every easement must have a reasonable purpose (Art. 175/1 PA). If an easement loses its reasonable purpose, the owner of the servient immovable may request the court to revoke it (Art. 242/1 PA).
628. Stipković in *Property Law II*, 8-13; Klarić / Vedriš in *Civil Law*, 316–317.
629. Article 182 PA. Easements are indivisible. They can neither be changed nor divided by a change of their forms, surface areas or extent of the development of the servient immovable (Art. 183/1 PA). When a servient immovable is divided, and an easement is exercised only on an individual part of the servient tenement, revocation of the easement may be requested in relation to other particle of the immovable (Art. 183/2 PA). If there is an easement in favour of the immovable (real easement), and the dominant immovable is divided, the easement remains in favour of all parts of the immovable but may be exercised only in such a way that the total burden for the owner of the servient immovable is not increased (Art. 183/3 PA).
630. Articles 324,27 LRA.
631. Article 174/2 PA. The rights and entitlements that derive from some kind of easement may be given until the moment of revocation (so-called apparent easement; *prividna služnost*). Then, the powers and duties granted by an easement may be granted until repeal, in which case they are assessed by the appropriate application of the rules on easement (Article 184/1 PA).
632. Article 177/2 PA. The costs of maintaining and repairing the servient immovable are borne by the holder, unless provided otherwise (Art. 181/1 PA).
633. Article 178/2 PA.
634. Article 177/3 PA.

172. Easements are divided into real and personal easements depending on their purpose and on whether an immovable is encumbered by an easement in the interest of its everyday owner of another immovable or in the interest of a particular individual.[635]

II. Real Easements

A. *Concept*

173. A real easement (*stvarna služnost*) is the property right of an everyday owner of a particular immovable (the so-called dominant immovable; *povlasna nekretnina*) to carry out for the needs of that certain immovable action on another's immovable (the so-called servient immovable; *poslužna nekretnina*) whose everyday owner is bound to suffer or omit certain actions he would normally be entitled to perform.[636,637] Real easements exist in the interest of an immovable (a dominant immovable), but they encumber another's immovable (a servient immovable). Real easements do not expire with the change of owner of either the servient or the dominant immovable. They exist in favour of the dominant immovable and are its appurtenances.[638] Therefore, they may not be separated from the ownership of the dominant immovable but are transferred together with the immovable.[639] When someone acquires ownership of a dominant immovable, the acquirer acquires the immovable in whose interest the right of real easement exists. When someone acquires ownership of a servient immovable, he acquires it encumbered with the right of real easement, which is its encumbrance. Every owner of a dominant immovable is authorized to exercise the content of servitude, and every owner of a servient immovable is bound to suffer such encumbrance. When the owner of a dominant immovable changes, the real easement which existed in favour of the immovable remains so that the new owner is authorized to use the servient immovable within the content of the existing real easement in the same way that the previous owner did. In the same way, when the owner of a servient immovable changes, its new owner is bound to sufferance based on the fact that the owner of the dominant immovable exercises real easement on his immovable. Both the owner of the dominant and the servient immovables may establish easements of any possible and permitted content.[640]

---

635. Article 167 PA. An immovable may be encumbered with several easements but a more recent easement may not limit the enforcement of those preceding it in order of priority (Art. 180/1 PA). The order of priority of more easements is determined in accordance with their order of registration in the land register. If several easements have the same order of priority, and the enforcement of one of them hinders the enforcement of another, each holder may file an action with the court to regulate enforcement equitably in the interest of all holders (Art. 180/2 PA).
636. Article 186/1 PA.
637. Stipković in *Property Law II*, 31; Klarić / Vedriš in *Civil Law*, 319.
638. Article 186/2 PA.
639. Article 186/2 PA.
640. Article 188/1 PA.

174. The content of a real easement is determined by the owners of both the dominant and the servient immovables. They may establish a real easement of any content that is possible and permissible.[641] The PA thus provides for particular real easements and their contents, but the parties may contract real easements of different contents. Depending on whether a real easement is established in the interest of a dominant immovable intended for agriculture or of a property with a building, real easements are divided into rural and urban easements.

B. Rural Easements

175. Rural easements (*poljske služnosti*) are established to serve property intended for agriculture,[642] such as the right-of-way (the right of transit passage, the right to drive cattle, the right to use a roadway), the right to water (the right to draw water, the right to water cattle, or the right to lead or lead off water), the right of pasture, timber easement (the right to cut timber and gather dead wood and the like). Separate rules for particular easements are specified in Articles 190–198 of the PA.[643]

C. Urban Easements

176. Urban easements (*kućne služnosti*) are established in order to serve a piece of property with a building,[644] such as the right to support one's building, insert a support beam or rafter in the wall of another, the right to have a window in the wall of another for light or for a view, to have a part of one's building in the neighbour's air space, the right to direct smoke or other gases through the neighbour's chimney, the right to cause rainwater to drip and drain onto the property of another, and the like. Special rules for individual real easements are specified in Articles 190–198 of the PA.[645]

D. Irregular Easements

177. An irregular easement (*nepravilna služnost*), which in its nature is a real easement, may be established on a servient immovable in favour of a particular person. The provisions on personal easements appropriately apply to such easements.[646] Irregular easements may also be established on the basis of separate acts,

641. Article 188/1 PA.
642. Article 188/3 PA.
643. For more, *see* Stipković in *Property Law II*, 32-34; Klarić / Vedriš in *Civil Law*, 321–322.
644. Articles 188/4,5 PA.
645. For more details *see* Stipković in *Property Law II*, 34–36; Klarić / Vedriš in *Civil Law*, 322–323.
646. Article 189/2 PA.

such as the RA, which expressly determine the way of establishing easements, their transfer to other persons, etc.[647]

III. Personal Easements

A. Concept

178. A personal easement is a property right individually authorizing a particular person to use in a certain way another's immovable (servient immovable) which its everyday owner is bound to suffer.[648,649] Personal easements encumber an immovable which the everyday owner of the servient immovable is bound to suffer. Personal easements exist in the interest of a particular individual person, and they encumber a particular immovable (servient immovable). Unless determined otherwise, personal easements expire on their holder's death.[650] Personal easements may not be transferred to other persons, and they are not inheritable, except for easements that are also expressly established for the holder's successors.[651] On the death of a person for whose benefit a personal easement was established, it ceases to exist without passing onto his successor unless it was also established for the successors.[652] A personal easement exists when a servient immovable changes owner. A person who acquires ownership of a servient immovable acquires it encumbered with a personal easement. Personal easements may exist on the entire immovable, as well as on a proportional (ideal) share, if it is possible to exercise them on a proportional share, taking into account the content of the easement.[653] The types of personal easements are listed in the PA.[654] Personal easements are the right to usufruct, the right to use and the right to habitation.

B. Usufruct

179. Usufruct (Latin (Lat). *ususfructus*; *pravo plodouživanja*) is a personal easement that entitles its holder (the usufructuary) to use another's property (servient immovable) in accordance with its purpose in such a way that its substance is preserved.[655,656,657] The usufructuary is entitled to use the servient immovable according to its purpose, to possess it, to utilize it for himself, to keep the net income but

647. For further details on easements on public roads, *see* Part I, Ch. 7, §4. Roads.
648. Article 199/1 PA.
649. Stipković in *Property Law II*, 36-37; Klarić / Vedriš in *Civil Law*, 324–325.
650. Article 201 PA. A personal easement may also be established for a particular period of time. It terminates on the expiry of the term for which it was established (Art. 240/1 PA).
651. Articles 202/1,2 PA.
652. Article 202/3 PA.
653. For example, usufruct may be established on a proportional (ideal) share of an immovable. All personal easements may be established on a proportional share of an immovable which is in the legal regime of condominium (Art. 200/2 PA).
654. Article 199/2 PA.
655. Article 203 PA. The right of usufruct, besides on an immovable, may also exist on a non-consumable movable and on a right yielding fruits or other benefits (Art. 203/2,3 PA). Usufruct may

to preserve its fundamental purpose.[658] The usufructuary may not transfer his right of usufruct to another person because usufruct is strictly a personal easement. However, the usufructuary may empower another person in a legal transaction to enforce his entitlements on the basis of the easement of usufruct.[659] The usufructuary is entitled to use the servient immovable in accordance with its purpose, and he is also authorized to keep all the fruits and other benefits derived from the servient property.[660] He bears the costs and other encumbrances regarding the use and utilization of the servient immovable.[661] The usufructuary is also responsible for keeping the servient immovable in the condition in which he received it, and he bears all the costs of its regular maintenance.[662] The owner of the immovable encumbered with usufruct is bound to exercise his ownership in such a way as not to disturb the usufructuary in exercising his rights. The owner is bound to do extraordinary repairs on the servient property.[663] When the easement of usufruct terminates, the usufructuary must return the immovable to its owner in the condition in which he received it.[664]

C. Use

180. The right of use (Lat. *usus*; *pravo uporabe*) authorizes its holder (the person having the right of use) to use someone's immovable (servient immovable) for his needs and the needs of his household in accordance with its purpose and in preserving its substance.[665,666,667] The person having the right of use is authorized to use the servient immovable for his needs by holding it in his possession to the determined extent, using it and gathering its revenues while at the same time preserving its substance.[668] Such a person is not entitled to transfer the exercise of his powers

---

also be established on a consumable (so-called quasi usufruct). In this case, after the termination of the usufruct, the usufructuary is bound to pay the owner of the consumable its pecuniary countervalue (Art. 211 PA).

656. Several persons may simultaneously enjoy the right of usufruct on the same servient immovable. Each of them is then an independent holder of his share of the usufruct. Unless it is determined otherwise, each of them is entitled to the same portion of the usufruct (Art. 203/5 PA).
657. Stipković in *Property Law II*, 37; Klarić / Vedriš in *Civil Law*, 325.
658. Article 204 PA.
659. Article 204/2 PA.
660. Articles 204, 205 PA. The revenues derived from the servient immovable include all fruits and other benefits derived from the immovable. The usufructuary acquires such fruits upon their separation from the servient immovable (Art. 205/2,3 PA).
661. Article 205/5 PA.
662. Article 205/6 PA.
663. Article 206 PA.
664. Article 210 PA.
665. Article 212 PA. Besides on an immovable, the right of use may exist on a movable, as well as on a right that yields fruits and other benefits (Art. 212/2,3 PA).
666. The rules on the right of usufruct apply accordingly to the right of use, unless the provisions of the PA determine otherwise for the right of use (Art. 212/6 PA).
667. Stipković in *Property Law II*, 42; Klarić / Vedriš in *Civil Law*, 327.
668. Article 213 PA.

based on the right of use to another person.[669] The owner of the servient immovable is bound to suffer the exercise of such a person's powers on his immovable, and he may not exercise his ownership in a way which would infringe the right of use. The owner is bound to bear all regular and extraordinary costs and burdens on the servient immovable, and he is responsible for maintaining it in good condition at his own cost.[670]

D. *Habitation*

181. The right of habitation (Lat. *habitatio*; *pravo stanovanja*) empowers its holder (resident) to use another's residence or a part thereof aimed for habitation (servient tenement) in accordance with its purpose and in preserving its substance.[671,672] The rules on the right of use apply accordingly to the right of habitation.[673]

IV. Establishment of Easements

A. *Legal Titles for the Establishment of Easements*

182. In Croatian law, easements may be established on several different legal titles. There is a distinction between the legal titles for the establishment of real easements and the legal titles for the establishment of personal easements. Real easements can be established by contract with the owner of the servient immovable, by decision of the court or another competent authority or on the basis of law.[674] Personal easements may be established only voluntarily by the owner of the servient immovable.[675] Personal easements may be acquired by contract *inter vivos* (e.g., a contract on the establishment of a personal easement) and on the basis of a will (e.g., a clause in the will by which the testator establishes a personal easement to someone's benefit). Regardless of the possible legal titles for acquisition, an easement is established only when all the necessary conditions provided by law are fulfilled.[676] The conditions for the establishment of easements on property are determined differently depending on the legal titles for their acquisition.

669. Article 213/2 PA.
670. Article 216/1 PA.
671. Article 217 PA.
672. Stipković in *Property Law II*, 43; Klarić / Vedriš in *Civil Law*, 328.
673. Article 217/2 PA.
674. Article 218/1 PA.
675. Article 218/2 PA.
676. Article 218/3 PA.

B. Establishment by Contract

183. In order to establish an easement by contract, three conditions must be fulfilled: ownership of the servient immovable,[677] a valid contract aimed at acquiring easement,[678] and a valid *modus* of acquisition, i.e., registration in the land register.[679,680,681] A contract for the establishment of an easement is made by the owner of the dominant immovable and the owner of the servient immovable (in the case of real easements), or the owner of the servient property and a person for whose benefit the personal easement is established. The contract aimed at establishing an easement on a servient property must be made in writing.[682] Both real and personal easements may be acquired by the contract.[683] Real easements are entered as a charge in the land register file where the servient property is registered and in the land register file where the dominant property is entered.[684] Personal easements are entered as a charge in the land register unit where the servient immovable property is registered.[685,686]

C. Establishment on the Basis of a Decision of a Court or Another Competent Authority

184. Real easements are established on the basis of a court decision or a decision rendered by another competent authority in the cases specified in the provisions of the PA.[687] Real easements are established in the procedure of establishing a way of necessity, necessary conduits and other equipment, in the procedure of division in inheritance proceedings, and in other cases established by law.[688] Only real and not personal easements may be acquired on the basis of decisions rendered

677. An easement from a non-owner on the basis of contract may be acquired only if, in favour of a fair acquirer, the conditions for the protection of trust in the reliability and completeness of the land register are met (Art. 221 PA).
678. Article 219/1PA. When an immovable encumbered by an easement is co-owned or jointly owned by more persons, they may all agree to encumber the entire immovable with an easement (Art. 219/5 PA).
679. Article 220/1 PA. An easement is entered by registration or conditional registration (Art. 220 PA, Art. 30/2,3 LRA.
680. When an immovable is not entered in the land register, an easement is acquired by depositing with the court a legalized document suitable for registration in the land register (Art. 220/3 PA).
681. For more details, *see* Part III, Ch. 2, §5. Acquisition of Easements by Contract *Inter Vivos.*
682. Article 219/4 PA. A contract must contain all the general and specific conditions required for registration.
683. Articles 218/1,2 PA.
684. Articles 21,24,37 LRA.
685. Article 24 LRA.
686. Stipković in *Property Law II*, 18; Klarić / Vedriš in *Civil Law*, 329.
687. For more details, *see* Part III, Ch. 3, §3. Acquisition of Real Easements on the Basis of a Court Decision or the Decision of Another Competent Authority.
688. Article 223/1 PA.

by a court or another competent authority.[689] A real easement may also be established by an administrative body in expropriation or land consolidation proceedings. A real easement is acquired on the day a court decision or the decision of an administrative body becomes final, i.e., without an entry in the land register.[690] Until an easement acquired on the basis of a court decision or a decision rendered by another competent authority is entered into the land register, the land register status is incomplete, and the legal effects of the protection of trust in the completeness of the land register may be set in favour of a bona fide acquirer. A real easement not registered in the land register may not oppose the right of the person who, having relied on the information in the land register, registered his right on the property in good faith. It will terminate on account of the operation of the protection of confidence in the land register.[691,692]

D. *Establishment of Real Easements on the Basis of Law*

185. Real easement on the basis of law is acquired by acquisitive prescription when the possessor of a dominant immovable exercises the content of real easement over a period of twenty years, and the owner of the servient immovable has not opposed it.[693] A real easement is acquired by means of the period necessary for the acquisitive prescription without an entry in the land register.[694,695]

V. Protection of Easements

186. Easements are protected by a special action filed by the persons in whose favour the easements are established. The municipal court in whose territory the servient immovable is located has jurisdiction over such actions.[696] The content of the claims for the protection of the right of easement differs and depends on the type of infringement of the right of easement.[697]

187. Protection from disturbance and obstruction of the right of easement is exercised by an action for the respect of the right of easement (Lat. *actio confessoria*). With such a claim, the owner of the servient immovable or any other person

689. Article 218/1 PA.
690. Article 223/3 PA.
691. Articles 27, 230, 243 PA.
692. Stipković in *Property Law II*, 19–22; Klarić / Vedriš in *Civil Law*, 329.
693. Article 229 PA. If easement, by its nature, may only rarely be enforced, a person claiming that the easement was established in favour of his immovable property by acquisitive prescription must prove that in a period of not less than twenty years, the situation of enforcement of such easement occurred at least three times, and that he or his predecessor each time enforced its content (Art. 229/3 PA).
694. For more details, *see* Part III, Ch. 5, §3. Acquisition of Easements on the Basis of Law.
695. Stipković in *Property Law II*, 22; Klarić / Vedriš in *Civil Law*, 329.
696. Article 56 CPA.
697. Stipković in *Property Law II*, 24; Klarić / Vedriš in *Civil Law*, 332.

who negates the claimant's right of easement disturbs him or obstructs its enforcement is requested to admit and suffer another's right of easement.[698] In court proceedings, the claimant must prove his right of easement[699] and the defendant's conduct by which the enforcement of the right of easement is obstructed or disturbed.[700] The right to protection terminates after a period of twenty years from the time when the holder of the easement was deprived of the possession of the right of real easement.[701]

188. When easement is violated by an invalid entry in the land register, it is protected by a cancellation action. With such an action, the holder of the right of easement requests that such an invalid entry, violating his right of easement, be cancelled.[702] The rules on the cancellation action, by which other rights entered in the land register are also protected, apply to such an action.

VI. Termination of Easements

189. The right of easement terminates upon the destruction of the dominant or servient immovable,[703] when the ownership of the dominant and the servient immovable belongs to the same person,[704] by a waiver of the holder of the real easement,[705] on the expiry of the term for which it is established or by the fulfilment of the dissolution condition under which it was established[706] if the real easement has not been exercised for a period of twenty years, i.e., if the owner of the servient immovable objected to its enforcement and the holder did not exercise real easement for a continuous period of three years,[707,708] by a court decision when easement loses its reasonable purpose,[709] and by the protection of another's trust[710] on

---

698. Article 233 PA.
699. As a rule, the right of easement is proven by an excerpt from the land register where the easement is registered.
700. Article 234 PA.
701. For another competent authority proves the legal title and the truthful way of acquiring the possession of the right of easement (Art. 235 PA).
702. Article 236 PA.
703. Article 237 PA.
704. Article 238 PA.
705. Article 239 PA. The right of easement terminates upon a valid waiver by its holder. However, if the dominant immovable is encumbered by usufruct or a lien, the owner of the dominant tenement may not waive the easement without permission given by all other persons exercising this right (Art. 239/3 PA).
706. Article 240 PA.
707. Article 241 PA. Easements are the only property rights in Croatian law which terminate by virtue of the statute of limitations, i.e. by omission to enforce them within the statutory time limit. All other property rights are not subject to the statute of limitations, i.e. they do not terminate by the fact that they were not enforced for a specified period of time.
708. The right of easement that, by its nature, may only seldom be enforced, terminates by virtue of the statute of limitations only if the person having the right of easement has failed to enforce it on three occasions when its content should have been enforced (Art. 241/2 PA).
709. Article 242 PA. When an easement loses its reasonable purpose, the owner of the servient tenement may request the court to render a decision on the revocation of the easement. Thus, the court will,

the basis of a law or a decision rendered by an administrative authority.[711] Personal easements terminate on the death of their holders unless the law provides otherwise.[712,713]

190. An easement entered in the land register terminates in each of the listed cases only when it is deleted from the land register.[714] An easement is deleted on the proposal of the owner of the servient tenement and on the basis of a public and a certified document proving that one of the reasons for the termination of easement referred to in Articles 237–245 of the PA has become effective.

§2. Real Burdens

I. Concept

191. A real burden (*stvarni teret*) is a property right on another‘s immovable, authorizing its holder to repeatedly receive things or to have acts done as a charge on the value of the property, which form the content of the real burden.[715,716] A piece of immovable, or several such immovables together, may have a real burden on them if they are suitable to be the subject matter of a lien.[717] Real burdens are entered in the land register unit where the charges immovables are entered, indicating their content and scope.[718] A real burden may be established in favour of an immovable or in favour of a person.

192. A real burden binds the owner of the encumbered immovable to fulfil the content of the burden in favour of its beneficiary, for which the owner is held accountable against the value of the property.[719] The content of a real burden is an act of giving or performance (possible, permitted, determined or at least determinable) to which the beneficiary is entitled on the basis of the value of the encumbered property. This act of giving or performance may consist of the repeated giving of a thing or money or of some acts which have a pecuniary value (e.g., the payment of rent and the like). The everyday owner of an immovable encumbered with a real burden is bound to such an act or performance because a real burden may not

---

on the request of the owner of the servient immovable, revoke a way of necessity or any other right-of-way if it establishes that there is a more suitable passage, or an equally suitable passage causing less damage to the owner of the servient immovable (Art. 242/2 PA).

710. Article 243 PA. For example, an easement acquired on the basis of a court decision or a decision rendered by some other authority, or by means of an acquisitive prescription, terminates if a fair acquirer acquired the immovable prior to such an easement being entered in the land register.

711. Article 245 PA.

712. Articles 201/1, 244 PA.

713. Stipković in *Property Law II*, 25–31; Klarić / Vedriš in *Civil Law*, 334.

714. Cf. Arts 238/2, 239/5, 240/3, 241/5, 242/5, 245/4 PA.

715. Article 246 PA.

716. Gavella in *Property Law II*, 60–61; Klarić / Vedriš in *Civil Law*, 361–362.

717. Article 247/1 PA.

718. Articles 24, 37 LRA.

719. Article 251/1 PA.

be separated from the immovable which it encumbers.[720] When the owner of an immovable that is encumbered with a real burden changes, the real burden remains so that the new owner acquires the immovable encumbered with a real burden and is bound to fulfil the content of the burden.[721] When an immovable in whose favour a real burden is established (praedial real burden), such a real burden is transferred together with the immovable, and the new owner of the dominant tenement acquires the immovable along with the real burden established in its favour. However, when a real burden is established in favour of a particular person (personal real burden), it may not be transferred to another[722] but expires upon the death of the beneficiary.[723]

II. Real Burden in Favour of an Immovable

193. A real burden in favour of an immovable (praedial real burden; *predijalni stvarni teret*) gives the everyday owner of such an immovable a limited property right to repeatedly receive acts or performances that are the content of the real burden. The everyday owner is accountable for such acts of giving or performance against the value of such property.[724,725]

III. Real Burden in Favour of a Person

194. A real burden in favour of a person (personal real burden; *personalni stvarni teret*) as a limited real right on an encumbered immovable authorizes this person to repeatedly receive acts of giving or performance that are the content of that real burden. The everyday owner of the encumbered immovable is accountable for such acts of giving or performance against the value of such property.[726,727]

---

720. Individual due obligations of the acts of giving and performance must be enforced by the owner of the encumbered immovable at the time of their maturity (Art. 252/1 PA). The right of claiming the fulfilment of individual due obligations is barred by the statute of limitations three years from the maturity of each individual obligation (Art. 252/3 PA). The everyday owner is liable for all mature individual obligations and for the acts of giving and performance not barred by the statute of limitations against the value of the encumbered real property (Art. 254/1 PA). A person who was the owner of the encumbered immovable at the time of the maturity of a particular individual obligation is personally liable for it (with his personal property), and it does not expire on the termination of the ownership of the encumbered immovable (Art. 53/1 PA). The real liability of the owner of the encumbered immovable and the personal liability of the person who was the owner of the immovable at the time of the maturity of an individual obligation are joint and several (Art. 254/2 PA).
721. Articles 251/3, 255 PA.
722. Articles 255/2, 259/2 PA.
723. Article 278/1 PA.
724. Article 256/1 PA.
725. Gavella in *Property Law II*, 50; Klarić / Vedriš in *Civil Law*, 364.
726. Article 259/1 PA.
727. Gavella in *Property Law II*, 50; Klarić / Vedriš in *Civil Law*, 364.

IV. Establishment of Real Burdens

A. *Legal Titles for the Establishment of Real Burden*

195. Real burdens are established by contract *inter vivos*, on the basis of a court decision[728] and by the operation of law (so-called real burdens of public law).[729] A real burden is established when all the conditions laid down by law are fulfilled.[730] The conditions for the acquisition of real burdens differ depending on the legal foundation of their acquisition.[731]

B. *Establishment by the Contract*

196. For the establishment of a real burden by the contract, three conditions must be fulfilled: ownership of the servient immovable,[732] a valid contract aimed at the establishment of a real burden made in writing,[733] and a valid modus of acquisition, i.e., an entry in the land register.[734,735,736] A contract on the establishment of a real burden is made between the owner of the dominant immovable and the owner of the encumbered immovable (in the case of praedial real burdens), or between the owner of the encumbered immovable and the persons in whose favour a personal real burden is established. The contract aimed at the establishment of a real burden must be made in writing.[737] Praedial real burdens are entered in the land register file where the encumbered immovable is entered and in the land register unit where the dominant immovable is entered.[738] Personal real burdens are entered into the land register unit where the encumbered immovable is entered.[739]

728. Article 261/1 PA.
729. Articles 162/2, 266 PA.
730. Article 261/3 PA.
731. Gavella in *Property Law II*, 68; Klarić / Vedriš in *Civil Law*, 365.
732. A real burden may be acquired from a non-owner on the basis of a legal transaction only if, in favour of a fair acquirer, all the conditions for the protection of trust in the truthfulness and completeness of the land register are fulfilled (Art. 264 PA).
733. Articles 262/1,3 PA. When an encumbered immovable is in the co-ownership or joint ownership of more persons, they may all agree to encumber it with a real burden (Art. 262/4 PA).
734. Articles 263/1,2 PA. Real burdens are entered in the land register by means of registration or conditional registration (Art. 263 PA, Art. 3/2,3 LRA).
735. When an immovable is not entered in the land register, a real burden is acquired by depositing with the court a certified document suitable for the registration of the right in the land register (Art. 263/3 PA).
736. For more details, *see* Part III, Ch. 2, §6. Acquisition of Real Burdens by Contract *Inter Vivos*.
737. Article 262/2 PA. A contract must contain all the general and special conditions required for registration.
738. Articles 21, 24, 37 LRA.
739. Article 24 LRA.

C. Establishment on the Basis of a Court Decision

197. Real burdens are established by a court decision in partition and probate proceedings if the court is authorized to establish easement in such proceedings and also in other cases provided by law.[740,741] The rules on the establishment of easements by a court decision apply accordingly to the establishment of real burdens.[742] A real burden is acquired when a court decision becomes final without an entry in the land register. Entry in the land register is made on the basis of a decision by which a real burden is established or upon the proposal of the person in whose favour it is established.[743] Prior to the registration of the non-registered real burden, the land register status is incomplete, and the fair acquirer, who did not know and had no reason to suspect that there was a non-registered real burden, is protected. A real burden not having been entered in the land register prior to the registration made by a fair acquirer terminates on account of the legal effects of the protection of trust in the completeness of the land register.[744]

D. Establishment on the Basis of Law

198. Real burdens of public law are established on the basis of law by the fulfilment of the conditions laid down by law.[745] Real burdens are effective for any third person by virtue of law.[746] Therefore, a real burden of public law becomes effective for any acquirer of an encumbered immovable even without being entered in the land register, and no one will be able to claim they did not know or had no reason to know about it.[747]

V. Protection of Real Burdens

199. Real burdens are protected by special actions filed by authorized persons in whose favour the real burdens have been established. The municipal court in whose territory the servient tenement is located has jurisdiction over such actions.[748,749]

---

740. Article 265/1 PA.
741. For more details, *see* Part III, Ch. 3, §4. Acquisition of Real Burdens on the Basis of a Court Decision.
742. Article 265/1 PA.
743. Article 15/3 LRA.
744. Article 277 PA.
745. Article 266/1 PA.
746. Article 266/2 PA.
747. For more details *see* Part III, Ch. 3, §4. Acquisition of Real Burdens on the Basis of Law.
748. Article 56 CPA.
749. Gavella in *Property Law II*, 69-71; Klarić / Vedriš in *Civil Law*, 366.

200. Protection against the infringement of a real burden is conducted by a special action filed by the authorized beneficiary of the real burden.[750,751] With such an action, the beneficiary requests that the owner of the encumbered immovable recognize and suffer the real burden imposed on property.[752] An action may be filed to oblige any third person interfering with the enforcement of the real burden to recognize and suffer a real burden imposed on an immovable and to put an end to the interference.[753] An action seeking such protection of the real burden is not subject to the statute of limitations.

201. When a real burden is violated by an invalid entry in the land register, it is protected by a cancellation action. By filing such an action, the beneficiary of a real burden requests the cancellation of an invalid land register entry violating his right.[754] All the rules on the cancellation action by which other rights entered in the land register are protected apply accordingly to such an action.

202. By filing a separate action, the beneficiary of a real burden may request that individual due obligations arising from a real burden be fulfilled. The claim and model of liability for the obligations arising from a real burden will depend on whether, upon the maturity of the obligations, the owner of the encumbered immovable has changed or not. If the owner is the same, i.e., if the same person was the owner of the immovable at the moment of the creation of the obligation and at the moment of filing an action, the defendant is invited to fulfil the due obligation. In order to fulfil the obligation, the defendant provides as a guarantee all his assets and the encumbered immovable. If the owner does not fulfil his obligation, the beneficiary of the real burden, in order to collect payment, may start enforcement proceedings on the entire property of the owner or may seek the amount to be paid from the encumbered immovable in accordance with the rules governing liens.[755] However, if the owner of the encumbered immovable has changed after the maturity of the obligation, the beneficiary of the real burden has different requests towards the person who was the owner of the encumbered immovable at the time of the maturity of an individual claim and towards the person who was the owner of the immovable at the moment of filing an action. The person who was the owner at the moment of the creation of the obligation continues to be liable for the obligations arising from the real burden maturing during the time he was the owner of the encumbered immovable, although it is no longer his.[756] Such a person may be requested to fulfil the claims that had not been fulfilled while he was the owner of the encumbered immovable. In order to fulfil these claims, such a person is personally responsible

750. The beneficiary of a real burden is a person in whose favour a personal real burden is established or the owner of a dominant tenement in whose favour a real burden is established.
751. The beneficiary of a real burden proves his authorization to file an action by submitting an excerpt from the land register where the real burden is entered.
752. Article 268/1 PA.
753. Article 268/2 PA.
754. Article 272 PA.
755. Article 270/4 PA.
756. Article 253/1 PA.

with his entire property.[757] The claim is governed by the statute of limitations of three years after the maturity of each individual obligation.[758] In addition, the fulfilment of the matured obligations may be requested from a person who is the owner of the encumbered immovable at the moment of filing the action. However, the owner will then be liable only with the encumbered immovable and may be requested only to suffer coverage of the matured but unpaid individual obligations arising from the real burden with the value of the encumbered immovable in accordance with the rules on settling the right of lien.[759]

VI. Termination of Real Burdens

203. Real burdens terminate with the destruction of the dominant immovable or the encumbered immovable,[760] with the beneficiary's waiver,[761] on the expiry of the term and fulfilment of the dissolution condition,[762] by revocation,[763] with the protection of another's confidence,[764] with the termination of the existence of the beneficiary in the case of personal real burdens,[765] and by the operation of law or a decision rendered by administrative authorities.[766,767]

204. A real burden entered in the land register terminates only after it has been cancelled from the land register.[768] It is cancelled on the proposal of the owner of an encumbered immovable, on the basis of a public, or certified, document by which it is proven that one of the reasons for the termination of the real burden has set in.[769]

757. Article 269 PA.
758. Article 252/3 PA.
759. Article 270 PA.
760. Article 273 PA.
761. Article 274 PA. A real burden terminates with a valid unilateral waiver by its beneficiary. However, the owner of a dominant immovable encumbered by the right of usufruct or lien may not waive a real burden established in his favour without the permission of the persons having these rights (Art. 274/4 PA).
762. Article 275 PA.
763. Article 276 PA. Real burdens terminate by revocation when they lose their reasonable purpose. The decision on revocation is rendered by a court on the proposal of the owner of the encumbered immovable (Art. 276/3 PA).
764. Article 277 PA. For example, a real burden acquired on the basis of a court decision or a decision of some other authority terminates if a fair acquirer acquires an immovable prior to the real burden being entered in the land register.
765. Article 278 PA.
766. Article 279 PA.
767. Gavella in *Property Law II*, 58–60; Klarić / Vedriš in *Civil Law*, 373.
768. Cf. Arts 274/5, 275/2, 276/3, 279/2 PA.
769. Articles 272–279 PA.

§3. THE RIGHT TO BUILD

I. Concept

205. The right to build (*pravo građenja*) is a limited property right on another's land authorizing its holder to have his own building on the surface of the land or below it, and the everyday owner of that land is bound to sufferance.[770,771] With the establishment of the right to build, the land is legally separated from the building erected on it. When the right to build is established on a piece of land, the building erected by the holder of this right is not considered to be a part of the land, and it does not share its legal destiny. The building is an appurtenance to the right to build which is equated with the immovable. The owner of the building is then the holder of the right to build, while the owner of the land is another person.[772]

206. Buildings and other constructions that are legally separated from the land by the establishment of the right to build are not considered to be part of the plot of land.[773] As long as the right to build exists, the structure built on or under the surface of the land and the land itself are subject to different legal relations and legal regimes.[774] Therefore, in legal transactions involving land, a plot of land may be disposed of independently of the building and vice versa. A building erected by the holder of the right to build may be transferred, together with the right to build, to other persons, and it may be inherited or encumbered.[775] Ownership of the building affixed to the right to build is transferred together with the right to build. However, the right to build is a charge on the plot on which it is established and it is inseparably connected to it. Therefore, if someone acquires ownership of the land after the right to build has been established, he acquires the plot encumbered with the right to build.[776]

207. The holder of the right to build is entitled to erect a building on another's land and be its owner for as long as the right to build exists. The owner of the land is another person bound to suffering.[777] The holder of the right to build is the owner of the building which is an appurtenance to his right. Regarding the land on which the building is erected, the holder of the right to build has the rights and the duties

770. Article 280/1 PA.
771. Gavella in *Property Law II*, 79-80; Klarić / Vedriš in *Civil Law*, 368–370.
772. Articles 280/2,3 PA. The right to build may be established on any pieces of land which can be subject to legal transactions and on which ownership and other property rights may exist. It may be established on the privately owned pieces of land and on those owned by the state or other public law bodies.
773. Article 9/4 PA.
774. The principle of the legal unity of immovables does not apply to the plot of land on which the right to build is established, according to which an immovable consists of a plot of land including everything that is reasonably permanently affixed to it, on its surface, or below it (Art. 9/1 PA). For more details on the legal unity of immovables Part I, Ch. 1, §2. Legal Unity of Real Property (the principle of *superficies solo cedit).*
775. Articles 285/2,3 PA.
776. Article 283 PA.
777. Article 280/1 PA.

of a usufructuary.[778] The holder of the right to build is bound to pay monthly compensation for the land in the amount of an average rent for such land unless it is otherwise determined.

208. The right to build is entered in the land register with a double entry. It is entered as a charge of the land it encumbers and as a separate entry in a newly established land register file.[779] When the building is finished, it is registered as if erected on the right to build.[780] The right to build established on the land where other charges are already registered may be entered in the land register only if other beneficiaries of previously entered limited real rights, for whom the right to build would be detrimental, have given their permission.[781]

II. Establishment of the Right to Build

A. *Legal Titles for Establishment*

209. The right to build is established by contract or a court decision. It is established when all the necessary conditions laid down by law are met. The conditions for the establishment of the right to build are determined differently depending on the legal title for its acquisition. Besides the PA, the establishment of the right to build is also regulated by separate acts.[782,783]

B. *Establishment by the Contract*

210. Three conditions must be fulfilled for the establishment of the right to build by the contract: ownership of the land on which the right to build is established,[784] a valid contract aimed at the establishment of the right to build,[785] and a valid modus of acquisition, i.e., entry in the land register.[786,787,788] The contract on the establishment of the right to build is made between the owner of the immovable encumbered

---

778. Article 281/1 PA.
779. Article 288/1 PA.
780. Article 288/3 PA.
781. Article 288/2 PA.
782. For example: Roads Act, Forests Act, Waters Act. For more details *see* Part I, Ch. 5, §3. II. D. Establishment on the Basis of Separate Acts.
783. Gavella in *Property Law II*, 79; Klarić / Vedriš in *Civil Law*, 367.
784. The right to build may be acquired from a non-owner only if the conditions for the protection of trust in the truthfulness and completeness of the land register for the benefit of a fair acquirer have been fulfilled.
785. Article 287/1 PA. When the land is co-owned by more persons (co-owners or joint owners), they must all agree to encumber it with the right to build (Art. 287/4 PA).
786. Article 228 PA. The right to build is entered in the land register by registration or conditional registration (Art. 288/5 PA, Art. 34/2,3 LRA).
787. When an immovable is not entered in the land register, the right to build is acquired by depositing with the court a certified document suitable for the registration of the right in the land register (Art. 288/5 in connection with Art. 220/3 PA).
788. For more details, *see* Part III, Ch. 2, §7. Acquisition of the Right to Build by Contract *Inter Vivos*.

with the right to build and the person for whose benefit the right to build is established. Such a contract must be made in writing.[789,790]

211. The right to build may be established by the owner of an immovable in his own favour. The owner of the land may establish the right to build in his own favour with the express declaration of his will made in writing.[791] The same person will then be the owner of the land encumbered with the right to build and the holder of that right. In this case, the same conditions for the establishment of the right to build are required (ownership of the plot of land, a unilateral legal transaction establishing the right to build, and an entry in the land register). After the owner of the land has established the right to build in his own favour, he may transfer it to another person by contract.[792]

C. Establishment on the Basis of a Court Decision

212. The right to build is established on the basis of a court decision when the court establishes it in partition or probate proceedings.[793,794] The court may render a decision on the establishment of the right to build if it is authorized to establish easement in these proceedings[795] and in other cases provided by law. The rules on the establishment of easements by court decisions apply accordingly to the establishment of the right to build.[796,797]

D. Establishment on the Basis of Separate Acts

213. The establishment of the right to build is regulated by numerous separate acts providing for the use and management of publicly owned immovables.[798] The right to build is a particularly important instrument of activating the economic value of an immovable when a separate act prohibits the alienation of state-owned property.[799] Every single regulation providing for the disposal of state-owned land stipulates specific conditions for the establishment of the right to build.

---

789. Article 287/2 PA. A contract must contain all the general and special conditions necessary for registration.
790. Gavella in *Property Law II*, 89; Klarić / Vedriš in *Civil Law*, 372.
791. Article 284/2 PA.
792. Article 285 PA. For more details, *see* Part I, Ch. 5, §3. III. Disposal of the Right to Build.
793. Article 289 PA.
794. Part III, Ch. 3, §5. Acquisition of the Right to Build on the Basis of a Court Decision.
795. Article 226 PA.
796. Article 289/2 PA.
797. Gavella in *Property Law II*, 51; Klarić / Vedriš in *Civil Law*, 372.
798. Public ownership is the ownership of the state, towns, counties or municipalities (Art. 35 PA). In principle, the state and other entities governed by public law have the same position regarding ownership as private owners, unless otherwise provided by law (Art. 35/1 PA).
799. For more details, *see* Part I, Ch. 7. Special Legal Regimes Regulating Immovables.

214. The establishment of the right to build on state-owned forest land is provided for in the FsA.[800] The right to build on forest land may be established to build a camp, a golf course or other recreation facilities or to build and maintain infrastructural objects.[801] The land then remains in state ownership. The right to build is then in favour of a natural or legal person for whose benefit the objects are built. [802] The content of the right to build is established by the general provisions on the right to build of the PA.[803] The right to build may be established on state-owned agricultural land.[804]

215. The right to build may be established on the immovables owned by the Republic of Croatia, which, pursuant to the Waters Act (WA),[805] are considered to be public good (e.g., rivers, lakes, land next to rivers and lakes, etc.). The right to build on public water domain is established in favour of natural and legal persons for the construction of water facilities in order to exercise economic and personal needs,[806] but only if this will not have an adverse impact on the exercise of the basic purpose of a public water asset. A contract on the establishment of the right to build is made by the public institution *Hrvatske vode* in the name of the Republic of Croatia (RC).[807] Water facilities built on the basis of the right to build are not considered to be part of a public water domain.[808] Other conditions for the establishment of the right to build on a public water domain are provided for in the general provisions on the right to build of the PA.[809]

216. The right to build may also be established on public roads that are owned by the Republic of Croatia.[810] This may be established only for the purposes laid down in the RA to build municipal, water and energy structures or electronic or other infrastructure on a public road.[811] The right to build is established in favour of the investor in the construction of such facilities.[812] A contract on the establishment of the right to build is made between the holder of the right to build and the legal person authorized for the management of public roads.[813] Regarding the content and method of establishing the right to build, the general provisions on the right to build of the PA apply. The RA expressly provides to whose favour the right to build may

800. OG Nos. 68/18, 115/18, 98/19, 32/20, 145/20.
801. Articles 51, 53 Forests Act.
802. Articles 51/7, 53 Forests Act.
803. For more *see*: Belaj in *Property Law III*, 177.
804. Articles 77-79. Agricultural Act, OG Nos 20/18, 115/18, 98/19.
805. OG Nos 66/19, 84/21.
806. Articles 12/10, 18 of WA.
807. Article 18/4 of WA.
808. Article 12/10 of WA.
809. For more *see*: Jug in *Property Law III*, 294.
810. Article 3/1 of the Roads Act, OG Nos 84/11, 18/13, 22/13, 54/13, 94/14, 110/19.
811. Article 3/3 RA.
812. Article 25/4 RA.
813. Articles 25/6, 8 RA.

be transferred. The transfer is allowed only in favour of a person who, according to a separate act, is authorized to manage infrastructural objects built on public roads.[814,815]

217. The right to build may also be established in projects of public-private partnerships in conformity with the Public-Private Partnership Act (PPPA). Within the framework of public-private partnership, a public partner may, among other things, establish the right to build on an immovable in public ownership for a private partner.[816] The obligation of establishing the right to build is assumed by the public partner by virtue of the contract on public-private partnership made between public and private partners, whereby the rights and obligations of the contractual parties are stipulated for the purpose of implementing a public-private partnership project.[817] The general provisions on the right to build of the PA apply to the conditions for the establishment of the right to build and its content since the PPPA does not contain any specific provisions regulating this issue.[818] A private partner acquires the right to build if all the general conditions stipulated for the establishment of the right to build on the basis of a legal transaction are fulfilled.

III. Disposal of the Right to Build

A. General Remarks on the Disposal of the Right to Build

218. The right to build is an alienable and inheritable right,[819] just like immovables in legal transactions. The right to build may, just like an immovable, be an independent subject to various property disposals. It may imply charges or no charges for the transfer to other persons and may be encumbered by easements and real burdens. It may also be the subject of liens and other property securities.[820] If a building is already erected on the right to build, the object of legal disposals will always be the right to build together with the building erected on this right.[821] The building is considered to be an appurtenance to the right to build as if it were a plot of land itself,[822] and it may not be disposed of separately from the right to build.[823]

219. The basic rule is that the provisions on the acquisition of ownership of immovables apply accordingly to legal disposals of the right to build and to its

814. Article 25/5 RA.
815. For more *see*: Josipović in *Property Law III*, 439.
816. Article 2/7 of PPPA (OG 78/12, 152/14, 114/18).
817. Article 4 of PPPA.
818. The PPPA specifically sets forth the procedure for entering into a contract on PP by which, among other things, the obligation of the right to build may also be obtained (Art. 4 of PPPA). Thus, the PPPA expressly provides for the procedure of selecting a private partner, procuring consent to the final draft of the contract from the competent authorities, etc. (Arts 9-15 of PPPA).
819. Article 285/1 PA.
820. Article 285/2 PA.
821. Article 285/3 PA.
822. Article 280/3 PA.
823. Gavella in *Property Law II*, 81–82; Klarić / Vedriš in *Civil Law*, 370.

transfer to other persons.[824] The provisions of the acquisition of these rights apply accordingly to the acquisition of limited property rights on the right to build unless it is otherwise determined or unless it ensues from the legal nature of the right to build. These rules are derived from the provision of the PA, pursuant to which the disposal of the right to build is legally equated with the immovable.[825]

B. Transfer of the Right to Build

220. The holder of the right to build may dispose of his right in the same way as any owner disposes of his immovable.[826] Regardless of whether or not a building is erected on the right to build, the holder of such right may transfer his right to build to other persons by contract *inter vivos*. The provisions on the acquisition of the right of ownership of property by contract *inter vivos*, court decision or by succession apply accordingly to the transfer of the right to build unless otherwise provided or unless it arises differently from the legal nature of the right to build.[827]

221. The right to build on the basis of a legal transaction is acquired by the transfer to another person of an already established right to build if the conditions are fulfilled which are normally required for the acquisition of ownership of property by a contract.[828] A person who alienates the right to build must be its holder.[829] The parties must enter into a legal transaction in writing, its goal being to transfer the right to build to a new acquirer,[830] and the acquirer must be entered in the land register as the holder of the right to build by registration or conditional registration.[831] The right to build is transferred by succession to the heirs at the time of the testator's death.[832]

222. A new acquirer of the right to build assumes the legal position of the previous holder of the right to build regarding the essential and obligatory content of such right stipulated by law, as well as regarding the limitations to the right to build made public by being entered in the land register. The time limit for establishing the right to build in favour of the first acquirer will thus continue running even after the second acquirer acquires the right to build. The time which has elapsed up to the moment of transfer of the right to build will be taken into account. If at the time

---

824. Article 290/1 PA. In order to dispose of the right to build, its holder does not need any special permission of the owner of the plot of land unless this is expressly determined in an agreement between the owner of the land and the holder of the right to build.
825. Article 280/2 PA.
826. Article 285/1 PA.
827. Article 290/1 PA.
828. Articles 115 PA.
829. Article 115/2 in connection with Art. 290/1 PA.
830. Article 115/1 in connection with Art. 290/1 PA.
831. Articles 119 et seq. in connection with Art. 290/1 PA. The entry will be made in the land register unit where the right to build is entered as if it were an immovable.
832. Article 128 in connection with Art. 290/1 PA.

of the transfer of the right to build, a building has already been erected together with the right to build, the acquirer also becomes the owner of the building erected on the right to build.[833]

C. *Establishment of Ownership of an Individual Part of a Building Erected on the Right to Build (Condominium on the Right to Build)*

223. The holder of the right to build may establish ownership of an individual part of a building erected on the right to build (condominium on the right to build) with the corresponding application of the rules on the establishment of ownership of an individual part of immovable property.[834,835] The holder of the right to build who establishes ownership of an individual part of a building erected on the right to build may continue to dispose of that ownership and transfer it to other acquirers by contract. By being entered in the land register, these acquirers then acquire the corresponding co-ownership shares of the building erected on the right to build with which the ownership of an individual part of the building is connected.[836] In the part in which they become the co-owners of the building, they also become the co-holders of the right to build towards the owner of the land, and they are bound to fulfil all the obligations towards him ensuing from the right to build.

224. Ownership of an individual part of a building erected on the right to build will last only as long as the right to build. The right to build with a building on which the ownership of an individual part is established may terminate based on all legal foundations on which the right to build normally terminates.[837] With the termination of the right to build with a building, the co-ownership of the building of all co-owners also terminates. The owner of the land becomes the owner of the building free of all limitations ensuing from the establishment of ownership of an individual part of an immovable unless the owner of the land has determined otherwise.

---

833. Articles 285/3, 290/2 PA.
834. Articles 66/3, 75/1 PA. The establishment of ownership of an individual part of a building erected on the right to build is possible when the building is finished and entered in the land register file where the right to build is already entered as if it were an immovable.
835. The establishment of condominium on the right to build is carried out with the corresponding application of the rules on the establishment of condominium on the immovable referred to in Arts 71–75 PA. For such an establishment, all conditions normally required for the establishment of ownership of an individual part of an immovable must be fulfilled. Ownership of an individual part of an immovable will be established by registration in the land register (Art. 72 PA). For more details, *see* Part I, Ch. 3, §III. G. Establishment of Ownership on an Individual Part of Immovable Property.
836. All the rules on the rights and obligations of flat owners of the individual parts of the immovable apply accordingly to the rights of owners of individual parts of the building erected on the right to build (building with the right to build, Arts 85–93 PA).
837. Articles 292, 293 PA.

D. Establishment of Securities on the Right to Build

1. Lien (Mortgage) on the Right to Build

225. The holder of the right to build may encumber it with a lien (mortgage)[838] in the same way as can be done by an owner who encumbers his plot.[839,840] The object of a mortgage may be the right to build before a building is erected,[841] as well as the right to build with a building. If a mortgage is established only after a building has been erected, the object of the mortgage may only be the right to build together with the building.[842] Any type of mortgage may be established on the right to build under the same conditions as when a mortgage is established on the plot of land.[843] A mortgage on the right to build is entered in the land register file, where the right to build is entered as an immovable.

226. Special rules apply to mortgages on the right to build if the right to build terminates. These rules are different depending on whether or not a building is erected on the encumbered right to build. When the right to build on which no building has been erected terminates, the mortgage established on the right to build also ceases to exist.[844] With the termination of the right to build a building, the mortgage is transferred to the compensation that the owner of the land is bound to pay the holder of the right to build for the increased value of his immovable on account of the erected building.[845] The enforcement of the claim secured by the mortgage is then governed by the provisions on the enforcement of a lien on the right to build (lien a pecuniary claim).[846]

2. Fiduciary Transfer of the Right to Build

227. In order to secure a particular claim, the holder of the right to build may make a fiduciary transfer of his right to the creditor. The provisions of the EA on the judicial/notarial fiduciary transfer of ownership of an immovable for security

838. Article 285/2 PA.
839. The right to build may be the object of enforcement, and the claims secured by a mortgage on the right to build may be settled by the application of the provisions of the EA providing for enforcement of immovables in enforcement proceedings (Art. 129/3 PA).
840. In order to encumber his right to build, the holder does not need to obtain the prior permission of the owner of the land, unless it was otherwise agreed.
841. When, after encumbering the right to build, a building is erected, the previously established lien on the right to build extends to include the building erected on the right to build.
842. Article 285/3 PA.
843. For more details on the types of liens (mortgages) established on immovables, *see* Part VI, Ch. 4, §1. Mortgage: Lien on Immovables.
844. Article 296/1 PA.
845. Article 296/2 PA.
846. It is possible, however, that the owner of the land agrees that the mortgage continues to encumber the immovable even after the termination of the right to build. *See* Gavella in *Property Law II*, 94.

apply accordingly.[847] [848] On the basis of a security agreement by means of transferring the right to build,[849] a transfer of the right to build is carried out in the land register in favour of the creditor of the security with recordation that the transfer was made in order to secure a particular claim.[850,851]

228. Judicial or notarial transfers of the right to build for security purposes bring about the effects of an unconditional transfer of the right to build to the creditor.[852] The creditor then becomes the holder of the right to build with the content, limitations and duration provided in the land register. Unless agreed otherwise, the creditor is not entitled to possession of the land encumbered with the right to build and of the building erected on the right to build.[853] The possessor of the encumbered land and the building continues to be a debtor who has made a fiduciary transfer of the right to build. If the debtor pays the secured claim, the creditor is bound to transfer again the right to build to the debtor.[854] If the claim is not paid when due, the creditor is entitled to exercise his rights, i.e., he is entitled to initiate notary public proceedings for the collection/sale of the right to build.[855] If the right to build is not sold within the time limits laid down in the EA, the creditor becomes a valid holder of the right to build.[856]

IV. Protection of the Right to Build

229. The right to build is protected by special court actions filed by the person in whose favour the right to build is established. The municipal court on whose territory the encumbered immovable is located is competent for such actions.[857] The right to build is protected differently depending on whether or not a building has already been erected on the right to build.[858,859]

230. Before a building is erected, the right to build is protected under the rules on the protection of easement, which apply accordingly.[860] When a building is

847. Articles 309–327 of EA.
848. For more details, *see* Part VI, Ch. 4, §2. Judicial or Notarial Security of Claim by Transfer of Ownership.
849. Article 310 of EA.
850. Article 312 of EA.
851. Gavella in *Property Law II*, 94–95.
852. *See* Dika in *Enforcement Law*, 784–822.
853. Article 315 of EA.
854. Article 323 of EA.
855. Articles 317, 322 of EA. The rules on the sale of immovables where fiduciary transfers for security purposes have occurred apply accordingly to the collection of the claim secured by a transfer of the right to build.
856. Article 322/7 of EA.
857. Article 56 CPA.
858. The actions by which the right to build is protected are not subject to the statute of limitations.
859. Gavella in *Property Law II*, 92; Klarić / Vedriš in *Civil Law*, 366.
860. Article 291/1 PA. For more details, *see* Part I, Ch. 5, §1. V. Protection of Easements.

erected, the ownership of the building erected on the right to build enjoys protection under the rules on the protection of the right of ownership, which apply accordingly.[861]

231. When the right to build is infringed by an invalid entry in the land register, it is protected by an action for cancellation. With such an action, the holder of the right to build seeks cancellation of the invalid land register entry by which his right to build has been violated.[862] All the rules governing the action for cancellation that protect other rights entered in the land register apply accordingly.

V. Termination of the Right to Build

232. The right to build terminates with the destruction of the thing, with the holder's waiver, upon the expiry of the period of time for which it is established, with the fulfilment of the dissolution condition, with the death of the beneficiary, by relief and by revocation on the basis of a court decision.[863] The court renders a decision on the revocation of the right to build at the request of the owner of the land unless a building is erected within twenty years from the establishment of the right to build.[864] At the request of the owner of the land, the court revokes the right to build if the building erected on the right to build is destroyed to such an extent that it cannot be used for the purpose for which it was intended unless it is rebuilt within a time limit of six years to an extent necessary to make it suitable for the previous purpose.[865]

233. In any of the aforementioned cases, the right to build terminates only when deleted from the land register.[866] The right to build will be deleted on a proposal made by the owner of the encumbered immovable on the basis of a document proving that one of the grounds for the termination of the right to build referred to in Article 292 of the Obligations Act (OA) existed.

234. When the right to build terminates, the building erected on the right to build becomes an appurtenance of the land, and its owner becomes the owner of the land.[867] With the termination of the right to build, a legal unity of the land and the building is established, and the land and the building are considered a single immovable. After the right to build ceases to exist, the owner of the land is bound to give compensation for the building to the person whose right to build has terminated. The compensation is determined in an amount equal to the augmented value of his property in legal transactions on account of the building erected on it.[868] The lien which

861. Article 291/2 PA. For more details, *see* Part I, Ch. 3, §4. Protection of Ownership.
862. Articles 168, 236 in connection with Art. 291 PA.
863. Articles 292–296 PA.
864. Article 294/1 PA.
865. Article 294/2 PA.
866. Articles 292/2, 294/4 PA.
867. Article 295/1 PA.
868. Article 295/3 PA.

encumbered the right to build after its termination encumbers the compensation which the owner is bound to pay to the person whose right to build has terminated,[869] and easements and real burdens continue to exist as easements and real burdens encumbering the land with the building based on the order of priority applicable until such time.[870]

§4. MORTGAGE

I. Concept

235. A mortgage is a limited property right on a particular immovable (*založno pravo na nekretnini, hipoteka*) authorizing its holder (lien creditor, mortgagee, *založni vjerovnik*) to have a particular claim settled against the value of the immovable if the claim is not settled when due, and its everyday owner (lien debtor, mortgagor, *založni dužnik*) is bound to sufferance.[871,872]

236. The mortgagee does not have the right of possession of the mortgaged immovable or the right to collect the fruits and other benefits derived from it.[873] The mortgagor remains in possession of the mortgaged immovable. The mortgagor is bound to maintain its value.[874] If the mortgagor endangers the value of the immovable, the mortgagee is authorized to request forced payment of the secured claim even before it is due.[875]

237. If the debtor does not pay his debt when it is due, the mortgagee is entitled to recover it against the value of the mortgaged immovable.[876] The mortgagee exercises his right to settlement from the value of the mortgaged immovable, i.e., from the value realized by selling the mortgaged immovable in court (court auction). The mortgagee must exercise his right to enforcement through the court in accordance with the rules on enforcement (enforcement actions) of pecuniary claims.[877] After the mortgaged immovable is sold and the mortgagee's claim is settled, the amount in excess of his claim is returned to the mortgagor.[878]

869. Article 296/2 PA.
870. Articles 296/2,3 PA.
871. Article 297/1 PA. For more details, *see* Part VI, Ch. 4. Securities on Immovable Property.
872. Gavella in *Property Law II*, 121–122.; Klarić / Vedriš in *Civil Law*, 335–336.
873. Article 329/1 PA.
874. Article 330 PA.
875. Article 330/1 PA.
876. Article 336 PA.
877. Articles 79–132i5 of EA.
878. For more details on the settlement of a mortgagee, *see* Part VI, Ch. 4, §1. V. Enforcement of a Secured Claim.

II. Types of Mortgages

238. In Croatian law, there are several types of mortgages: voluntary mortgage, voluntary judicial or notarial mortgage, compulsory mortgage and statutory mortgage.[879]

III. Creation of a Mortgage

239. A mortgage is acquired on the basis of a legal transaction (voluntary mortgage), a court decision (judicial mortgage) or by law (statutory mortgage). It is deemed acquired when all conditions laid down by law are fulfilled.[880] The conditions for the acquisition of a mortgage are provided for differently depending on the legal title for acquisition.[881]

IV. Protection of Mortgages

240. Mortgages are protected by special court actions filed by the creditor (mortgagee). The municipal court on whose territory the encumbered immovable is located is competent to decide upon such actions.[882]

241. The mortgagee is authorized to protect his mortgage against third persons and against the owner of the encumbered immovable (mortgagor). A mortgagee may require that the mortgagor, or a third party, does not perform, regarding the mortgaged immovable, anything that would endanger it or diminish its value.[883,884]

242. When a mortgage is infringed by an invalid entry in the land register, it is protected by an action for cancellation. With such an action, the mortgagee requires the invalid entry infringing his mortgage to be cancelled from the land register.[885] The rules on the cancellation action protecting all other rights entered in the land register apply accordingly to such an action.

V. Termination of a Mortgage

243. A mortgage terminates if the mortgaged immovable is destroyed,[886] if the mortgagee renounces the mortgage,[887] with a lapse of time and the fulfilment of the

879. For more details on types of mortgages, *see* Part VI, Ch. 4, §1. II. Types of Mortgages.
880. Article 305/2 PA.
881. For more details on the establishment of mortgages, *see* Part VI, Ch. 4, §1. II. Types of Mortgages.
882. Article 56 CPA.
883. Article 332/1/ind. 2 PA.
884. For more details on the action for the protection of mortgages, *see* Gavella in *Property Law II*, 166.
885. Article 129 LRA, Art. 332/1/ind. 1 PA.
886. Article 343 PA.
887. Article 344 PA.

dissolution condition,[888] with the termination of the secured claim (the entire secured claim, all accessory claims to interest and costs),[889] by protecting the trust in land register of another,[890] if the mortgagee ceases to exist,[891] by revocation,[892] by relief on the basis of the operation of law, or with a decision of an administrative authority.[893]

244. In each of the aforementioned cases, the mortgage expires only with deletion from the land register.[894] Deletion of a mortgage is entered on the basis of a document proving that the claim has ceased to exist or that a circumstance has occurred because of which a mortgage must be deleted from the land register.

---

888. Article 345 PA.
889. Article 346 PA. Before the mortgage is deleted from the land register, the owner of an immovable may transfer the undeleted mortgage to a new claim (Art. 347/2 PA).
890. Article 349 PA. A mortgage on an immovable which is not entered in the land register terminates when the encumbered immovable is acquired by a person who did not know and had no reason to know that it existed.
891. Article 350 PA.
892. Article 351 PA.
893. Article 352 PA. For more details on the termination of a mortgage, *see* Part VI, Ch. 4, §1. VI. Termination of Mortgage.
894. Cf. Arts 344/5, 345/2, 347/1, 351/2, 352/2, 353 PA.

Chapter 6. Leasehold Interests

§1. Rental

I. Concept

245. Under a rental contract (*ugovor o najmu*), the lessor undertakes to deliver to the lessee a specified thing for use, and the lessee undertakes to pay the lessor a specified rent therefor.[895] General provisions on a rental contract are set forth in Articles 550–578 of the Obligations Act (OA). These provisions lay down the lessor's[896] and the lessee's[897] obligations, sublease,[898] the legal effects of the alienation of the rented thing[899] and termination of a rental contract.[900] The provisions of the OA on a rental contract apply to the rentals of movables and immovables. For renting immovables, the OA lays down only some rules.[901] A rental contract must be made in writing.[902] A rental contract entered into for a fixed term is deemed tacitly renewed for the same period of time unless either of the parties to the contract, not later than thirty days before the expiry of the period, notifies in writing the other party that it does not wish to enter into a next fixed-term contract.[903] A rental contract for an immovable entered into for an indefinite time may be terminated with a cancellation notice made in writing.[904] If the deadline for the cancellation notice is not stipulated in the contract, it is thirty days.[905]

246. The provisions of the OA on the rental contract apply subordinately to the rental of immovables governed by special laws.[906] The most common rental contracts entered into under Croatian law are those regulated by the Residential Lease Act (RLA).[907]

---

895. Klarić / Vedriš in *Civil Law*, 524–530.
896. Articles 553–560 of OA.
897. Articles 561–566 OA.
898. Articles 567–569 OA.
899. Articles 570–573 OA.
900. Articles 574–578 OA.
901. The parties to the contract may agree that the rental be entered in the land register. It is entered either by registration or conditional registration (Art. 35/1 LRA) in the land register file in which the rented immovable is entered (Art. 24,43 LRA). Entering a rental in the land register has an absolute effect against any third parties. It is of particular importance in the case of enforcement involving the rented immovable. A rental entered in the land register prior to the commencement of enforcement proceedings does not terminate with the sale of the immovable, so that the purchaser at an auction assumes the rights and obligations of the lessor (Art. 88/1 of EA). A rental not entered in the land register terminates in the case of the sale of the immovable as a result of enforcement proceedings (Art. 88/3 of EA).
902. Article 552 of OA.
903. Article 575 of OA.
904. Article 576/3 of OA.
905. Article 576/2 of OA.
906. Article 551 of OA.
907. OG Nos 91/96, 48/98, 66/98, 22/06, 68/18, 105/20.

II. Residential Lease Contract

A. Concept

247. A residential lease contract (*ugovor o najmu stana*) imposes an obligation on the lessor (owner of a flat) to cede the flat to the lessee for a stipulated rent.[908,909] A residential lease contract is governed by the RLA. It stipulates the rights and obligations concerning the lease or the use of a flat or part of a flat.[910] Pursuant to this Act, a flat consists of rooms meant for habitation with all the necessary facilities which make a complete architectural unit and have a separate entrance.[911] Other rooms and areas in the building which the lessee uses (garages, laundry rooms and the like) may also be subject to the lease contract, but a separate rent must be paid for their use.[912] A residential lease contract, in order to be valid, must be made in writing.[913] It may be entered into for a definite or indefinite term.

248. The residential lease contract lays down the relations between the lessor and the lessee regarding the rented flat. It specifically identifies the parties to the contract (the lessor and lessee) and contains a description of the flat, the amount of rent and how it is to be paid, the costs that must be covered and the means of their payment, the names of the persons who are to use the flat together with the lessee, the length of the lease, provisions on the maintenance of the flat and the use of common areas, as well as the provisions on the handover of the flat.[914]

B. Rights and Obligations of the Lessor

249. The lessor is entitled to request from the lessee the payment of rent in the amount, means and time of payment as stipulated in the contract.

250. The lessor is bound to hand over the flat to the lessee in the way and at the time stipulated in the lease contract.[915] The flat must be handed over in a habitable condition. The lessee is accountable for any defects or possible damage to the lessor in accordance with the rules on obligations (liability for material defects). The lessor is responsible for maintaining the flat in a habitable condition in accordance

908. Article 3/1 of RLA.
909. Klarić / Vedriš in *Civil Law*, 527–530.
910. The Residential Lease Act also provides for the legal position of persons whose tenant's rights on flats under so-called social ownership terminated when this Act became effective. On the day when the Act entered into force, they acquired the rights and obligations of lessees (so-called protected lessees, *zaštićeni namjmoprimci*).
911. Article 2/1 of RLA.
912. Article 2/2 of RLA.
913. Article 4/2 of RLA.
914. Article 5 of RLA.
915. Article 12 of RLA.

with the residential lease contract.[916] The lessor is bound to bear the costs of necessary repairs in the flat and in the common particle of the building.

C. Rights and Obligations of the Lessee

251. The lessee is entitled to use the rented flat for habitation together with the persons specified in the residential lease contract and may use common areas, particles and devices in the building necessary for the use of the flat, as well as the accompanying land.[917] The lessee is entitled to use other common areas, parts and devices of the building if this is specifically stipulated in the contract. The lessee may sublease the flat or its part to a third person only with the permission of the lessor.[918]

252. The lessee is bound to pay rent.[919] It may be protected rent (*zaštićena najamnina*) or freely contracted rent. Protected rent is determined on the basis of the conditions and measures stipulated by the Republic of Croatia.[920] In other cases, when it is not stipulated that the lessee pays protected rent, the lessee is bound to pay the rent agreed upon freely by the parties to the residential lease contract.[921] The lessee must use the flat without damaging it.[922] The lessee is liable to the lessor jointly and severally with the members of his household for any damage caused by him or any other occupant either in the flat or in the common part or to the devices in the building.[923] The lessee is not allowed to make any changes to the flat or to any of the common parts of the building without the lessor's written permission.[924] Upon the termination of the residential lease contract, the lessee must hand back the flat to the lessor in the condition in which he received it, taking into account the changes that occurred during the regular occupancy of the flat.[925]

D. Termination of the Residential Lease Contract

253. The residential lease contract terminates upon the expiry of a definite period of time for which it is rented, with a cancellation notice, the dissolution of the lease contract, upon the agreement of the parties, and in other cases regulated

916. Article 13 of RLA.
917. Article 18/1 of RLA.
918. Article 28/1 of RLA.
919. Articles 6–11 of RLA.
920. Article 7 of RLA. Protected rent is paid by persons who use flats built with the funds allocated for the housing care of indigent persons, persons who use flats pursuant to the regulations on the rights of Croatian homeland war veterans, persons who used to be holders of tenant's rights on flats under so-called social ownership in the previous housing regime (now in private ownership), as well as other persons specified in separate laws (Art. 8 of RLA).
921. Articles 9–11 of RLA.
922. Article 14 of RLA.
923. Article 15/1 of RLA.
924. Article 14/2 of RLA.
925. Article 17 of RLA.

by law. A residential lease contract made for an indefinite time expires with a cancellation notice. When a lease contract is terminated with a cancellation notice, the grounds on which the lessor may terminate the contract must be observed. There are special provisions governing the cases where a residential lease contract is cancelled by the lessee.

254. The lessor may terminate the contract entered into for a definite or indefinite time if the lessee or other occupants use the flat contrary to the RLA or the residential lease contract.[926] The residential lease contract may also be terminated if the lessee does not pay rent or other expenses within the terms stipulated in the contract, if the lessee sublets the flat without the lessor's permission, if the lessee disturbs other lessees or occupants of the building, or if the lessee does not use the flat for habitation but for other purposes.[927] The residential lease contract entered into for an indefinite period of time may be terminated by the lessor if he or his children or parents intend to move in.[928]

255. The lessee may terminate the residential lease contract entered into for an indefinite period of time without giving any reasons for termination. The lessee is bound to notify the lessor at least three months prior to the date when he intends to move out.[929]

256. In the case of the death or change of the lessor, the lessor's rights and obligations referred to in the contract are transferred to his heir or legal successor.[930] In the case of the death of the lessee, or when the lessee leaves the flat, the lessee's rights and obligations are transferred to his spouse or child, stepchild or adoptee specified in the residential lease contract.[931]

§2. Lease

I. Concept

257. Under a lease contract (*ugovor o zakupu*), the lessor undertakes to deliver to the lessee a specified thing for enjoyment in exchange for a rent that the lessee undertakes to pay.[932] General provisions on the lease contract are provided for in Articles 519–549 of the OA. These provisions lay down the obligations of both the

926. Article 19/1 of RLA.
927. When any of the grounds for termination are met, the lessor must first notify the lessee and ask him to eliminate, within thirty days, the ground for the cancellation of the contract (Art. 19/2 of RLA). The lessor must send to the lessee a reasoned cancellation notice in writing (Art. 22/1 of RLA). The eviction deadline is three months (Art. 22/2 of RLA). If the lessee does not move out of the flat after the expiry of this deadline, the lessor may file an action for eviction with the competent court.
928. Article 21 of RLA.
929. Article 23 of RLA.
930. Article 24/1 of RLA.
931. Article 24/2 of RLA.
932. Klarić / Vedriš in *Civil Law*, 515–524.

lessor[933] and the lessee,[934] the conditions of the sublease,[935] the legal effects of the alienation of the leased thing[936] and the termination of the lease contract.[937] The provisions of the OA apply to the lease of both movables and immovables.[938] The provisions of the OA apply subsidiarily to the lease of immovables governed by special regulations.[939] The most common lease contracts made in Croatian law are commercial lease contracts regulated by the Commercial Lease Act (CLA)[940] and contracts of lease of agricultural land owned by the state provided for in the Agricultural Land Act (ALA).[941]

II. Commercial Lease

A. Concept

258. With a commercial lease contract (*ugovor o zakupu poslovnih prostorija*), the lessor is obliged to hand over to the lessee specific business premises, and the lessee is bound to pay the contracted rent.[942,943] A lease contract is provided for in the CLA. This Act stipulates the commencement and the termination of the lease of business premises and the mutual rights and obligations of the lessor and the lessee. According to the CLA, commercial premises include a building, particular space used for business purposes, and a garage or a parking place in a garage.[944] A business building is a building intended for the execution of business activities if it is largely used for that purpose.[945] The space used for business is a single room or several rooms in a business or residential building intended for business activities which, as a rule, makes up an architectural unit and has a separate entrance.[946]

933. Articles 521–531 of OA.
934. Articles 532–536 of OA.
935. Articles 537–540 of OA.
936. Articles 541–544 of OA.
937. Articles 545–549 of OA.
938. The contractual parties may agree that the lease be entered in the land register. The entry of a lease in the land register and the legal effects of such an entry in relation to third parties in enforcement proceedings are subject to the same rules as when residential lease is entered in the land register. For more details, *see* Part I, Ch. 6, §1. I. Concept.
939. Articles 551, 520 of OA.
940. OG 125/11, 65/15, 112/18.
941. OG 20/18, 115/18,98/19 .
942. Article 5/1 of CLA.
943. Klarić / Vedriš in *Civil Law*, 521–524.
944. Article 2/1 of CLA.
945. Article 2/2 of CLA.
946. Article 2/3 of CLA. When commercial premises are owned by the Republic of Croatia or by counties, municipalities, towns or the City of Zagreb, or by legal persons owned, or predominantly owned by them, a commercial lease contract is entered into on the basis of a public bidding procedure (Art. 6 of CLA).

259. For a commercial lease contract to be valid, it must be made in writing.[947] It contains the names of the parties to the contract, a description of the business premises, the data on the activities to be performed on the premises, the provisions regarding the use of common devices and areas in the building and provisions regarding common services and the terms of their payment, the deadline for the handover of the business premises to the lessee, the period of time for which the contract is made, the amount of rent and the terms of payment, as well as provisions on the termination of the lease contract and the place and time of its conclusion.[948] The amount of rent is freely agreed upon by the parties to the contract. A commercial lease contract may be entered into for definite or indefinite periods of time.

B. Rights and Obligations of the Lessor

260. The lessor is entitled to the rent that the lessee is bound to pay in the amount, method and time stipulated in the contract. On the basis of the commercial lease contract, the lessor is bound to hand over to the lessee the premises within the time limit and in the condition stipulated in the contract[949] and to maintain them in the conditions stipulated therein, i.e., in the conditions suitable for the activities specified in the contract.[950] The lessee is bound to carry out any repairs necessary for the maintenance of the business premises for the duration of the lease contract.

C. Rights and Obligations of the Lessee

261. The lessee is entitled to carry out the activity for which the business premises are leased and which is specified in the lease contract. The lessee must pay the contracted rent in accordance with the term laid down in the contract,[951] pay the expenses for the use of common devices and for the common services carried out in the building where the business premises are located,[952] bear the costs of regular maintenance of the business premises[953] and pay for any damage caused by him within the business premises.[954] The lessee may not sublease the business premises or any of their parts unless otherwise stipulated in the lease contract.[955] Without permission given by the lessor, the lessee is not allowed to make any changes to the business premises by which the construction, arrangement, surface area, purpose or the external looks of the business premises would be substantially changed.[956] Upon

947. Article 4/3 of CLA.
948. Article 5/2 of CLA.
949. Article 8 of CLA.
950. Article 11 of CLA.
951. Article 16 of CLA.
952. Articles 17,18 of CLA.
953. Article 18/1 of CLA.
954. Article 18/3 of CLA.
955. Article 19/1 of CLA.
956. Article 15/1 of CLA.

the termination of the lease contract, the lessee is bound to hand back the business premises in the condition in which they were received.[957]

D. Termination of the Commercial Lease Contract

262. A commercial lease contract entered into for a definite period of time terminates upon the expiry of the period for which it was made.[958] A commercial lease contract entered into for an indefinite period of time expires with a notice of cancellation[959] after the expiry of the cancellation term.[960] If not otherwise stipulated in the contract, the cancellation term is thirty days, and a notice may be given only on the first or the fifteenth of the month.[961] A commercial lease contract must always be cancelled in writing by registered mail or through a notary public when a lease contract is made in the form of a notarial act. [962] A commercial lease contract may be cancelled by either party to the contract, regardless of whether it was made for a definite or indefinite time if the other party does not fulfil its obligations.[963]

263. Regardless of the provisions on the length of the lease, the lessor may terminate the contract at any time[964] if the lessee, despite a written warning, uses the premises in contravention of the contract, or causes substantial damage by using them without due care, if the lessee fails to pay the due rent within fifteen days' notice of a written reminder by the lessor, if the lessor needs the premises to perform his activity because he, by not being responsible for the reasons, can no longer use the premises in which he used to perform his business activity.

264. The commercial lease contract does not terminate if a third party purchases or otherwise acquires the lessor's business premises.[965] In such a case, the third party enters into the rights and obligations of the lessor. The commercial lease contract does not terminate with the death of the lessee since his heirs take over his rights and obligations unless otherwise stipulated in the contract.[966]

III. The Lease Contract of Agricultural Land

265. A contract on the lease of agricultural land owned by the Republic of Croatia is provided for in the ALA. State-owned agricultural land is sold or leased

957. Article 20 of CLA.
958. Article 22 of CLA.
959. Article 23 of CLA.
960. A lease contract may not terminate with a cancellation notice earlier than one year from the date of its conclusion, unless otherwise stipulated in the contract (Art. 23/2 of CLA).
961. Article 24 of CLA.
962. Article 25 of CLA.
963. Articles 26,289 of CLA.
964. Article 26 of CLA.
965. Article 30 of CLA.
966. Article 31 of CLA.

on the basis of a public bidding procedure.[967] Any natural or legal person engaged in agricultural activities may participate in the bidding procedure for the lease of agricultural land.[968] State-owned agricultural land is leased for a period of twenty-five years with the possibility to be extended for the same period of time. [969]

266. Based on the decision on the selection of the most advantageous bid offered in the sale or lease bidding process, the head of the municipality or the mayor concludes a sale or lease contract with the bidder.[970] The lessee must pay annual rent.[971] The lessee may neither transfer his rights under the lease contract to another person nor sublease the agricultural land.[972]

267. The lease contract of agricultural land terminates upon the expiry of the term for which it was concluded, by mutual consent or with the change of the purpose of the agricultural land.[973] The lessor must cancel the lease contract if the lessee fails to pay rent, does not use the agricultural land as a good manager, cultivates the agricultural land contrary to the provisions of the concluded contract, subleases the leased agricultural land, undertakes construction works on the agricultural land which goes beyond the boundaries of usual management practice, changes the use of the agricultural land without the approval of the lessor or carries out activities in contravention of the provisions on the protection of nature.[974]

268. Upon the termination of the lease contract, the lessee is bound to hand back the land to the owner's possession but is entitled to harvest the crops or collect the fruits.[975] The lessee is entitled to take away his objects and buildings erased on the land.[976]

§3. CONCESSIONS

269. The Concessions Act (CA) provides for the method of commercial exploitation of immovables considered common goods (e.g., maritime domain) and immovables in public ownership (e.g., public roads). A concession contract (*ugovor*

967. Article 31 of ALA.
968. Articles 35,36 of ALA.
969. Article 31 of ALA. The same period of lease is awarded for state-owned land intended for fish ponds (Art. 52 of ALA).
970. Article 38/1 of ALA. The lease contract must be made in writing (Art. 38/1 of ALA). It must contain provisions concerning the subject of the lease, its length, the amount of rent, the rights and obligations of the lessee, the intended use of the land and reasons for the cancellation and termination of the contract (Art. 42 of ALA).
971. Article 40 of ALA.
972. Article 41 of ALA.
973. Article 43/1 of ALA.
974. Article 43/4 of ALA. Where not regulated by the provisions of this Act, the termination of a contract for the sale or lease of state-owned agricultural land is governed by legislation regulating civil obligations (Art. 47 of ALA).
975. Article 43/8 of ALA.
976. Article 46 of ALA.

o koncesiji) is regulated by the Concessions Act.[977] The Concessions Act provides for the process of granting concessions, terminating concessions and legal protection in granting and terminating concessions. A concession contract is a specific contract having public and private law elements. A concession contract is entered into, upon a public bidding procedure and a decision on the selection of the most advantageous bidder, by a concession grantor[978] and a concessionaire (a natural or a legal person).

270. A concession on an immovable may be awarded in various fields and for various activities, such as the exploitation of mineral raw materials, the exploitation of the public water domain, maritime domain, agricultural land, protected natural areas, public roads, ports and the like.[979] The conditions, procedure, method and other important issues for awarding concessions in individual fields and for various activities are governed by special regulations.[980] When a concession is governed by a special regulation, the Concessions Act applies subordinately.

271. With a concession contract, the concessionaire acquires the right to exploit a particular immovable which is considered to be a common or public good.[981] A concession contract is entered into after a public bidding procedure where the most advantageous bid is selected.[982] A concession contract specifies the rights and obligations of the concession grantor and concessionaire in accordance with the provisions of the CA and other special regulations governing the particular concession.[983] The concessionaire must pay a fee for the concession in the amount stipulated in the concession contract.[984] The concession contract terminates with the

977. OG No. 69/17, 107/20.
978. A concession grantor may be the Croatian Parliament, the Government of the Republic of Croatia, central state administration bodies on behalf of the Republic of Croatia, the competent bodies of local and regional self-government and legal persons authorized to award concessions under special regulations (Art. 7/1 of CA).
979. Article 8 of CA.
980. Article 8/3 of CA. For example: the Agricultural Land Act (OG No. 20/18, 115/18, 98/19), the Roads Act (OG Nos 84/11, 22/13, 54/13, 148/13, 93/14, 110/19), the Cultural Heritage Act (OG Nos 66/99, 151/03, 157/03, 100/04, 87/09, 88/10, 61/11, 25/12, 136/12, 136/12, 157/13, 152/14, 98/15, 44/17, 90/18, 32/20, 62/20), the Waters Act (OG Nos 66/19, 84/21), the Maritime Domain and Ports Act (OG Nos 158/03, 100/04, 141/06, 38/09, 123/11, 56/16, 98/19), the Nature Protection Act (OG Nos 80/13, 15/18, 14/19, 127/19), the Railway Act (OG Nos 32/19, 20/21), the Hunting Act (OG Nos 99/18, 31/19, 32/20), the Mining Act (OG No. 56/13, 14/14, 52/18, 115/18, 98/19) and others. For more details, *see* Part I, Ch. 7. Special Legal Regimes Regulating Immovable Property.
981. Article 3 of CA. A concession contract may serve as a basis for the legal separation of land from the building erected on the land awarded by concession (Art. 9 PA). For more details, *see* Part I, Ch. 1, §2. Legal Unity of Real Property (the Principle of *Superficies Solo Cedit*).
982. Articles 54 of CA.
983. Article 56 of CA.
984. Article 57 of CA. A concession is entered in the land register in accordance with the rules on the registration of a lease (Art. 24/2 LRA). A concession is entered in the land register file where the immovable on which the concession is awarded is entered.

fulfilment of the legal conditions,[985] with the cancellation of the concession contract in the public interest, by termination of the concession contract by consent and by a court decision whereby the concession contract is annulled.[986]

985. The CA stipulates that the concession terminates upon the expiry of the period for which it was awarded, with the death of the concessionaire, with the unilateral cancellation of the concession grantor if the concessionaire fails to settle the concession fee, if he fails to take the measures necessary for the protection of the general or public good, if the concessionaire does not perform the concession contract, etc. (Art. 70-73 of CA).

986. Articles 70-73 of CA. Concessions are entered into a special register of concessions kept by the ministry responsible for finance (Art. 79 of CA).

Chapter 7. Special Legal Regimes on Immovables

§1. Concept

272. The general property regulation of the PA covers all immovables in the Republic of Croatia unless otherwise provided by law.[987] Legal relations on property are governed by a special regime laid down in a separate act, while the provisions of the PA providing for rights, their protection, exercise and termination apply subsidiarily unless otherwise provided by a separate act or unless these provisions are contrary to this special regime. In the Republic of Croatia, separate acts provide for the legal regime governing immovables under special protection of the state. Because of their purpose and importance for the protection of the environment, nature, national security, people's health and the like, many pieces of property are proclaimed by a separate act to be goods of special significance to the Republic of Croatia.[988] The domains of interest to the Republic of Croatia are the sea, seashore, islands, waters, airspace, mineral resources and other natural assets, as well as land, forests, flora and fauna, other components of the natural environment, property and items of particular cultural, historical, economic or ecological significance.[989] The manner in which any assets of interest to the Republic of Croatia may be used and exploited by holders of rights thereto and by their owners are regulated by law.[990] Some obligations regarding their maintenance are also imposed on the owners, or they are prohibited from behaving in certain ways so as not to distort the particular characteristics of these things for which they are proclaimed to be of interest to the Republic of Croatia. Owners and persons authorized to exercise other rights related to the aforementioned things may exercise these rights for their use and utilization in accordance with the procedure laid down by law.[991], [992]

§2. Agricultural Land

273. Agricultural land (*poljoprivredno zemljište*) in the territory of the Republic of Croatia is subject to a special legal regime laid down in the ALA. Agricultural land in terms of the ALA includes plough fields, gardens, meadows, pastures, orchards, olive groves, vineyards, fish farms, as well as any other land that can be used for agricultural purposes.[993] Agricultural land is an asset of interest to the

987. Article 1/5 PA.
988. Article 52 of the Constitution of the RC, Art. 4 PA.
989. Article 52/1 of the Constitution of the RC.
990. Article 52/2 of the Constitution of the RC.
991. Article 4/2 PA.
992. For more, *see* Gavella in *Property Law III*, 5 et seq.
993. Article 3 of ALA.

Republic of Croatia and enjoys its particular protection.[994] Ownership of agricultural land may not be acquired on the basis of contract by foreign legal or natural persons unless otherwise provided in a treaty.[995]

274. Agricultural land may be in private or public ownership. Both domestic natural, private law and public law persons may be owners of agricultural land. With the entry into force of the ALA, the Republic of Croatia became the owner of agricultural land, which, prior to the entry into force of this Act, had been in social ownership.

275. The particularities of the legal regime governing agricultural land in the ALA laid down to secure maximum protection of agricultural land as an asset of interest for the Republic of Croatia are twofold. Special restrictions of ownership are imposed on private owners of agricultural land. For the Republic of Croatia, as the owner of agricultural land, there are separate rules governing the disposal of such land.

276. Owners of agricultural land, pursuant to the general rules on the disposal of the rights on immovables, also dispose of their agricultural land. They may, in legal transactions *inter vivos* and in the case of death, alienate their agricultural land with or without charging it, they may encumber it by limited rights, lease it, or they may limit their ownership on the basis of a contract by prohibiting alienation, encumbrance or the like. The ALA lays down many limitations imposed on owners of agricultural land regarding its use, as well as special obligations in the case of the change of purpose of such land. Owners are bound to use agricultural land in the way provided for in the ALA.[996] The owner's rights are also limited when the purpose of the land is changed to non-agricultural. Such alteration is allowed only if it is in accordance with physical planning documents and if the owner pays a one-time charge on account of degrading the value and the area of agricultural land.[997]

277. The ALA provides, in particular, for the model of management of agricultural land owned by the Republic of Croatia.[998] The Republic of Croatia disposes of its agricultural land according to the general regulations governing the disposal of immovables unless otherwise laid down in the ALA.[999] The state may sell, lease its agricultural land, common pastures and fish farms, give agricultural land for temporary exploitation, swap state-owned agricultural land for private agricultural land

994. Article 2/1 of ALA.
995. Article 2/2 of ALA.
996. Articles 4–7 of ALA. For example, the owner is bound to keep and maintain agricultural land in a state suitable for agricultural production (Art. 4 of ALA), protect agricultural land from pollution in accordance with the provisions of the ALA (Arts 5 and 6 of ALA), and observe the necessary agro-technical measures (Art. 4/6 of ALA).
997. Articles 18-26 of ALA.
998. Articles 27-82 of ALA.
999. Article 27 of ALA.

and establish the right to build and the right of servitude on state-owned agricultural land.[1000] The lease of state-owned agricultural land and fish farms is carried out through a public tendering procedure.[1001] Based on the decision on the selection of the best bid in the tendering procedure for the lease of such land, *općinski načelnik odnosno gradonačelnik*, on behalf of the Republic of Croatia, enters into a lease agreement.[1002 ,1003] State-owned agricultural land and fish farms are leased for a period of up to twenty-five years with the possibility of extending it for the same period of time. [1004]

§3. Forests and Forest Land

278. A special legal regime governing forests and forest land (*šume i šumsko zemljište*) is provided in the FsA.[1005] Forests are assets of interest to the Republic of Croatia, enjoying its special protection.[1006] The FsA lays down provisions concerning the management, use, utilization and protection of forests and forest land. Forests and forest land in Croatia may be in private or public ownership. Their owners may be domestic natural or legal persons. Foreign natural persons who are not nationals of the Republic of Croatia or of another EU Member State and legal persons seated outside the Republic of Croatia or any other EU Member State may not acquire ownership of forests or forest land unless this is otherwise provided in international treaties.[1007] Any forests or forest land not privately owned are owned by the state.[1008] Forests and forest land which used to be in social ownership were transferred to the ownership of the Republic of Croatia when the FsA became effective.

279. Forests and forest land in private ownership are managed by their owners under the conditions and in the way laid down in the FsA.[1009] State-owned forests and forest land are managed by *Hrvatske šume* d.o.o, founded by the Republic of Croatia.[1010] Private owners manage their forests in accordance with the Programme for Forest Management. [1011] This Programme lays down the measures and actions to be taken by the owners in their forests or on their forest land.

280. Private owners of forests and forest land legally dispose of their immovables in accordance with the general regulations governing the disposal of property.

1000. Articles 27/2 of ALA.
1001. Articles 31/2, 59/1 of ALA.
1002. Article 38/1 of ALA.
1003. For more details, *see* Part I, Ch. 6, §2. III. The Lease Contract on Agricultural Land.
1004. Article 31/1 of ALA.
1005. Forests Act, OG Nos 68/18, 115/18, 98/19, 32/20, 145/20.
1006. Article 2/1 of FsA.
1007. Article 56/6 of FsA.
1008. Article 16/1 of FsA.
1009. Articles 9-25 FsA.
1010. Article 17 of FsA.
1011. Articles 23, 25, 27 FsA.

The FsA does not contain any special limitations regarding the legal disposal of forests and forest land. The owner may alienate his forest land in chargeable or non-chargeable legal transactions *inter vivos* and in the case of death or encumber it with rights and obligations. However, the FsA provides for some limitations regarding the management of forests, their use or change of purpose.[1012] In privately owned forests and on private forest land, only forest infrastructure may be built.[1013]

281. State-owned forests and forest land may not be alienated from the ownership of the state[1014] except in the cases expressly stipulated in the FsA.[1015] A state-owned forest may be transferred to another person's ownership, encumbered with an easement or the right to build in order to be used only for the purpose expressly provided for in the FsA, such as to build military facilities or to control the country's border. [1016] State-owned forests may be encumbered by easements and the right to build for the purpose of building infrastructural objects,[1017] and they may be leased for the purpose of carrying out various forest management plans.[1018,1019]

§4. Roads

282. A special legal regime for roads (*ceste*) is provided for in the RA.[1020] Public roads are a public asset in general use owned by the Republic of Croatia.[1021] Public roads are classified into state roads and county roads depending on their social, traffic or economic importance. Neither may public roads be alienated from the ownership of the Republic of Croatia[1022] nor may rights be acquired on them, except in cases provided for in the RA.[1023]

1012. For example, owners of forests and forest land are obliged to ensure the unified biological reproduction of forests in the way prescribed by law, take various measures aimed at protecting forests and forest land, refrain from particular activities which are prohibited for the protection of forests, including activities altering the purpose of forest land, participate in the provision of funds to cover the costs of developing and implementing management programmes for forests with the right of ownership, and the like (Arts 10, 36 et seq. of FsA).
1013. Article 47 of FsA.
1014. Article 56/1 of FsA.
1015. Articles 51,52 of FsA.
1016. Article 51. of FsA.
1017. Articles 53, 58 of FsA.
1018. Article 59 of FsA.
1019. For more, *see* Belaj in *Property Law III*, 157–178.
1020. Roads Act, OG Nos 84/11, 22/13, 54/13, 148/13, 92/14, 110/19.
1021. Article 3/1 RA.
1022. Management, construction and maintenance of public roads is entrusted to companies founded by the Republic of Croatia, or to institutions founded by counties. Public roads are managed by a limited company called *Hrvatske ceste d.o.o.* (Art. 82 RA). Motorways are managed by a limited company called *Hrvatske autoceste d.o.o.* (Art. 81 of RA). County roads are managed by the county road administration (Art. 107 of RA).
1023. Article 3/2 RA.

283. The right of easement and the right to build for the purpose of building infrastructural objects (communal, water supply, energy supply, telecommunications and other facilities) may be established on a public road.[1024] Easements or the right to build are established for the benefit of the investors of such objects, and their transfer is permitted only to persons who are authorized, by separate laws, to manage such objects.[1025]

284. The only way for the commercial exploitation of public roads is by means of concessions.[1026] Through a concession, the right of commercial exploitation, construction and maintenance of a state road is acquired, as well as the right of management of motorways and objects and facilities on areas along such roads.[1027] Concessions may be granted to domestic or foreign natural or legal persons fulfilling the conditions specified by the holder of a concession in a public bidding procedure. A concession decision is rendered on the basis of such a procedure and is granted for a period of sixty years.[1028] A concession on a state road is entered into the land register on the basis of a concession contract in accordance with the rules on the registration of leases. It is entered in a special register of concessions kept by the Ministry of Finance.[1029,1030]

§5. Maritime Domain

285. The legal status of maritime domain, deciding the limits thereof, and the management and protection of maritime domain are provided for in the Maritime Domain and Ports Act (MDPA).[1031] Maritime domain enjoys particular protection from the Republic of Croatia.[1032] It consists of internal sea waters and territorial sea, their seabed and subsoil, and a part of land that is by its nature intended for general use or has been designated as such, as well as anything that is permanently attached to such a part of land on its surface or underneath it.[1033] Buildings and other facilities on maritime domain that are permanently associated with it are considered to be constituent parts of maritime domain.[1034]

286. Maritime domain is a common good. Neither ownership nor any other property right may be acquired on maritime domain on any grounds.[1035] Maritime domain may not be subject to any legal transactions because no one may acquire

1024. Article 3/3 RA.
1025. Articles 25/4,5 RA.
1026. Articles 75–80 RA.
1027. Article 75/1 RA.
1028. Article 75/3 RA.
1029. Article 79 of the Concessions Act.
1030. For more, *see* Josipović in *Property Law III*, 405–449.
1031. Maritime Domain and Ports Act, OG Nos 158/2003, 100/2004, 141/2006, 38/2009, 123/2011, 56/16, 98/19.
1032. Article 3/1 of MDPA.
1033. Article 3/2 of MDPA.
1034. Article 5/1 of MDPA.
1035. Articles 3/1, 5/2 of MDPA.

ownership on it.[1036] Maritime domain is managed, and the care and responsibility for it are taken by the Republic of Croatia directly or through units of regional self-government or units of local self-government.[1037]

287. Commercial exploitation of maritime domains is granted through concessions[1038] and concession approvals.[1039] Concessions on maritime domain may be granted upon deciding their limits and by recording them in the land register.[1040] They may be granted to natural and legal persons registered for business activities.[1041] Concessionaires may be both domestic and foreign natural or legal persons. Concessions may be granted for a period ranging from five to ninety-nine years.[1042] Concessions for the commercial exploitation of maritime domain and for the use and construction of objects of importance for the county, granted by a county assembly for a period of up to twenty years, may exceptionally be extended for a maximum of thirty years.[1043] Concessions for the commercial exploitation of maritime domain, including the construction of objects of importance for the Republic of Croatia, granted by the Government of RC for a period of fifty years, may exceptionally be extended to sixty years in total.[1044] Upon the collection of public bids and the submission of a request for a concession, on the basis of a decision on a concession, the concession grantor and the concessionaire enter into a concession contract.[1045] On the basis of the concession contract, the concession is entered into a special register of concessions on maritime domain.[1046,1047,1048]

1036. Maritime domain is always entered into the land register (Art. 15/1 of MDPA). Prior to its being entered in the land register, the boundaries of the maritime domain have to be determined. The criteria and procedure of determining the boundaries of the maritime domain are regulated by a special Regulation on the Procedure of Determining the Limits to Maritime Domain (OG Nos 8/2004, 82/2005).
1037. Article 10/1 of MDPA.
1038. Articles 16–37 of MDPA.
1039. Articles 38–39 of MDPA.
1040. Article 7/4 of MDPA.
1041. Article 16/1 of MDPA.
1042. Article 20/1 of MDPA.
1043. Article 22/1 of MDPA.
1044. Article 22/2 of MDPA.
1045. Article 25 of MDPA.
1046. Article 36 of MDPA. Natural and legal persons registered for business activities may be granted approval for carrying out such activities on maritime domain by which its general use is neither excluded nor limited. Such approval is granted at the request of a concessionaire for a period of up to five years (Art. 38 of MDPA).
1047. The Republic of Croatia may undertake any actions for the protection of maritime domain and may file lawsuits for its determination, compensation of damage or acquisition without any legal foundation against persons who use or have used maritime domain without a concession or concession approval and have thus gained particular benefits or have caused damage by their activities (Art. 37a of MDPA).
1048. For more, *see* Jug in *Property Law III*, 253–274.

§6. Other Special Regimes on Immovables

288. The legal status of railway infrastructure (*željeznička infrastruktura*) is provided for in the Railway Act (RwA).[1049] Railway infrastructure is owned by the Republic of Croatia.[1050] Immovables constituting railway infrastructure are a public asset in general use and must be registered accordingly in the land register.[1051] Railway infrastructure may not be alienated from the ownership of the Republic of Croatia. The railway infrastructure manager is appointed by the Government of the Republic of Croatia. The right to build and the right to servitude may only be exceptionally established on the railway infrastructure under the condition that its railway traffic and the maintenance of the railway infrastructure are not obstructed. The utilization of the railway infrastructure and access to railway services are provided by the Railways Act in compliance with the EU regulations on the establishment of a single European railway area. [1052]

289. The legal regime of cultural goods (*kulturna dobra*) is laid down in the Cultural Heritage Act (CHA).[1053] Under the CHA, cultural heritage includes movables[1054] and immovables[1055] of special artistic, historical, archaeological, anthropological and scientific importance, archaeological sites and zones, landscape or its part containing historically characteristic structures evidencing man's presence in that area, and possessing artistic, historical and anthropological significance, immaterial cultural assets and man's spiritual creativity in the past, as well as documentation and bibliographical heritage, and facilities or spaces used permanently to keep or exhibit the cultural heritage and documentation about it.[1056] Cultural goods are of interest to the Republic of Croatia and enjoy special protection, including preventive protection and registration in accordance with the CHA.[1057]

1049. Railway Act, OG Nos 32/19, 20/21.
1050. Article 71/1 of RwA.
1051. Article 71/5 of RwA.
1052. Article 2 of RwA.
1053. Cultural Heritage Act, OG Nos 69/1999, 151/2003, 157/2003, 100/2004, 87/2009, 88/2010, 61/2011, 25/2012, 136/12, 157/13, 152/14, 98/15, 44/17, 90/18, 32/20, 62/20.
1054. Movable cultural goods include collections of objects in museums, galleries, libraries and other institutions, in the possession of other legal persons and state and administrative bodies, and also in the possession of natural persons, church inventories and objects, archive materials, records, documents, letters and manuscripts, films, archaeological finds, anthological works of fine art, applied art and design, ethnographic objects, old and rare books, money, securities, postage stamps and other printed material, documentation on cultural heritage, theatre props, sketches, costumes and the like, items of use (furniture, clothes, weapons, etc.), communication and means of transport and facilities, objects that are important evidence of the development of science and technology (Art. 8 of CHA).
1055. The following can be declared as culturally significant immovables: towns, villages, settlements or their parts, buildings or their parts, buildings with their surroundings, elements that are historical accessories of a settlement, areas, places, monuments and memorials connected to historical events and persons, archaeological sites and archaeological zones, including underwater sites and zones, areas and places with ethnological and toponymic contents, landscape or its part containing historically characteristic structures evidencing man's presence in that particular area, gardens and parks, technical facilities with equipment and other similar structures (Art. 7 of CHA).
1056. Article 2 of CHA.
1057. Articles 2/1,3 of CHA.

The status of cultural goods is established by the Ministry of Culture. A decision on the termination of the status of a cultural good is also rendered by the Ministry of Culture.[1058] Cultural goods may be in private or public ownership. The owner of a cultural good is limited in the possession, use[1059] and disposal of the cultural good in order to ensure its protection and preservation.[1060] Ownership of cultural goods and their disposal is limited by the right of pre-emption in favour of the town or municipality on whose territory a particular cultural good is located, the county, the City of Zagreb or the Republic of Croatia.[1061] Concessions may be granted for cultural goods owned by the Republic of Croatia, its counties, the City of Zagreb, as well as its towns and municipalities.[1062] With a concession, the right of commercial exploitation of an immovable cultural good, or the right of carrying out economic activities in connection with immovable cultural goods, is acquired. A concession is granted for a maximum of thirty years on the basis of a public bidding procedure announced by the owner of the cultural good. The concessionaire is bound to take the necessary measures to protect and preserve the cultural goods in conformity with the CHA.[1063]

290. Protected areas of nature (*zaštićeni dijelovi prirode*), i.e., strict reserves, national parks, special reserves, nature parks, regional parks, natural monuments, important landscapes, forest parks and monuments of park architecture of interest to the Republic of Croatia enjoy its special protection laid down in the NtPA.[1064] The procedure and the powers for the designation of protected areas differ depending on the type of protected areas.[1065] Immovables designated as protected areas may be in private or public ownership. When privately owned immovables within protected areas are sold, the Republic of Croatia, the county, or the City of Zagreb

---

1058. Article 15 of CHA.
1059. If the owner does not act in conformity with the limitations aimed at the protection and preservation of a cultural good and thus risks damaging or destroying it, a temporary manager of the cultural good is appointed. The temporary manager undertakes actions for the protection of the cultural asset (Art. 31 of CHA). For more details, *see* Part V, Ch. 3, §5. Administration of Cultural Goods.
1060. Articles 28–40 of CHA.
1061. The owner must first offer the cultural good for sale to the town or municipality on whose territory the cultural asset is located. The right of pre-emption then belongs to the county or the City of Zagreb, and if they do not wish to exercise this right, the right of pre-emption is conferred on the Republic of Croatia (Art. 37/2 of CHA). If the owner sells the cultural good without offering it first to the legal persons having the pre-emptive right ninety days from acquiring information on the existence of the contract, and not later than five years from its conclusion, its annulment may be sought (Art. 39 of CHA).
1062. Articles 43a–43i of CHA.
1063. For more details, *see* Josipović in *Property Law III*, 373–399.
1064. Nature Protection Act, OG Nos 80/13, 15/18, 14/19, 127/19.
1065. For example, a national park or a nature park is designated by an Act adopted by the Croatian Parliament (Art. 123/1 of NtPA); strict and special reserves are designated by a decree of the Government of the RC upon the proposal of the ministry competent for the protection of nature (Art. 123/2 of NtPA); and regional parks, important landscapes and forest parks are designated by a county assembly (Art. 123/3-4 of NtPA).

has the right of pre-emption.[1066] A concession may be granted for the commercial exploitation of natural assets in protected areas.[1067,1068]

291. The legal regime governing waters and water assets (*vode i vodno dobro*) and their management are laid down in the WA.[1069] Waters are common goods which, because of their natural characteristics, may not be the objects of ownership rights.[1070] The water estate is a set of land plots which include water-bearing and abandoned channels of inland surface waters, flood-plain areas and islands formed in a water-bearing channel.[1071] The water estate is an asset of interest to the Republic of Croatia and enjoys special protection.[1072] Any land considered to belong to the water estate may be in private or public ownership, i.e., the ownership of the Republic of Croatia. A privately owned water asset is disposed of in accordance with the general rules of disposal of immovables. In the case of sale, the Republic of Croatia is entitled to pre-emption.[1073] A state-owned water asset is called a public water estate in general use.[1074] The public water estate is inalienable from state ownership.[1075] No one may acquire the right of ownership or any other property right over the public water estate by acquisitive prescription or in any other way except for the right of easement and the right to build.[1076] The use of the public water estate is accomplished by the right of lease, the right of easement or the right to build in accordance with the conditions stipulated by law.[1077] Commercial exploitation of waters is granted by concessions.[1078,1079]

1066. Article 165 of NtPA.
1067. Articles 178–193 of NtPA.
1068. For more, *see* Gliha in *Property Law III*, 333–369.
1069. Waters Act, OG Nos 66/19.
1070. Article 8 of WA.
1071. Article 9 of WA.
1072. Article 9/6 of WA.
1073. Article 22 of WA.
1074. Article 12 of WA.
1075. Article 12/9 of WA.
1076. Article 12/10 of WA.
1077. Article 18 of WA.
1078. Articles 91 of WA.
1079. For more, *see* Jug in *Property Law III*, 277–299.

Chapter 8. Acquisition of Immovables by Foreigners

§1. CONCEPT

292. The legal position of foreign nationals in property transactions in the Republic of Croatia is regulated by Articles 354–358b of the PA. In principle, domestic and foreign nationals are on an equal footing in terms of the application of general property regulations and other acts applicable to the acquisition, exercise and protection of property rights and obligations concerning immovables (the so-called principle of equal legal conditions for domestic and foreign nationals). The provisions of the PA on the acquisition, change, cessation, exercise and protection of property rights also applied when the holders of such rights were foreign natural and legal persons.[1080] There were exemptions only when it was so stipulated in a separate legal act or an international treaty.

293. However, the principle of equal treatment of foreign and domestic persons did not apply when foreign natural or legal persons acquired ownership of immovables in the territory of the Republic of Croatia. They could acquire ownership of immovables[1081] only if, besides some general conditions for such acquisition, specific requirements stipulated in Articles 355–357 of the PA were fulfilled.[1082] At the same time, the PA and some separate laws expressly provided that foreign nationals could not become owners of specific types of immovables in the Republic of Croatia and that they could not acquire immovables on any legal grounds.

§2. SPECIAL CONDITIONS FOR THE ACQUISITION OF OWNERSHIP OF IMMOVABLES

294. The special conditions for the acquisition of property are different depending on the legal basis of their acquisition, i.e., whether it involved inheritance, contract, court decisions or another body's decision or laws.

295. A special condition for the acquisition of property by way of inheritance is the principle of reciprocity.[1083] A foreign national can become the owner of property by succession if the law of the state on foreign citizenship allows Croatian

1080. Article 354/1 of the PA.
1081. A foreign natural person is a person who does not have the citizenship of the Republic of Croatia unless otherwise prescribed by the law (Art. 355/1 of the PA). A foreign legal person is a legal person having its registered seat outside the territory of the Republic of Croatia, unless otherwise prescribed by the law (Art. 355/3 of the PA). According to the valid Croatian legislation, the legal position of companies established (registered) in the Republic of Croatia is not different in any way if established by domestic or foreign capital. In order for a company to have the status of a domestic legal person, it is sufficient that it is lawfully established and in accordance with the law of the Republic of Croatia and that it has its registered seat in the Republic of Croatia.
1082. Special regulation of the acquisition of real property by foreigners is based on Art. 48/3 of the Constitution of the Republic of Croatia.
1083. Article 356/1 of the PA.

nationals to inherit immovables abroad. Reciprocity as a special condition for the acquisition of ownership of property by inheritance should exist at the moment of death, i.e., at the moment when all other general conditions for the acquisition of ownership by inheritance must be fulfilled as stipulated in the PA.

296. As for other legal bases (e.g., legal transactions, court decisions, laws), a foreign national was allowed to acquire ownership if two special prerequisites were fulfilled: reciprocity[1084] and consent obtained by the minister of justice.[1085] If the minister of justice refuses to grant consent, a foreign natural or legal person is not allowed to be the holder of ownership on immovables. The minister of justice decides whether to grant consent on the basis of discretionary powers. The granting or refusing the consent by the minister of justice is an administrative act against which court protection may be sought by way of an administrative action.

297. The minister's refusal had manifold legal implications for a foreign national acquiring property in the Republic of Croatia. The PA expressly stipulated that without the consent granted by the minister of justice, a legal transaction resulting in the acquisition of ownership was invalid.[1086] Before such consent was granted, no rights or obligations could be exercised by the contractual parties. Without the minister's consent, ownership could not be entered into the land register. Therefore, the land register court had to establish whether the acquirer was a domestic or a foreign national and whether the minister of justice had granted consent or not. If no consent was granted and the application for the acquisition of ownership was refused, five years had to pass before a new application could be submitted to apply for the minister's consent.[1087]

298. In the PA and in some other regulations, it is expressly stipulated in which immovable property it is impossible to acquire ownership. A foreign national cannot own property in some specific areas.[1088] Foreign persons may not acquire ownership of agricultural land. Foreign persons may acquire ownership of agricultural land by inheritance. The exceptions to these rules are possible only on the basis of international treaties.[1089] Foreign natural and legal persons who are not nationals of another EU Member State or whose seat is not in another EU Member State may not acquire ownership on forests and forest land. The exceptions to these rules are possible only on the basis of international treaties.[1090]

1084. The condition of reciprocity exists if a Croatian citizen is recognized the right, in the state of a foreigner's citizenship, to acquire ownership of immovables on any of the permitted grounds, or if a Croatian legal person is recognized such right in a state where a foreign legal person is established and registered.
1085. Article 356/2 of thc PA.
1086. Article 357/1 of the PA.
1087. Article 357/3 of the PA.
1088. Article 358/1 of the PA. Specific areas are those where, according to the law, foreign persons may not acquire ownership of immovables because the interests and the security of the Republic of Croatia must be protected.
1089. Articles 2/2,3, of the ALA.
1090. Article 56/2 of the FA.

299. When foreign nationals may not acquire immovables by inheritance, the PA separately provides for the right to compensation on the basis of the regulations governing expropriation.[1091] Compensation is granted on the basis of a final decision on inheritance. The Republic of Croatia is obliged to pay compensation by becoming the owner of the immovable that a foreign person may not inherit. Such a person is entitled to receive compensation, instead of the immovable, established on the basis of the market value of the immovable in question, which is transferred *ex lege* to the ownership of the Republic of Croatia. Any secured rights on such immovables are transferred to the compensation the heir is entitled to claim from the Republic of Croatia[1092] while all other encumbrances remain attached to the property.[1093]

§3. Treatment for EU Nationals Since 1 February 2009

300. Since 1 February 2009, full liberalization of immovable property transactions for national and legal persons from the European Union was introduced in the Republic of Croatia with the amendments to the PA of 2008.[1094] In the Act on Amendments to the Act on Ownership and Other Property Rights Property of 2008 (PA/2008), a dual regime for the acquisition of ownership is established depending on whether immovable is acquired by nationals and legal entities from the Member States of the European Union or by nationals and legal entities from countries which are not members of the European Union. Liberalization was introduced to include only nationals and legal entities from the European Union.[1095] As for the nationals and legal entities from other countries, the already existing system stipulated in the PA is kept both with regard to special requirements for the acquisition of ownership on immovables and the type of immovables that foreign nationals are not allowed to acquire.

301. In Article 358a of the PA, it is strictly prescribed that the PA provisions regarding special conditions for the acquisition of ownership by foreign nationals do not include nationals and legal entities from the Member States of the European Union. It is expressly provided that nationals and legal entities from the Member States of the EU acquire ownership on immovables under the same conditions as citizens of the Republic of Croatia and the legal persons seated in Croatia.[1096] It means that since 1 February 2009, foreign nationals and legal entities from the Member States of the EU are on a fully equal footing with Croatia's own citizens regardless of the grounds on which they acquire ownership (e.g., contracts, inheritance, courts' decisions, laws). All foreign nationals and legal entities from the Member States of the European Union who have entered into legal transactions to

1091. Article 358b of the PA. A foreign national, despite the fact that he may not inherit such real property, has the legal status of an heir.
1092. Article 358b/2 of the PA.
1093. Article 358b/3 of the PA.
1094. Act on Amendments to the OA, OG 146/2008 (OA/2008).
1095. Article 358a of the PA.
1096. Article 358a/1 of the PA.

acquire ownership of real property in the Republic of Croatia, no matter when the transaction was made and whether or not they had applied for the consent according to the previous regulations, or the consent was refused. Since 1 February 2009, they have been allowed to enter their ownership in the land register just like any other citizen of Croatia.

302. Equal treatment is established not only *pro futuro*, i.e., for the acquisitions of immovables that will take place in the years to come, but also for all cases where foreign nationals and legal entities from the European Union had entered into legal transactions to acquire ownership or had applied to obtain consent from the minister of justice before 1 February 2009. Such equal treatment for the acquisition is established by a twofold intervention by the PA. First, it is strictly prescribed that all legal transactions aimed at the acquisition of ownership of immovable property by nationals of the Member States of the European Union entered into before 1 February 2009 are valid (convalidation) regardless of the fact that the consent of the minister of justice has not been obtained.[1097] Second, it is strictly prescribed that any procedures to obtain consent initiated before the PA/2008 entered into force must be stalled ex officio.[1098]

303. From the provisions for equal treatment, only the following property has been excluded: agricultural land and protected areas of nature.[1099] Nationals and legal entities from the Member States of the European Union were still not allowed to acquire such immovables.

304. Where the EU nationals are not allowed to acquire immovables on the grounds of inheritance, in these exempted areas, they have the same right to compensation as any other foreign nationals who may not acquire immovables.[1100] The same rules concerning compensation apply as in the case of any other foreign nationals who may not acquire immovables.[1101]

§4. Treatment of EU Nationals after Accession to the EU

305. After Croatia acquired the status of a full member of the EU (1 July 2013), the EU nationals have the same treatment as Croatia's nationals when acquiring ownership of immovables. The only difference with regard to the position of EU nationals prior to the accession lies in the fact that after the accession, there are no limitations for the acquisition of protected areas of nature and forest land. Upon accession, the EU nationals are not able to acquire agricultural land because in the Accession Agreement, concerning agricultural land, a seven-year postponement of

1097. Article 6 of the PA/2008.
1098. Article 5 of the PA/2008.
1099. Article 358a/2 of the PA.
1100. Article 358b of the PA.
1101. Article 358b of the PA. Such a person is entitled to receive a compensation, instead of an immovable, established on the basis of the market value of the immovable in question which has been transferred *ex lege* to the ownership of the Republic of Croatia.

the implementation of the rules on the free movement of capital referred to in the Treaty on the Functioning of the European Union is laid down. It is expressly agreed that notwithstanding the obligations under the Treaties on which the European Union was founded, Croatia may, for seven years from the date of the accession, maintain the restrictions laid down in its ALA, which was in force on the date of the signature of the Treaty of Accession regarding the acquisition of agricultural land by the nationals of other Member States, by the nationals of the states which are party to the European Economic Area Agreement (EEAA), and by legal persons formed in accordance with the laws of another Member State or an EEAA state.[1102,1103] In 2020, a seven-year moratorium on the acquisition of agricultural land was extended for additional three years. It expires on 30 June 2023. For all other types of immovables, the same treatment is provided which applies to Croatia's own nationals.

§5. Acquisition of Limited Rights on Immovables

306. In the acquisition of some limited property rights (e.g., easements, security rights, right to build), foreign nationals are on a fully equal footing with domestic citizens. This rule applies regardless of the legal basis on which such limited property rights are acquired (e.g., inheritance, contract, law or a decision by competent authorities) and regardless of whether it is a foreign national from the EU or a non-EU country. Foreign nationals can acquire limited property rights in immovables in which ownership cannot be acquired as a result of a separate regulation and also in immovables where the consent for acquiring the ownership was denied (no consent was given by the minister).

307. The principle of equal treatment of foreign and domestic nationals is applied in cases of the acquisition of leasehold interests in immovable property authorizing their holder to use immovables (rental, lease, concession). No special requirements have to be fulfilled in acquiring the leasehold interests in favour of foreign persons.

1102. *See* ANNEX V – a list referred to in Art. 18 of the Act of Accession: Transitional Measures, http://eur-lex.europa.eu/LexUriServ/LexUriServ.do?uri=OJ:L:2012:112:0067:0086:EN:PDF.

1103. The exception does not apply to self-employed farmers who are nationals of another Member State and who wish to establish themselves and reside in Croatia. When it comes to the acquisition of agricultural land, the same rules and procedures applying to the nationals of Croatia also apply to them.

Part II. Movable Property and Personal Property

Chapter 1. Movable Property

§1. CONCEPT

308. Movables (*pokretnine*) are things that may be moved from one place to another without their substance being damaged.[1104] The most important feature of movables is their movability.[1105,1106] In Croatian law, there are no separate provisions for rights on movables which would differ from those established on immovables. The same rules concerning rights apply to both movables and immovables. The subject matter of rights may be any movables except those that the law expressly lays down as not being in circulation (*res extra commercium).* As a rule, all movables are subject to legal transactions. It is possible, however, that the circulation of some movables is restricted by law (weapons, medicaments, poisons, etc.).[1107] Any natural or legal person, domestic and foreign, may be a holder of rights on movables. There are no special conditions for the establishment of rights on movables, as is normally the case with immovables.[1108]

309. Because of their natural characteristics, movables may be divided into commercially interchangeable (*res fungibiles*) and non-interchangeable things (*res non fungibiles*). Interchangeable things are those that are in circulation determined by their kind, number or measure. They are usually called generic. Non-interchangeable things are those that in circulation appear as strictly individual species. Movables are also divided into consumable (*res consumptibiles*) and non-consumable (*res non consumptibiles*). Consumable things are those that are extinguished by single use or where their substance is significantly decreased. Non-consumable things are those that are not extinguished as the result of common use and where their substance is not decreased. Movables are also classified as divisible (*res divisibiles*) and indivisible (*res indivisibiles*). Divisible things are those that may be divided into several identical parts without their original substance being

1104. Article 2/4 PA.
1105. Gavella in *Property Law I*, 78.
1106. In the case of doubt whether a thing is a movable or immovable, it is deemed a movable (Art. 2/7 PA).
1107. Klarić / Vedriš in *Civil Law*, 74.
1108. Article 354/2 PA.

destroyed or their values disproportionally diminished. Indivisible things are those whose substance would be destroyed by division or their values disproportionally diminished.[1109] Movables are further distinguished depending on whether they are simple or assembled. Simple things are those which, when in circulation, are considered as constituting a unity, and assembled things are those which come into existence when simple things are assembled, i.e., individual things which, by being assembled, become a new whole whose parts do not lose their physical existence.[1110]

310. In Croatian law, property rights on movables are not divided into legal interests and equitable interests, as is the case in Anglo-Saxon legal orders. All property rights which may exist on movables are governed by the same rules as provided in the PA. The same rules governing immovables apply accordingly to property rights on movables, excluding those that can apply only to immovables because of their specific nature.[1111]

§2. Property Rights on Movables

311. Property rights which may be established on movables are those which, taking into consideration the characteristics of movables and the content of property rights, may be established on movables. Property rights which by their content and their holders' rights may be established only on immovables may not be established on movables (e.g., the right to build, real burdens, real easements). The right of ownership may exist on movables (individual ownership, co-ownership, joint ownership). Movables may be encumbered by personal easements[1112] or liens.[1113]

312. The same rules concerning property rights which apply to immovables also apply to movables. The PA provides for property rights uniformly without making any distinction between immovables and movables. Only exceptionally, when necessary because of some specific characteristics of movables or immovables, does the PA lay down different rules regarding property rights. The most common differences exist when it comes to conditions for the acquisition of some property rights on movables or immovables, such as the conditions for the acquisition of ownership by contract *inter vivos*, the acquisition of ownership by acquisitive prescription, the acquisition of liens, and the like.[1114] In principle, the content of entitlements belonging to the holders of property rights does not differ depending

1109. Klarić / Vedriš in *Civil Law*, 75–81.
1110. Klarić / Vedriš in *Civil Law*, 81–82.
1111. Things that by their nature are considered to be movables are legally considered as immovables if they are appurtenances to immovables or if by law equal status is extended to them as to immovables (Art. 2/4 PA).
1112. Article 199 PA.
1113. Article 289 PA.
1114. For further details, *see* Part III. Acquisition of Property Rights.

on whether this is a property right on a movable or an immovable. Only exceptionally, when absolutely necessary, does the PA provide for separate and different powers of property right holders depending on whether the property right is established on a movable or an immovable.[1115]

1115. For further details, *see* Part VI. Security Rights.

Chapter 2. Patrimonial Rights

§1. Concept

313. As a rule, patrimonial rights (*imovinska prava*) may not be the object of property rights. The rules of the law on obligations apply to patrimonial rights. However, a particular type of patrimonial rights may be equated with things by virtue of law. In this case, the provisions on property rights applying to movables also apply to such rights. If these rights are connected with the ownership of immovables or if they constitute their encumbrances, the provisions on property rights on immovables apply to them.[1116] In Croatian law, patrimonial rights may be subject to liens and other property securities.[1117] The object of a lien may be a particular, individual patrimonial right which is suitable for a creditor to settle his claim against it.[1118]

1116. Article 2/6 PA.
1117. Article 298/2 PA.
1118. For further details, *see* Part VI. Security Rights, Ch. 6. Securities on Rights.

Chapter 3. Limited Property Rights

314. In Croatian law, limited property rights on movables are not expressly and separately regulated. In principle, the same rules applying to limited property rights on immovables also apply to movables. Movables, however, because of their characteristics, may not be encumbered by all the property rights which apply to immovables but only by those which, taking into consideration their content, may be established on movables.

315. Personal easements, such as usufruct[1119] and the right to use,[1120] may be established on movables. The right of usufruct may exist on a movable that is non-consumable.[1121,1122,1123] The right to use may also exist only on a movable that is non-consumable.[1124,1125,1126] The right of usufruct and the right to use on movables are established by contract *inter vivos* by being surrendered into the acquirer's possession.[1127,1128] If the acquirer has entered into several legal transactions on the establishment of usufruct or the right to use regarding the same movable, easement is established in favour of the person into whose possession the movable has been surrendered.[1129] The provisions on the protection and termination of the right of usufruct and the right to use involving immovables apply accordingly to the protection and termination of the same rights involving movables. If the owner has entered into several legal transactions on the establishment of the right of usufruct or the right to use on the same movable easements that may not simultaneously exist on the same thing), easement is established in favour of the person into whose possession the movable has been surrendered.[1130]

1119. Articles 203/2, 211 PA.
1120. Article 212 PA.
1121. Article 212/2 PA.
1122. The object of the right of usufruct may be the whole movable or only one of its ideal parts. In any case, an object of the right of usufruct is a movable with all its component parts, such as appurtenances and the like (Art. 203/4) PA). An object of usufruct may be several movables taken together (Art. 203/1 PA).
1123. The content of the right of usufruct on a movable is the same as the content of the right of usufruct on an immovable (Arts 204 et seq. PA).
1124. Article 212/2PA.
1125. The right to use may exist on several movables (Art. 212/2 PA).
1126. The content of the right to use on a movable is the same as the content of the right to use on an immovable (Arts 213 et seq. PA).
1127. Article 222/1 PA.
1128. The relationships between the owners of movables and other persons with whom a contract on the establishment of the right of usufruct or the right of use have been entered into are regulated by the provisions of the law on obligations (Art. 222/3 PA).
1129. Article 222/2 PA.
1130. Article 222/2 PA.

316. Personal easements (the right of usufruct, Article 203/3 PA and the right to use, Article 212/3) may also be established on patrimonial rights. The right of usufruct may exist only on a right yielding fruits or other benefits (e.g., a claim accruing interest).[1131] The right to use may also exist only on a property right which yields fruits or other benefits.[1132,1133]

1131. The provisions on the right of usufruct on movables apply accordingly to the right of usufruct established on a patrimonial right because this right is then considered to be a movable thing (Art. 203/3 PA).

1132. Article 212/3 PA.

1133. The provisions on the right to use on movables apply accordingly to the right to use established on patrimonial rights (Art. 212/3 PA).

Chapter 4. Securities on Movables and Patrimonial Rights

317. Movables and patrimonial rights may also be objects of liens and other property securities.[1134] Any movables or patrimonial rights that are in circulation and can be converted into cash in order to settle a creditor's claim may be objects of security rights. The modus of establishment of security rights on movables and patrimonial rights depends on the type of security right (lien, fiduciary transfer of ownership or of a right), on the legal basis for the establishment of a security right, on the type of movable or patrimonial right, as well as on whether a registrable security right has been established. In principle, the same rules which apply to security rights on immovables also apply to security rights on movables and patrimonial rights unless it is otherwise stipulated because of the particular characteristics of movables of patrimonial rights.[1135]

1134. Articles 298/1,2 PA, Arts 262, 274 EA, Art. 6 of the Register Act, Art. 3a of the Financial Collateral Act (OG 76/07, 59/12).

1135. For more details, *see* Part VI. Security Rights.

Part III. Acquisition of Property Rights

Chapter 1. General

318. Property rights (*stvarna prava*) on immovables and movables may be acquired on the basis of several legal titles. They may be acquired by contract (transfer of establishment of property rights by contract *inter vivos*), on the basis of a court decision or the decision of another competent authority, by inheritance (transfer of establishment of the property rights upon death), or on the basis of law. In each of these legal titles for acquisition, property rights are acquired or established only when all the conditions stipulated by law have been met. The PA lays down the conditions for the acquisition of each property right and for each legal title.[1136]

1136. Articles 114–160 PA (ownership), Arts 218–230 PA (easements), Arts 261–264 PA (encumbrances), Arts 286–289 PA (the right to build), Arts 305–318 PA (liens).

Chapter 2. Acquisition by Contract *Inter Vivos*

§1. General

319. The acquisition of property rights by contract *inter vivos* is a voluntary transfer of ownership to the new acquirer or the voluntary establishment of limited property rights on a thing for the benefit of another person. It takes place on the basis of the will of the former owner of a thing. This is why one of the basic principles of acquisition by contract *inter vivos* states that it is not possible to transfer more rights to another than a person already has (the principle *nemo plus ad alium transferre potest quam ipse habet*). The PA expressly provides that ownership by contract may be acquired only within the limits of the owner's powers to dispose of the thing.[1137] With the provisions on the acquisition of limited property rights, the PA expressly lays down that these rights are derived from the ownership of a thing.[1138] An exception to the rules contained in these provisions is envisaged only in the cases of acquisition of property rights in good faith when a bona fide acquirer enjoys protection.[1139]

§2. Principle of Causal Tradition

320. In Croatian law, the acquisition of property rights by contract *inter vivos* is governed by the principle of causal tradition (*načelo kauzalne tradicije*). This means that for the acquisition by contract, two components must always exist: a valid contract (*titulus*) and the corresponding modality (*modus*) of acquisition of a property right. A contract is only the legal basis for acquisition (*titulus*), and on its conclusion, the acquirer does not yet obtain a property right. The contract is the manifestation of the acquirer's legal request and the seller's obligation to transfer the ownership or to establish a limited property right for the acquirer. The acquisition of the right takes place only after the appropriate modus of acquisition is made (e.g., the transfer of possession of a movable, registration in the land register or other public register, and the like). How a property right is acquired and what the modus of acquisition primarily depends on whether the property right is acquired on movable or immovable property.[1140] In some cases, the modus of acquisition depends on the type of contract by which a property right is acquired and in what kind of procedure it is acquired.[1141]

1137. Article 115/2 PA.
1138. Articles 219/2, 262/1, 287, 306/1 PA.
1139. For further details, *see* Part III, Ch. 2, §4. III. Acquisition of Ownership from Non-owners.
1140. In the case of immovables, the modus of acquisition is, as a rule, an entry in the land register (registration, conditional registration) and, in the case of movables, the transfer of a movable into the possession of the acquirer. For more details, *see* Part III, Ch. 2. Acquisition by Contract *Inter Vivos*.
1141. Thus, for example, a lien established on movables acquired on the basis of a court register or a notarial act is acquired by an entry in a register and not by the transfer of a movable into the possession of a lienor. For more details, *see* the Part VI, Ch. 5. Securities in Movable Property.

321. The principle of causal tradition provides for the acquisition of property rights by contract *inter vivos*. This means that for the acquisition of property rights, both conditions for acquisition must be fulfilled cumulatively – a valid contract and the appropriate modus of acquisition. If the contract, as the basis for the acquisition of a property right, is not valid, the acquisition will not occur.[1142] The acquisition of property rights by contract depends on a valid contract governed by the law of obligations by which the owner of a thing is bound to transfer ownership or to establish some other property right in favour of the other party to the contract. Such a contract is a *causa* for the acquisition of a property right, and if it is not valid, there is no legal basis for the acquisition of a property right by contract. This rule is valid even when, despite the invalidity of a contract, the appropriate modus of acquisition has already been accomplished (e.g., a movable has been transferred to the acquirer, or the acquirer has already been registered as the owner of the immovable).

§3. Conditions for Acquisition on the Basis of Contract *Inter Vivos*

322. The principle that it is not possible to transfer more rights to another than a person already has (the principle *nemo plus ad alium transferre potest quam ipse habet*) and the principle of causal tradition provide for the acquisition of property rights by contract *inter vivos* by stating that three conditions must always be met: ownership, i.e., the owner's capacity to dispose of an immovable/movable belonging to a predecessor, a valid contract aimed at transferring or establishing a property right, and a corresponding modus of its acquisition. This rule applies accordingly to the acquisition and establishment of all property rights on movables and immovables. Possible differences may occur because sometimes, depending on

1142. The conditions for the validity of a contract aimed at acquiring property rights are subject to the rules of the law on obligations (Obligation Act (OA)):

(a) capacity of parties to enter into contracts – the parties must possess legal and business capacity. In order to enter into a contract that is valid, a party to the contract must have the contractual capacity required for the conclusion of a contract (Art. 276/1 of OA);

(b) mutual and valid assent – the parties must express mutual and valid assent to enter into a contract. The statement of assent must be made freely and in a serious manner (Art. 249/3 of OA). If the expression of will is invalid, or if there is no genuine assent (so-called defect of will or intention), for example in the case of simulation, threat, fundamental mistake, fraud or misunderstanding, the contract is, dependent upon the reason why the assent is invalid, considered null and void or void (Arts 282, 285, 330 of OA);

(c) the subject of the obligation – the performance must be possible, admissible and determined or determinable (Art. 269/2 of OA). If performance is impossible, inadmissible, not determined or not determinable, the contract is null and void and does not have any legal effects (Art. 270/1 of OA);

(d) the form of the legal transaction if it is stipulated by law that particular contracts, in order to be valid, must be made in a particular form (the so-called prescribed form of a contract, Art. 286/1 of OA), or if the parties to a contract have agreed to use a special form only as proof of validity of their contract (the so-called prescribed form of a contract, Art. 289 of OA). A special form, being a condition for the validity of a contract, is laid down in various regulations. All contracts concerning property rights on immovables, in order to be valid, must always be made in writing (Art. 115/3 PA). In some specific cases, contracts must be made in the form of public documents (notarial acts, solemnized private documents, court records). For more details, *see* Part III, Ch. 2. Acquisition by Contract *Inter Vivos*.

the type of a particular property right, the contract by which such a right is acquired, or its object, different forms of contract validity and different forms of the modus of acquisition are required.

§4. ACQUISITION OF OWNERSHIP BY CONTRACT *INTER VIVOS*

I. Conditions

323. Ownership passes from the former owner to the acquirer on the basis of a valid contract whose aim is the acquisition of ownership in accordance with the modus laid down by law.[1143] The conditions for the acquisition of ownership by contract *inter vivos* are the following:

- ownership of the predecessor (vlasništvo prednika); ownership by contract may be acquired only from a person who is the owner of a thing. The owner of a thing is the person who is registered as such in the land register.[1144,1145,1146] The owner of a movable is the person who is its independent possessor;[1147,1148]
- a valid contract (titulus) whose aim (causa) is the transfer of ownership,[1149] such as a contract of sale, a contract of exchange, a contract of donation, etc.[1150] When ownership of a movable is acquired by contract, no special form is normally required in order for a contract on the transfer of ownership of movables to be valid. A contract of transfer of ownership of an immovable may be valid even if made orally. When ownership of an immovable is acquired by contract, in order

1143. Article 115/1 PA.

1144. Article 8/2 LRA.

1145. Ownership may be acquired from a person not entered in the land register as the owner only if the person is able to prove, on the basis of valid documents, a non-registered transfer of the ownership right from the registered owner to himself (Art. 41 LRA).

1146. If a person, who is not the actual owner of the immovable, is entered in the land register, the acquisition of ownership may take place only if the conditions are met for the protection of a bona fide third acquirer who acted in good faith having relied on the information in the land register (Arts 123, 124 PA). For more details, *see* Part III, Ch. 2, §4. III. Acquisition of Ownership from Non-owners.

1147. Article 11/3 PA.

1148. If a person, who is an independent possessor of the movable, is not the actual owner, the acquisition of ownership may take place only if the conditions are met for the protection of a bona fide acquirer, who did not know or did not have sufficient reasons to doubt, that the possessor was not the owner of the movable (Art. 118 PA). For more details, *see* Part III, Ch. 2, §4. III. Acquisition of Ownership from Non-owners.

1149. Article 115/1 PA.

1150. With a contract of sale, a seller undertakes to deliver to a buyer ownership of a thing, and the buyer undertakes to pay him the corresponding price (Art. 376/1 of OA). Contracts of sale are provided for in Arts 376–473 of OA. With a contract of exchange, one contracting party undertakes to deliver ownership of a thing to the other party (Art. 474/1 of OA). With a contract of exchange, rights and obligations arise for each contracting party, such as those which arise for the seller in a contract of sale. The contract of exchange is regulated in Arts 474, 475 of OA. A contract of donation is a contract where one contracting party (donor) undertakes to transfer to the other party (donee), without expecting anything in return, a thing or property, and the donee accepts it. The contract of donation is regulated in Arts 479–498 of OA.

for the contract to be valid, it must always be concluded in writing.[1151] A contract on the transfer of ownership of an immovable must, as a rule, be made in the form of a private written document signed by the owner (alienor) and the acquirer. In some cases, however, regardless of whether the ownership of immovables or movables is transferred, a special (qualified) form is required for the contract to be valid (court records, notarial act);[1152]

- a valid modality (modus) of acquisition, which differs depending on whether an immovable or a movable is acquired; when the ownership of a movable is acquired by contract, the modus of acquisition is delivery (tradition, tradicija) of a movable into the independent possession of the acquirer.[1153] The acquisition of a movable by delivery (traditio) may occur in various ways – by surrendering the thing to the acquirer, or by surrendering the means by which the acquirer exercises actual control over the thing (e.g., through the surrender of car-keys), by submitting a request for the transfer of the thing into direct possession (cessio vindicationis), and the like.[1154] The ownership of a movable is acquired at the moment when the acquirer becomes its independent possessor, regardless of whether the possession is direct or indirect.[1155] When the ownership of an immovable is acquired by contract, the statutory modus of acquisition is the entry in the land register, i.e., registration or conditional registration in favour of the acquirer.[1156,1157] The ownership of immovable property not entered in the land register is acquired by depositing a deed with the court which is competent for the registration of the right in the land register.[1158,1159,1160]

1151. Article 115/3 PA.
1152. For example, the Notaries Public Act provides that in order to be valid, the following contracts must be made in the form of a notarial act: contracts on disposal of assets belonging to persons under legal age and persons deprived of business capacity, contracts of donation without the direct transfer of a thing to the donee, all legal transactions *inter vivos* undertaken personally by the blind or deaf who cannot read, or the dumb who cannot write (Art. 106/2 of the Inheritance Act (IA)). The OA lays down that a contract on the cessation and division of property during a lifetime must be made in the form of court records, a notarial act or a solemnized private document (Art. 106/2 of IA). The OA lays down that a life-maintenance contract, a contract of support until death, a contract of donation without the transfer of things and a contract of donation in the case of death must be made in the form of a notarial act or court records (Arts 482/2, 491/1, 580/1, 589 of OA). A matrimonial agreement, by which the spouses regulate their matrimonial property relations, including immovables, is considered to be valid if the signatures of both parties to the contract are certified (Art. 255/3 of the Family Act).
1153. Article 116/1 PA.
1154. Articles 14, 15 PA.
1155. For more details, *see* General Introduction, VIII. Possession.
1156. Articles 119/1, 120, 121 PA.
1157. In order to acquire ownership resulting from a contract by registration or conditional registration, the entry must be valid and truthful: all the conditions required under the rules of land register law, as well as all other requirements for the acquisition of ownership on the basis of a contract, must be met (a valid contract, a predecessor).
1158. Articles 120/4, 121/5 PA.
1159. When this document is properly made and fulfils the requirements for registration, its deposition has the same legal effects as registration in the land register. When the document fulfils the requirements for conditional registration, its deposition has the same legal effects as conditional registration in the land register. For more details, *see* Part I, Ch. 2, §4. Land Register Entries.
1160. Gavella in *Property Law I*, 443–471, Klarić / Vedriš in *Civil Law*, 285–294.

II. Multiple Conclusion of Contracts on the Alienation of the Same Thing

324. The owner of a thing may make contracts on the transfer of the same thing with several persons. If all conditions have been met, all these contracts are deemed valid, and they have the same legal effects.[1161] Who acquires ownership by virtue of any of such contracts will depend on whether all the conditions for the acquisition of ownership laid down in the PA for multiple contracts on alienation have been met.

325. When multiple contracts on the alienation of the same movable are at issue, the PA expressly provides that of all the persons who have entered into various contracts with the owner on the alienation of the same thing; ownership will be acquired by the person into whose possession the thing was first surrendered.[1162] It is not decisive whether that person was the first to enter into a contract on alienation. The only important thing is that the person was the first to be given possession of the thing. All other persons who have concluded a contract on the acquisition of ownership with the same seller will not acquire ownership but will only make a claim to the seller, regulated by the law, on obligations, such as indemnification, return of the purchase price and the like.[1163,1164]

326. When several persons have made more contracts on the alienation of the same immovable with the same owner, ownership is acquired by the person who first applied for the ownership to be entered in the land register.[1165] It is not decisive whether that person was the first to have made a contract on alienation. What is important is whether that person was the first to have applied for ownership to be entered in the land register. The seller's relationship with other persons who have entered into contracts on the alienation of the same immovable is regulated by the rules of the law on obligations. However, the PA specifically provides for a situation where the acquirer, who was registered first as the owner in the land register, was a *mala fide* acquirer because, at the moment of the conclusion of the contract, he knew that the immovable had already been sold to another person and that it had been surrendered into his direct possession.[1166] In such a case, the person with whom a contract had previously been made and who is already in direct possession of the immovable may bring an action (*kvazibrisovna tužba*) requesting the deleting of the registration in favour of the *mala fide* acquirer and the registration of ownership in his favour. An action may be brought within a period of three years from the registration of a *mala fide* acquirer.

1161. The fact that a contract on the transfer of ownership has already been made does not in itself have an impact on the validity of subsequently made contracts on the alienation of the same thing.
1162. Article 117/1 PA.
1163. Article 117/2 PA.
1164. Gavella in *Property Law I*, 445, Klarić / Vedriš in *Civil Law*, 290.
1165. Article 125/1 PA.
1166. Article 125/2 PA.

III. Acquisition of Ownership from Non-owners

327. Croatian law expressly provides for cases of acquisition of ownership where the contract of transfer was concluded by a person who is not the owner of the thing (*stjecanje vlasništva od nevlasnika*). Although the contracting party is not the owner, a contract on the alienation of a thing belonging to another is valid, and it has all the effects of the law on obligations, and it binds the parties to the contract.[1167] Under some specific conditions expressly provided for in the PA, it is possible to acquire ownership on the basis of a contract on the alienation of a thing (so-called acquisition from non-owners). The acquisition of ownership from non-owners is regulated by special rules depending on whether the ownership of an immovable or a movable is acquired from a non-owner.

328. Ownership of a movable on the basis of a contract on the alienation of a movable belonging to another (contracts with non-owners) may be acquired by a bona fide acquirer to whom, on the basis of a payable contract (e.g., a contract of sale, a contract of exchange), the seller (possessor – non-owner) surrendered a movable into direct and independent possession.[1168] The acquirer is deemed to be in good faith if, at the moment of concluding the transaction and at the moment of accepting the thing into immediate possession, he did not know and did not have sufficient reason to doubt that the thing belonged to the seller.[1169] A bona fide acquirer cannot acquire ownership under these rules only if the owner ceased to possess the movable against his will, i.e., if the immovable was stolen or the owner lost or misplaced it.[1170] A bona fide acquirer becomes the owner of a movable at the moment the seller surrenders the movable into the acquirer's independent and direct possession.[1171,1172]

329. Ownership of an immovable on the basis of a contract entered into with a non-owner is acquired if all the conditions for the protection of trust in the truthfulness and completeness of the land register are met.[1173,1174] Ownership of an immovable deriving from a non-owner is acquired when a contract of alienation of such property is made with a person entered in the land register as the owner, although he is not the owner of the particular immovable because the legal status of the immovable entered in the land register is untruthful and incomplete. The

1167. Article 382 of OA expressly provides for the sale of a thing belonging to another person to be binding on the contracting parties, but the buyer who did not know or had no sufficient reason to doubt that the thing belonged to another may, if the purpose of the contract cannot be achieved, terminate the contract and request compensation for damage.
1168. Article 118/1 PA.
1169. Article 118/3 PA.
1170. Article 118/4 PA.
1171. Legal relations between the seller (a non-owner) and the former owner are regulated by the rules of the law on obligations. The former owner does not have any claims against the new owner. The former owner may request compensation for damage from the seller, the payment of an amount which corresponds to the value of the alienated thing or other forms of compensation.
1172. Gavella in *Property Law I*, 446–449, Klarić / Vedriš in *Civil Law*, 278.
1173. Articles 123, 124 PA.
1174. For more details *see* Part I, Ch. 2, §2. III. The Protection of Trust.

acquirer is deemed to have acted bona fide if he did not know and did not have sufficient reason to doubt that the person entered as the owner was not the owner (e.g., because someone else had acquired the immovable by acquisitive prescription but failed to enter his ownership in the land register). A bona fide acquirer of an immovable acquires ownership on the basis of a sales contract made with the seller (a non-owner registered as if being an owner) at the moment of his registration in the land register as the new owner.[1175] The possibilities of acquiring ownership of an immovable from a non-owner are greater than those of acquiring ownership of a movable from a non-owner because an immovable may be acquired from a non-owner both on the basis of a payable contract or of a contract free of charge.[1176]

§5. Acquisition of Easement by Contract *Inter Vivos*

330. The conditions for the acquisition of easements by contract *inter vivos* are based on the same principles as in the case of the acquisition of ownership. With a contract *inter vivos,* both real and personal easements may be acquired. The following three conditions must be fulfilled:

(1) ownership of the servient property.[1177] Easement is derived from the ownership of a thing which will be encumbered by easement. The person entered in the land register is considered to be the owner of the immovable.[1178,1179,1180] In the case of movables, the owner is the person who is the independent possessor of the movable;[1181,1182]
(2) a valid contract aimed at acquiring easement made by the owner of the dominant property and the owner of the servient property (in the case of real easements) or the owner of the servient property and a person for whose benefit

1175. Legal relations between the seller (a non-owner) and the former owner are regulated by the rules of the law on obligations. The former owner does not have any claims against the new owner. He may request compensation for damage from the seller, the payment of an equivalent amount for the value of the alienated thing, and similar compensations.
1176. Gavella in *Property Law I*, 464–470, Klarić / Vedriš in *Civil Law*, 293.
1177. Article 219/1 PA.
1178. Article 8/2 LRA.
1179. If a person is not entered in the land register as the owner of an immovable, easement may be established only if the person can prove, by valid documents for entering his ownership, an uninterrupted succession of acquisition without registration from the registered owner to himself (Art. 46RLA).
1180. If a person who is not a real owner is entered in the land register as the owner of an immovable, the establishment of easement may occur only if all the conditions are met for the protection of a bona fide third acquirer who acted in good faith by having trust in the land register (Art. 230 in conjunction with Arts 123, 124 PA). For more details, *see* Part I, Ch. 2, §2. III. The Protection of Trust.
1181. Article 11/3 PA.
1182. If a person who is an independent possessor of a movable is not the real owner, the establishment of personal easement may occur only if the conditions are met for the protection of a bona fide acquirer who did not know and did not have any sufficient reason to doubt that the possessor was not the owner of the movable (Art. 118 in conjunction with Art. 1/6 PA). For more details, *see* Part III, Ch. 2, §4. III. Acquisition of Ownership from Non-owners.

the personal easement is established. If the servient property is an immovable, the contract must be made in writing;[1183]

(3) a valid modus of acquisition. If the servient property is an immovable, easement must be entered in the land register.[1184] Easement is entered by registration or conditional registration.[1185] If an immovable is not entered in the land register, easement is acquired by depositing a legalized document with the court.[1186] When personal easement is established on a movable, the modality of acquisition is by surrendering it to the acquirer.[1187,1188,1189]

§6. Acquisition of Real Burdens by Contract *Inter Vivos*

331. By contracts *inter vivos,* praedial real burdens and personal real burdens may be established. Three conditions must be fulfilled:

(1) ownership of the servient immovable.[1190] Real burdens are derived from the ownership of an immovable, which will be encumbered. The person who is entered in the land register as the owner will be considered the owner of the immovable;[1191,1192,1193]
(2) a valid contract aimed at acquiring a real burden made by the owner of the dominant immovable and the owner of the servient immovable (praedial real burdens), or the owner of the servient immovable and the person for whose benefit the personal real burden is established. The contract must be made in writing;[1194]

1183. Article 219/4 PA.
1184. Article 220 PA.
1185. Article 220/1-2 PA.
1186. Article 220/3 PA.
1187. Article 222/1 PA.
1188. If the owner concludes several legal transactions in order to establish a personal easement on one and the same movable as servient, and such easements cannot exist simultaneously on one and the same movable, the easement with respect to which the movable was first surrendered into possession is deemed to be established (Art. 222/2 PA).
1189. Stipković in *Property Law II*, 18; Klarić / Vedriš in *Civil Law* 329.
1190. Article 262/1 PA.
1191. Article 8/2 LRA.
1192. A real burden may be acquired from a person not entered in the land register as the owner of an immovable only if such a person is able to prove an interrupted succession of acquisitions without registration from the registered predecessor to himself (Art. 46 LRA).
1193. If a person who is not a real owner is entered in the land register as the owner of an immovable, the establishment of easement may occur only if all the conditions are met for the protection of a bona fide third acquirer who acted in good faith having trust in the land register (Art. 264 in conjunction with Arts 123, 124 PA). For more details, *see* Part I, Ch. 2, §2. III. The Protection of Trust.
1194. Article 262/2 PA.

(3) a valid modus of acquisition, i.e., an entry in the land register.[1195] A real burden is established by registration or conditional registration.[1196] If the immovable is not entered in the land register, a real burden is established by depositing a legalized document with the court.[1197,1198]

§7. Acquisition of the Right to Build by Contract *Inter Vivos*

332. In order to acquire the right to build by a contract *inter vivos,* three conditions must be fulfilled:

(1) ownership of the immovable (plot) on which the right to build is established. A right to build is derived from the ownership of an immovable encumbered with the right to build.[1199] The owner of the immovable is the person who is entered in the land register as such;[1200,1201,1202]
(2) a valid contract aimed at acquiring the right to build made by the owner of the immovable encumbered with the right to build and the person for whose benefit the right to build is established. The contract must be made in writing;[1203]
(3) a valid modus of acquisition, i.e., an entry in the land register.[1204] A right to build is entered by registration or conditional registration.[1205] If an immovable is not entered in the land register, the right to build is acquired by depositing a legalized document with the court.[1206,1207]

§8. Acquisition of a Lien by Contract *Inter Vivos*

333. The conditions for the acquisition of a lien on the basis of a legal transaction (voluntary lien), apart from in the PA, are also provided for in other regulations

1195. Article 263 PA.
1196. Articles 263/1,2 PA.
1197. Article 263/3 PA.
1198. Gavella in *Property Law II*, 18; Klarić / Vedriš in *Civil Law*, 55.
1199. Article 287/1 PA.
1200. Article 8/2 LRA.
1201. The right to build may be acquired from a person not entered in the land register as the owner of an immovable, only if that person can prove, with valid documents for entering ownership, an uninterrupted succession of acquisition without registration from the registered predecessor to himself (Art. 41 LRA).
1202. If a person, who is not a real owner, is entered in the land register as the owner of an immovable, the acquisition of the right to build may occur only if all the conditions are met for the protection of a bona fide third acquirer who acted in good faith having trust in the land register (Art. 288/5 in conjunction with Arts 264, 123, 124 PA). For more details, *see* Part I, Ch. 2, §2. III. The Protection of Trust.
1203. Article 287/2 PA.
1204. Article 288 PA.
1205. Article 288/5 in conjunction with Art. 263/1,2 PA.
1206. Article 288/5 in conjunction with Art. 263/3 PA.
1207. Gavella in *Property Law II*, 89; Klarić / Vedriš in *Civil Law*, 372.

such as the EA, the Act on the Register of Secured Transactions Established in Movables and Patrimonial Rights before a Court or Notary Public (Register Act), and the like. The same principles apply as in the case of the acquisition of other property rights by contract *inter vivos* (the principles *nemo plus* and the principle of causal tradition). Therefore, for the acquisition of a lien by contract *inter vivos*, three basic conditions must be fulfilled, just as in the case of the acquisition of other property rights. They are the following:

(1) Ownership of the liened thing, i.e., the belonging of the right on which a lien is established.[1208] The person entered in the land register as owner is the owner of the immovable.[1209,1210,1211] The owner of a movable is the person who is an independent possessor of the movable.[1212,1213]
(2) A valid contract (*titulus*) whose aim is the establishment of a lien – a contract of lien.[1214] The form of the contract of lien depends on whether the lien is established on a movable, an immovable or a right. It also depends on whether the voluntary lien is established or whether it is a voluntary court or a notarial lien. A contract of lien by which a voluntary lien on a movable is established or on a patrimonial right equated with a movable is also valid if it is made orally. In order to be valid, a contract of lien by which a voluntary lien on an immovable is established or on a patrimonial right which is equal to the immovable (e.g., the right to build) must be made in writing.[1215] A contract of lien must then be made in the form of a written, private document signed by the owner of the immovable (lienee) and the lienor. A contract of lien, by which a voluntary court or a notarial lien is established, is made before the court in the form of court records and in accordance with the provisions of the EA.[1216,1217] A contract of lien establishing a voluntary notarial lien is made before a notary public in the form of a notarial act.[1218,1219]
(3) The valid modus of acquisition differs depending on whether the lien is acquired on a movable, an immovable or a patrimonial right, as well as on

1208. Article 306/1 PA.
1209. Article 8/2 LRA.
1210. A lien may be acquired from a person not entered in the land register as the owner of an immovable only if that person, in order to enter the fact of ownership, can prove with valid documents an uninterrupted succession of acquisition without registration from the registered predecessor to himself (Art. 41 of LRA).
1211. If a person who is not a real owner is entered in the land register as the owner of an immovable, the acquisition of lien may occur only if all the conditions are met for the protection of a bona fide third acquirer who acted in good faith having confidence in the land register (Art. 318 PA).
1212. Article 11/3 PA.
1213. If a person who is an independent possessor of an movable is not the real owner, the acquisition of lien may occur only if all the conditions for the acquisition of ownership from a non-owner are fulfilled (Art. 317 in conjunction with Art. 118 PA). For more details, *see* the Part III, Ch. 2, §4. Acquisition of Ownership from Non-owners.
1214. Article 306/1 PA.
1215. Article 307/6 PA.
1216. Articles 312/1, 313/1 PA, Arts 300–306 of EA.
1217. In the case of voluntary court liens, the form of court records is always required, regardless of whether liens on movables, immovables or patrimonial rights are established.
1218. Articles 300–309 of EA; Arts 53, 54, 59 of NPA.

whether a voluntary lien, a voluntary court, or a notarial lien is acquired. A voluntary lien on a movable is acquired by surrendering the movable to the direct possession of the lienor.[1220] A voluntary lien on an immovable is acquired by its being entered in the land register, i.e., by registration or conditional registration of the lien in favour of the lienor.[1221,1222] A voluntary lien on patrimonial rights such as claims is acquired by ceding the claim to the lienor and informing the debtor of the cession.[1223] A voluntary lien established on a patrimonial right equal to the immovable is acquired by an entry in the land register under the same rules which apply to voluntary liens on immovables.[1224] A voluntary court lien or a voluntary notarial lien on an immovable is acquired by being entered in the land register.[1225] Voluntary court and notarial liens on movables and patrimonial rights are acquired by being entered in the Register of Secured Transactions Established in Movables and Patrimonial Rights before a Court or a Notary Public kept by the Financial Agency.[1226] In this case, a liened movable is not surrendered into the lienor's possession, and the patrimonial rights are not ceded in favour of the lienor.[1227]

1219. In the case of voluntary notarial liens, the form of a notarial act is always required, regardless of whether liens on movables, immovables or patrimonial rights are established. A private document on a lien made by the parties and solemnized by a notary public is equal to a notarial act developed by a notary public (Art. 59 of NPA).
1220. Article 308/1 PA.
1221. Articles 309/1,2 PA.
1222. A lien on an immovable not entered in the land register is acquired by depositing with a court a document concerning the legal transaction which is the basis for the acquisition of ownership (Art. 309/3 PA). When such a document is properly made for registration, its deposition with the court has the same legal effects as the registration in the land register. When the document satisfies all the conditions for conditional registration, its deposition with the court has the same legal effects as conditional registration in the land register.
1223. Article 310/1 PA.
1224. Article 310/2 PA.
1225. Articles 309/1,2 PA.
1226. Article 17 of the Register Act.
1227. For more details on the powers of lienors with all these types of liens, *see* Part VI. Security Rights.

Chapter 3. Acquisition of Property Rights by the Decision of Competent Authority

§1. General

334. Property rights are acquired by a court decision or the decision of another competent authority in the cases provided for and specified by law. Property rights established on the basis of a court decision are acquired at the moment the court decision becomes enforceable. Property rights based on decisions by administrative authorities are acquired at the moment the decision reached in administrative proceedings becomes final. Property rights and the conditions for their acquisition on the basis of court decisions or decisions by administrative authorities are laid down in the PA and in some other regulations.[1228] The provisions of the PA and the corresponding regulations stipulate that ownership, easements, encumbrances and the right to build may be acquired on such a legal basis.[1229]

§2. Acquisition of Ownership by the Decision of Competent Authority

I. General

335. Ownership may be acquired on the basis of a court decision or the decision of another competent authority in cases prescribed by law and in accordance with the stipulated conditions. Ownership is acquired at the moment a court decision or the decision of another competent authority becomes enforceable unless it is otherwise stipulated in a separate act.[1230] Ownership is acquired by a court decision or by the decision of another competent authority only in cases where it is laid down in a separate regulation and when all the necessary conditions are met.[1231]

336. The PA expressly provides that through the acquisition of ownership on the basis of a court decision or the decision of another competent authority, other property rights (such as liens, easements), which have existed on a particular thing for the benefit of other persons, do not terminate.[1232] Only the rights specified in the

1228. For example, the Expropriation Act, the Roads Act, the Cultural Heritage Act, the Physical Planning Act, the Construction Act, the Waters Act, the Cemeteries Act, the Nature Protection Act, the Act for Compensation for Property Taken during the Communist Rule, and the like.
1229. Article 126 PA (ownership), Arts 223–226 PA (easements), Art. 265 PA (encumbrances), Art. 289 PA (the right to build).
1230. Articles 126/1,2 PA.
1231. These are mostly regulations providing for expropriation of immovable because of the need to build objects or execute works in the interest of the Republic of Croatia, or to protect and maintain particular immovables of interest to the Republic of Croatia.
1232. Article 126/3 PA.

decision by which ownership is acquired or stipulated in the law on which the decision is based cease to exist. The same is the case with the rights which by nature can no longer exist.[1233]

337. Ownership of immovable property acquired on the basis of a court decision, or the decision of another competent authority is entered in the land register on the acquirer's request. It is entered on the basis of a court decision or the decision of another competent authority by which it is acquired and at the request of its acquirer.[1234] However, entry in the land register is not then a condition for the acquisition of ownership. It is already acquired by virtue of a court decision or the decision of another competent authority without being entered into the land register. An entry in the land register is necessary for the protection of ownership against all third persons and for the subsequent free disposal of the immovable. Before the ownership of an immovable is entered into the land register in favour of the person who has acquired it on the basis of a court decision or the decision of another competent authority, the land registry status is incomplete. In the case of bona fide acquirers, the land register status is considered to be complete, and they enjoy protection if they have acted with trust in the land register.[1235] A bona fide acquirer who has acted in good faith by having trust in the land register acquires ownership from the registered owner, who is no longer the actual owner because his ownership terminates after a third person has acquired ownership by a court decision, or the decision of another competent authority.[1236] Therefore, Article 127/2 PA expressly stipulates that ownership of an immovable acquired by a court decision or the decision of another authority cannot oppose the right of the person who, having relied on the information in the land register, had entered his property right in good faith before the right acquired by a court decision, or the decision of another authority was entered in the land register. This actually means that the owner, having acquired ownership by a court decision or the decision of another competent authority, may be registered in the land register before the legal effects of the protection of trust in the completeness of the land register are established in favour of a third person acting in good faith.[1237,1238]

1233. Thus, in Arts 3/2, 41, the ExA expressly provides that on the day of the enforceability of the decision on expropriation by which an immovable falls under the ownership of the beneficiary of expropriation, all rights established on the immovable (such as mortgages, easements) terminate and the holders of these rights receive corresponding compensations.

1234. Article 127/1 PA.

1235. For more details, *see* Part I, Ch. 2, §2. III. The Protection of Trust.

1236. Article 124 PA.

1237. Because of the operation of the protection of trust in the completeness of the land register, after a bona fide acquirer has been registered as the owner of an immovable, the unregistered ownership acquired on the basis of a court or another body's decision terminates. Legal relations between the registered owner and the owner who has acquired the ownership on the basis of a court or another body's decision are dealt with in accordance with the rules of the law on obligations.

1238. Gavella in *Property Law I*, 471-492.

II. Acquisition of Ownership by Expropriation

338. The acquisition of ownership by expropriation is the most frequent type of acquisition on the basis of the decision of another competent authority. The general rules on the conditions and expropriation proceedings are laid down in the ExA.[1239] The expropriation of immovables because of their protection and maintenance (e.g., immovables of cultural heritage) or because of the construction of particular objects of interest to the Republic of Croatia (e.g., public roads) is laid down in a number of separate regulations.[1240] Separate regulations on expropriation take precedence in application, so the ExA applies subsidiarily if separate regulations do not expressly provide otherwise.[1241]

339. The basic condition for the adoption of a decision on expropriation of immovable is that objects are built, or works are carried out,[1242] in the interest of the Republic of Croatia, as well as the assessment that through such a use of a piece of immovable and being given a new purpose, a greater benefit will be achieved than the one achieved by its previous use.[1243] The decision that building an object, or carrying out works, is in the interest of the Republic of Croatia is passed by the Government of the Republic of Croatia on the proposal of a person in whose favour the expropriation takes place and who becomes the new owner of the immovable by virtue of the expropriation decision.[1244,1245] After the interest of the Republic of Croatia has been established, the person in whose favour the immovable is expropriated must submit a proposal for expropriation to the competent administrative body.[1246,1247] The proposal for expropriation is decided upon in administrative proceedings, and a decision on expropriation is adopted. Based on a final decision on expropriation, the person in whose favour the immovable has been expropriated acquires ownership of the immovable. At the same time, ownership of the former owner, as well as all other rights on the expropriated immovable, terminates. This creates an obligation for the new owner to pay compensation to the former owner

---

1239. OG 74/14, 69/17, 98/19.

1240. For example, the Roads Act, the Cultural Heritage Act, the Waters Act, the Cemeteries Act, the Nature Protection Act.

1241. Gavella in *Property Law I*, 479–484.

1242. Expropriation is carried out for the purpose of carrying out works or for building infrastructural objects (traffic, telecommunications, water supply, supply of energy), health, educational or cultural objects, as well as objects to meet the needs of the judiciary, the armed forces or the police, or objects used for research and exploitation of mineral and other riches (Art. 2/2 of ExA).

1243. Article 2/1 of ExA.

1244. Article 9/1 of ExA.

1245. A decision on the establishment of the interest of the Republic of Croatia does not need to be reached in cases where it is expressly provided in a separate act that the execution of particular works is in the interest of the Republic of Croatia (Art. 13/2 of ExA). Thus, the Roads Act expressly provides that the construction of public roads is in the interest of the Republic of Croatia (Art. 36/1 RA).

1246. Articles 25,26 of ExA.

1247. The state administration office of the county or of the City of Zagreb reaches decisions on expropriation, and the Ministry of Justice decides upon appeals against such decisions (Art. 16,17/1,2 of ExA). Court protection in expropriation proceedings is offered by the administrative court (Art. 17/3, 18 of ExA).

for the expropriated immovable in accordance with its market value.[1248] After the compensation has been duly paid, the new owner, on the basis of a final decision on expropriation, may be registered in the land register as the new owner[1249] and request that the immovable be surrendered into his possession.[1250]

§3. Acquisition of Real Easements by the Decision of Competent Authority

340. On the basis of court decisions or decisions of other competent authorities, only real easements may be acquired. A real easement is acquired on the day a court decision or a decision of an administrative body becomes final, i.e., without its entry in the land register.[1251] The acquirer of a real easement is authorized to request the entry of the real easement in the land register.[1252,1253] Before a real easement, acquired on the basis of a court decision or the decision of another competent authority, is entered in the land register, the land register is incomplete. A real easement not registered in the land register may not oppose the right of the person who, having relied on the information in the land register, registered his right on the property in good faith. It will terminate on account of the operation of the protection of trust in the land register.[1254,1255]

341. Real easements are established on the basis of a court decision in cases specified in the provisions of the PA. Real easements are established by a court decision in the procedure of establishing a way of necessity,[1256] necessary conduits and other equipment,[1257] in the procedure of division in inheritance proceedings[1258] and in other cases established by law.[1259]

1248. Articles 11,46,47 of ExA.
1249. Article 56 of ExA.
1250. Article 40 of ExA.
1251. Article 223/3 PA.
1252. Article 223/4 PA.
1253. An entry is made on the basis of a final court decision, or the decision of the competent authority by which the real easement was established.
1254. Article 227 PA. For more details, *see* Part I, Ch. 2, §2. III. The Protection of Trust.
1255. Stipković in *Property Law II*, 19; Klarić / Vedriš in *Civil Law*, 329.
1256. A way of necessity is established by a court decision rendered on the request of the owner of an immovable if there is no access or no suitable access to a public road and if the benefit of making the way of necessity is greater than the damage caused to the servient immovable. The owner of the immovable for whose benefit the way of necessity is established is bound to pay appropriate compensation to the owner of the servient immovable (Art. 224/1,4 PA).
1257. The easement of conduits and other equipment on another's servient immovable will be established by the court on the request of the owner who has no access or no appropriate access to the supplier of substances, energy sources or services delivered through such conduits and other equipment and if the benefit of installing such conduits is greater than the damage to the servient immovable. The owner of the immovable for whose benefit such easement is established is bound to pay compensation to the owner of the servient immovable (Art. 225/1 PA).
1258. The court conducting proceedings for the partition of co-ownership or joint ownership decides to establish an easement in agreement with the parties. In cases of the geometric partition of immovables, the court renders such a decision without the parties' permission (Art. 226/1 PA).
1259. Article 223/1 PA.

342. A real easement may also be established by an administrative body in expropriation or land consolidation proceedings.[1260] The most frequent case in the establishment of easements on the basis of a decision of an administrative body is that in expropriation proceedings.[1261]

§4. Acquisition of Real Burdens by the Decision of Competent Authority

343. Real burdens are established by a court decision in partition and probate proceedings if the court is authorized to establish easement in such proceedings and also in other cases provided by law.[1262] The rules on the establishment of easements by a court decision apply accordingly to the establishment of real burdens.[1263] A real burden is acquired on the day a court decision becomes final, i.e., without an entry in the land register.[1264] The acquirer of a real burden is entitled to seek entry of the real burden to his benefit in the land register.[1265,1266] A real burden not registered in the land register may not oppose the right of the person who, having relied on the information in the land register, registered his property right in good faith.[1267,1268]

§5. Acquisition of the Right to Build by the Decision of Competent Authority

344. The right to build is established on the basis of a court decision when the court establishes it in partition or probate proceedings.[1269] The court may render a decision on the establishment of the right to build if it is authorized to establish real easement in these proceedings[1270] and in other cases provided by law. The rules on the establishment of real easements by court decisions apply accordingly to the establishment of the right to build.[1271] The right to build is acquired on the day a court decision becomes final, i.e., without an entry in the land register.[1272] The acquirer of the right to build is entitled to seek the right to build to his benefit in the

1260. Article 223/2 PA.
1261. A real easement is established on the basis of a final decision on expropriation (Art. 4 of ExA). The owner of the encumbered land is entitled to compensation in the amount by which, because of the establishment of easement, the market value of his land is decreased (Art. 37 of ExA).
1262. Article 265/1 PA.
1263. Article 265/2 PA.
1264. Article 223/3 in conjunction with Art. 265/2 PA.
1265. Article 223/4 in conjunction with Art. 265/2 PA.
1266. An entry is made on the basis of a final decision of the court or a competent body by which a real burden was established.
1267. Article 227 in conjunction with Art. 265/2 PA. For more details, *see* Part I, Ch. 2, §2. III. The Protection of Trust.
1268. Gavella in *Property Law II*, 56; Klarić / Vedriš in *Civil Law*, 365.
1269. Article 289/1 PA.
1270. Article 226 PA.
1271. Article 289/2 PA.
1272. Article 223/3 in conjunction with Art. 289/2 PA.

land register.[1273,1274] However, the right to build not registered in the land register may not oppose the right of the person who, having relied on the information in the land register, registered his right on the property in good faith.[1275,1276]

1273. Article 223/4 PA.
1274. An entry is made on the basis of a final decision of the court or another competent body by which the right to build was established.
1275. Article 227 in conjunction with Art. 289/2 PA. For more details, *see* Part I, Ch. 2, §2. III. The Protection of Trust.
1276. Gavella in *Property Law II*, 91; Klarić / Vedriš in *Civil Law*, 372.

Chapter 4. Acquisition of Property Rights by Inheritance

345. Property rights are acquired by inheritance at the moment of initiation of inheritance proceedings, e.g., upon the testator's death. This rule applies regardless of whether an heir inherits from the testator by law or by a will. Strictly personal property rights, such as personal easements or personal real burdens, cannot be acquired by inheritance.[1277,1278]

346. An heir acquires ownership of inherited things at the moment of the initiation of inheritance proceedings unless otherwise provided by law.[1279] By acquiring ownership by descent, the property rights on the thing belonging to other persons do not terminate (e.g., liens, easements, real burdens etc.), save for those provided by law or which cannot continue to exist because of the nature of the thing.[1280] It is expressly laid down that the right to build is inheritable.[1281] There is no express provision governing the acquisition of other property rights by inheritance. However, all other property rights are inherited together with the ownership of the thing in whose favour they were established (e.g., real easements, praedial real burden). This ensues from the provisions of the PA, according to which real easements and real burdens are inseparably connected with the dominant immovable and are transferred together with the ownership of a dominant immovable.[1282] Any person who acquires ownership of a dominant immovable by inheritance also acquires all rights of real easement and encumbrance existing in favour of the respective immovable.[1283] As far as liens are concerned, a rule applies that the person who has inherited the claim secured by a lien also acquires the lien.[1284]

347. The fact concerning who has inherited which property rights by inheritance is established by a decision on inheritance. This is rendered in inheritance proceedings.[1285] With the final decision on inheritance, the heir proves in relation to all third persons which rights he has acquired and on which things. Based on such a decision, the heir is authorized to request the inherited immovable to be entered in the land register.[1286] The entry is not a condition for the acquisition of ownership by inheritance because the title was acquired at the time of the testator's death. However, the entry in the land register is necessary for further disposal of the immovable (sale, lien and the like) and for efficient protection and realization of ownership in relation to all third persons.

1277. Article 202 PA.
1278. The right of personal easement expires upon the death of the person having the right of easement (Art. 244/1 PA). It will not expire if it was established to expressly include the heir of the person having the right of personal easement (Art. 244/2 PA). However, personal easement may be established only for the heirs of the first authorized heir and not for any subsequent heirs.
1279. Article 128/1 PA.
1280. Article 128/3 PA.
1281. Articles 285, 290 PA.
1282. Articles 182/2, 255/2 PA.
1283. Articles 231, 267 PA.
1284. Article 319 PA.
1285. Inheritance proceedings are governed by the Inheritance Act. These are non-contentious proceedings conducted by the court or a notary public as the court's trustee.
1286. Article 128/2 PA.

Chapter 5. Acquisition of Property Rights on the Basis of Law

§1. General

348. Property rights are acquired on the basis of law in cases where acquisition does not take place on any other legal basis. This is acquisition of property rights regardless of the will of the former owner of the thing. When property rights are acquired by operation of law, some conditions must be fulfilled that do not concern a legal transaction, a court decision or the decision of another competent authority or inheritance. Property rights are acquired by operation of law when the statutory conditions are met. Both the possibilities for acquisition and the conditions to be met are expressly provided for in the PA. Therefore, the only property rights acquired on the basis of law are those expressly stipulated by law. The PA lays down that ownership,[1287] real easements,[1288] real burdens[1289] and liens[1290] are acquired on the basis of law.

§2. Acquisition of Property Rights on the Basis of Law

I. General

349. Ownership is acquired on the basis of law upon the fulfilment of the stipulated conditions. These conditions are provided for differently depending on particular cases of statutory acquisition. What is common to all these cases is the fact that ownership acquired by operation of law is acquired at the moment the statutory conditions are fulfilled.[1291] When ownership is acquired on the basis of law, all the previously existing property rights on a particular thing cease to exist, save for the ones that the acquirer knew about or should have known about.[1292]

350. When ownership is acquired by operation of law, no particular modality of acquisition is required that is normally needed when ownership is acquired by contract *inter vivos*. Ownership of a movable on the basis of law is acquired even if the thing is not surrendered to the acquirer. Ownership of an immovable on the basis of law is acquired even without it being entered in the land register. However, a person who has acquired ownership of a movable by operation of law is entitled to request its surrender into his possession. Likewise, a person who has acquired ownership of an immovable by operation of law is entitled to request its registration in the land register.[1293,1294] The registration of ownership acquired by operation of law

1287. Articles 129–160 PA.
1288. Articles 228–230 PA.
1289. Article 266 PA.
1290. Article 314 PA.
1291. Article 129/1 PA.
1292. Article 129/2 PA.
1293. Article 130/1 PA.
1294. An entry in the land register is made on the basis of a final court decision or another public document establishing the ownership of an immovable on the basis of law.

is important so that it can be proven and protected in relation to any third persons. If, prior to the acquisition of ownership on the basis of law, a fair acquirer obtains it from a person registered as the owner (although no longer being the actual owner because someone else has acquired ownership on the basis of law), the legal effects of the protection in trust in the completeness of the land register come into play. A fair acquirer becomes the owner of the immovable. At the same time, the ownership of the person who has acquired ownership on the basis of law but who has failed to have it registered terminates. Therefore, Article 130/2 of the PA expressly provides that ownership of an immovable by operation of law may not oppose the right of a person who, having relied on the information in the land register, registered his right on the property in good faith before the right acquired by operation of law was entered in the land register.[1295]

II. Appropriation

351. Ownership of a movable belonging to no one (*res nullius*) is acquired by appropriation (*prisvojenje*). A movable does not have an owner if it originally does not belong to anyone because it has never been owned by any person or if the owner of a movable has waived his ownership right.[1296] An owner is deemed to have waived his ownership of a movable when, in order to waive it, he actually abandoned its possession.[1297,1298] Ownership is acquired by appropriation when a movable is taken into possession with the aim of actually appropriating and owning it.[1299]

352. It is not possible to acquire ownership of immovables by appropriation. When the owner waives ownership of an immovable, it becomes the ownership of the Republic of Croatia by operation of law.[1300] In order for an immovable to be deemed waived, it is not sufficient for the owner to abandon the possession of the

1295. Before an entry in the land register is made in favour of the person who has acquired ownership by operation of law, the land register status is incomplete. It is incomplete because, even without being entered in the land register, the ownership acquired outside the land register is acquired at the moment all the conditions stipulated by law are fulfilled. Even when the land register situation is incomplete, it is considered to be complete in favour of fair acquirers, so they will be protected if they have acted with trust in the land register. A fair acquirer who has acted with trust in the land register acquires ownership of an immovable from a registered owner who is actually not a real owner in the case where the real owner is a non-registered person who acquires ownership by operation of law (Art. 124 PA). For more details, *see* Part I, Ch. 2, §2. III. The Protection of Trust.

1296. Article 132/1 PA.

1297. Article 132/2 PA.

1298. When abandoning ownership of a moveable, the owner must clearly express his intention of waiving it. When in doubt whether the owner has abandoned a movable or has just lost it, the movable is deemed to be no one's (Art. 132/2 PA).

1299. Article 131/1 PA.

1300. Article 133/2 PA.

immovable. The owner is deemed to have waived ownership of a particular immovable by making a statement on waiving the ownership in the form of a written document.[1301]

353. It is not possible to acquire ownership of things by appropriation if they may only be in public ownership (e.g., state ownership) by virtue of a separate law. However, things in public ownership may be acquired by appropriation if their purpose is appropriation (fish, animals, minerals, river waters, and the like) for which special permission is required by law or a permit issued on the basis of law. A person who has a permit for appropriation (e.g., a mining concession, a hunting license, and the like)[1302] acquires ownership of such things on the basis of such a permit.

III. Finding

354. Ownership of a lost movable is acquired by the act of finding it (*nalaz stvari*).[1303] The finder of a lost movable is obligated to hand it over to a lost and found office (*nalazni ured*).[1304] The lost and found office is bound to keep the lost movable and publish a notification of its being found.[1305] If within one year from the publication of the notification, the owner of the movable does not come forward, the lost and found office hands the movable over into the finder's possession.[1306,1307] The finder then acquires ownership of the lost thing under the conditions for the acquisition of ownership by acquisitive prescription.[1308] The ownership of a lost movable is acquired if it has been possessed for three years after the lost and found office has surrendered it into the finder's possession.[1309,1310,1311]

IV. Treasure Trove

355. Special rules apply in the case of treasure troves (*nalaz blaga*), such as money, valuables or other items of value hidden for a long time so that their owner

1301. On the basis of such waivers, ownership is deleted from the land register and the Republic of Croatia is registered as the owner (Art. 133/1 PA).
1302. The issuance of permits is provided for in a number of acts such as the Mining Act, the Waters Act, the Nature Protection Act, the Hunting Act, the Sea-Fishing Act, etc.
1303. Article 134/1 PA.
1304. Article 134 PA.
1305. Article 135 PA.
1306. Article 138 PA.
1307. If the lost and found office returns the lost movable to the owner, the finder is entitled to compensation amounting to 10% of the market value of the movable. The owner to whom the lost movable has been returned must pay the compensation to the finder (Art. 136 PA).
1308. Article 139 PA.
1309. Article 159/2 PA.
1310. If, in the meantime, the owner has requested the return of the lost movable, the finder must return it to the owner and is thereby entitled to compensation amounting to 10% of the turnover value of the movable, as well as to compensation of the costs of its maintenance.
1311. Gavella in *Property Law I*, 514–519; Klarić / Vedriš in *Civil Law*, 281–282.

can no longer be identified.[1312] If the owner of the treasure does not exist, it becomes the property of the Republic of Croatia.[1313] The finder is bound to notify the lost and found office of the treasure, and the office is then obligated to notify the competent state authority responsible for the protection of cultural heritage.[1314] The finder and the owner of the immovable where such treasure is found are entitled to an adequate fee from the Republic of Croatia and to compensation for costs incurred.[1315,1316]

V. Acquisition of Fruits

356. The fruits (*plodovi*),[1317] or whatever is separated from a thing, normally belong to the owner of the thing.[1318,1319] Any other persons, other than the actual owner, may exceptionally acquire ownership of the fruits borne by a thing belonging to another. Such persons acquire ownership of fruits by separation (*odvajanje*). In order for such persons to be able to acquire ownership of fruits by separation, they must exercise some right on the thing which bears these fruits that entitles them to these fruits. By way of separation from the main thing, ownership of fruits is acquired by a person who is entitled to the fruits from another's thing on the basis of some leasehold interest, such as that of a lessee.[1320] A person who, as a holder of a property right, possesses another's thing, such as a usufructuary, also acquires ownership of the fruits by separation.[1321] If one person has a property right and another person has a leasehold interest in the same thing, and both are entitled to collect fruits, the person having a leasehold interest has priority, and he will acquire the ownership of fruits by separation.[1322] For example, if a usufructuary has leased an immovable to which he has a personal easement of usufruct, the ownership of fruits is acquired by separation by the lessee.[1323,1324,1325]

1312. Article 140/1 PA.
1313. Article 140/2 PA.
1314. Articles 140/3,4 PA.
1315. Article 140/5 PA.
1316. Gavella in *Property Law I*, 519–521; Klarić / Vedriš in *Civil Law*, 281.
1317. Fruits are the products a thing yields naturally, or as the result of someone's work, as well as everything else the thing yields as part of its purpose (Art. 8/2 PA).
1318. Article 141/1 PA.
1319. The rule according to which the owner of a thing is also the owner of all the fruits it yields is applied accordingly to the person who, as an independent and bona fide possessor, possesses another's thing (Art. 141/2 PA).
1320. Article 143/1 PA.
1321. Article 142/1 PA.
1322. Article 142/3 PA.
1323. The rules according to which the holder of a property right or leasehold interest on another's thing acquires ownership of its fruits apply accordingly to the person who, as a bona fide possessor, possesses another's thing as if being the holder of a property right, or a leasehold interest (Arts 142/2, 143/2 PA).
1324. The rules on the acquisition of fruits by separation apply accordingly to fruits of animals and all other benefits they yield (Art. 144 PA).
1325. Gavella in *Property Law I*, 530; Klarić / Vedriš in *Civil Law*, 282.

VI. Merger, Confusion, Commixture

357. Any person who merges, confuses or commixes the movables of another with his own without any legal title will not be deemed to have acquired any rights to the property of such other person by merger, confusion or commixture (*prerada, sjedinjenje, miješanje*).[1326] If the things merged can be restored to the previous condition or separated without any excessive costs, each owner shall receive his own property.[1327] Each owner of the merged, confused or commixed things is entitled to request their separation.[1328,1329,1330]

358. If the result of such restoration is not a new thing but rather that one already existing thing has simply become a part of the main thing of another person and cannot be separated without excessive costs, the ownership of the main thing extends to the newly created component part.[1331] The owner of the component part is entitled only to seek compensation for his thing. The owner of the material, or of whatever has been built in, may seek compensation according to the rules of the law on civil obligations.

359. When, by merger, confusion or commixture, a movable ceases to exist independently, all limited property rights on that movable also terminate, as well as any rents or leases.[1332] An exception is envisaged only for the limited property rights which may exist regarding the compensation to which the owner of the movable which ceased to exist independently is entitled.[1333,1334,1335]

VII. Making a New Movable

360. When, by merger, confusion or commixture of other persons' movables, a new movable is created and its separation is not possible or allowed, all previous owners of these individual movables become co-owners of the newly created movable.[1336] They co-own the newly created movable in proportion to the values of their

1326. Article 148/1 PA.
1327. Article 148/2 PA.
1328. The rules of the law on civil obligations determine who is entitled to request compensation for damage and from whom (Art. 148/2 PA).
1329. If, by merger, confusion or commixture of another's things, a new thing is created of distinguished artistic or cultural value which would be destroyed by separation (restoration to the previous condition), the person who has merged the things belonging to other persons is entitled to request the court not to allow restoration to the previous condition (Art. 148/3 PA).
1330. Gavella in *Property Law I*, 554; Klarić / Vedriš in *Civil Law*, 283.
1331. Article 150/1 PA.
1332. Articles 151/1,2 PA.
1333. Article 151/1 PA.
1334. For example, if a movable which ceases to exist independently is charged a lien, the lien is transferred to the claim made by its owner against the person with whose thing his thing has been merged.
1335. Persons whose property rights, rentals or leases have terminated are entitled to compensation according to the rules of the law on civil obligations (Art. 151/3 PA).
1336. Article 149/1 PA.

movables and the useful work invested at the moment of the creation of the new movable.[1337] However, any co-owner of the newly created movable may, in relation to other co-owners whose fault is the creation of the new movable, request a dissolution of co-ownership (*razvrgnuće suvlasništva*). Such a co-owner may request that the newly created movable is surrendered into his ownership only or into the ownership of any other co-owner, with an obligation to compensate all other co-owners accordingly. If a new movable is created without anyone's fault, the co-owner whose movable is considered to be of the highest value is entitled to purchase the entire movable.[1338]

VIII. Building with Another Person's Material

361. When an owner erects a building on his plot by using material belonging to another or builds into his building a movable belonging to another, or if someone else does so, the owner of the immovable acquires ownership of whatever has been built or built into the building unless it can be separated from it without any excessive costs.[1339] The former owner of the material, or built-in movables, is entitled to compensation for the value of the material according to the rules of the law on civil obligations.[1340] All limited property rights, rentals or leases cease to exist on another's material or built-in things.[1341] Any liens encumbering the material, or built-in things, are transferred to the claim which their owner may seek from the owner of the immovable.

IX. Building on the Land of Another

362. A building erected on the land of another without the knowledge or will of the owner of such land becomes the ownership of the owner of the land (*građenje na tuđem zemljištu*).[1342,1343] The owner of the land is then entitled to request the plot and the building to be surrendered to his possession, and the builder may request compensation for the building from the owner of the land.[1344] The owner of the land, if he has any legal interest therein, may request restoration to the previous condition (e.g., tearing down the building). In that case, the builder is not entitled to compensation but is authorized to take all the material used for the construction of

1337. The rules of the law on civil obligations also provide whether an individual co-owner may request compensation and from whom (Art. 149/1 PA).
1338. Article 149/2 PA.
1339. Articles 150/2,3 PA.
1340. The rules on building with another person's material apply accordingly to the holder of the right to build who has built a building by using another's material (Art. 150/3 PA).
1341. Article 152/1 PA.
1342. Article 152/1 PA.
1343. This rule applies regardless of whether the builder was fair or unfair and regardless of whether he knew or could have known, or did not know or could not have known, that he was building on another's land. If the owner of the land did not know of the construction on his land, or did not permit the construction, everything built on the respective land belongs to its owner.
1344. Article 152/2 PA.

the building on the other's land.[1345] However, if the owner knew about the construction works being carried out on his land and did not immediately prohibit the builder, who knew that he was building on another's land, from doing further work, the owner is not entitled to request restoration to the previous condition.[1346] The builder is then obliged to bear the cost of restoration to the previous condition and to take his material built into the building, but not after the expiry of the time limit within which, following the enforceability of a court decision, he must surrender the land to the possession of the owner.[1347,1348,1349]

363. Although a basic rule lays down that whatever is permanently connected with a person's land belongs to its owner (the principle of the legal unity of real property),[1350] there is an exception to this rule aimed at the protection of a bona fide builder who builds on another's land without knowing or being aware that he is building on another's land. A bona fide builder is protected in cases where the owner was unfair, i.e., he knew about the construction but failed to immediately prohibit further construction.[1351,1352] If the builder was fair and the owner unfair, the land with the building comes into the builder's ownership. A fair builder, by building on another's land, becomes the owner of the immovable (the land including the building), and the former owner of the land is entitled to compensation of the market value of the land. The builder becomes the owner of the land at the moment of the construction of the building. The building is considered to be a structure more or less permanently affixed to the surface of the land or below it, and the building is in a condition to be used for the purposes for which such buildings are usually used.[1353,1354]

X. Additions, Adaptations, Reconstructions

364. The rules on the acquisition of ownership of an immovable by building on another's land do not apply to additions, adaptations, reconstructions or investments in another's building. Ownership is not acquired as a result of carrying out additions, annexes, adaptations and investments in another's building or in the rooms of another's building.[1355] Ownership is acquired in these cases only if the

1345. Article 152/2 PA.
1346. Article 154/1 PA.
1347. Article 154/2 PA.
1348. The rules on building on another's land apply accordingly to building on land encumbered by the right to build of another (Art. 157 PA).
1349. Gavella in *Property Law I*, 537; Klarić / Vedriš in *Civil Law*, 284.
1350. For more details, *see* Part I, Ch. 1, §2. Legal Unity of Real Property.
1351. Article 153 PA.
1352. For example, the owner did not warn the builder that he was building on another's land, he did not seek protection of ownership in court proceedings, did not request a temporary measure to stop the construction, or failed to take any similar steps.
1353. Article 152/5 PA.
1354. The rules on the acquisition of ownership by building on another's land apply accordingly when building on another's right to build (Art. 157 PA).
1355. Article 156 PA.

owner of the building expressly agrees to such alterations and if there is an agreement with the owner of the building that through additions, annexes, adaptations, reconstruction or investment, ownership or co-ownership of the entire immovable (land with the building) is acquired.[1356,1357]

XI. Crossing the Boundary Through Construction Works

365. If a boundary is crossed only as a result of construction and a part of the neighbouring land is encroached upon, the builder does not acquire ownership of the neighbouring land (*prekoračenje međe građenjem*). The owner of the neighbouring land is entitled to request restoration to the previous condition, and until it is carried out, the owner of the building is deemed to have real easement in respect of the part of his building on the neighbouring land.[1358,1359] The owner of the land on which a part of the building of another is erected is entitled to request that the owner of the building buys the entire land at the market price. The owner of the building, by being a fair builder, may also request to buy the entire land if the owner of the land claims restoration to the previous condition, which is not possible without substantial damages to the remaining part of the building, or without incurring excessive costs.[1360,1361]

XII. Sowing and Planting

366. Plants that have grown roots on a piece of land and where the seeds and seedlings belong to another person are the property of the owner of the land.[1362] The owner of the seeds and seedlings is entitled to request compensation for their value pursuant to the rules of the law on civil obligations.

XIII. Acquisitive Prescription

367. Acquisitive prescription (*dosjelost*) is the acquisition of ownership by possessing a thing over a particular period of time. Both movables and immovables

---

1356. The rules on additions, adaptations or reconstruction of another's building apply accordingly to additions, adaptations or reconstructions of a building built on another's right to build (Art. 157 PA).
1357. Gavella in *Property Law I*, 544.
1358. Articles 155/1,2, 196 PA.
1359. The owner of the land on which a part of another's building is erected is entitled to compensation in the amount of rent for the land encroached upon. The owner of the building is bound to pay for as long as the part of the building is on another's land. The owner of the land is also entitled to compensation (Art. 155/3 PA).
1360. Article 155/4 PA.
1361. Gavella in *Property Law I*, 542.
1362. Article 158 PA.

may be acquired by acquisitive prescription. Ownership is acquired by the independent possession of a thing[1363] over a period of time stipulated by law. In order to acquire ownership by acquisitive prescription, possession of a thing must meet certain conditions: it must be fair, lawful and truthful, or at least fair, and the possessor must be capable of being the owner of a thing.[1364] The quality of the possession is a condition to determine how long a thing must be possessed in order to be acquired by prescription.

368. A possessor who is fair, lawful and truthful (so-called qualified possessor) acquires ownership of a movable on the expiration of a period of three years and the ownership of an immovable after the expiry of ten years (so-called regular acquisitive prescription, *redovna dosjelost*).[1365] A possessor who is only a fair possessor acquires ownership of a movable on the expiration of ten years and the ownership of an immovable on the expiration of twenty years (so-called extraordinary acquisitive prescription, *izvanredna dosjelost*).[1366,1367,1368] The period of time required for acquisitive prescription begins on the day when the possessor assumes the independent possession of a thing, and it expires on the last day of the period necessary for acquisitive prescription to apply.[1369,1370] The period of acquisitive prescription also includes the period of time during which the possessor's predecessors continuously possessed the thing as qualified or fair independent possessors.[1371] A possessor becomes the owner upon the expiration of the period of time prescribed

1363. An independent possessor is a person who possesses a thing as if being its owner. Possession is deemed independent until it is proven otherwise (Art. 11/1,2 PA).

1364. Possession is lawful if the possessor has a valid legal title for the possession (Art. 18/1 PA). Possession is truthful if it was not obtained by force, covertly, by fraud or abuse of someone's trust (Art. 18/2 PA). Possession is fair if, at the time of acquisitive acquisition, the possessor did not know and did not have any reason to doubt his right to such possession (Art. 18/3 PA). The fairness of possession terminates as soon as the possessor finds out that he is not entitled to the right of possession. Possession is deemed fair until it is proven otherwise (Art. 18/5 PA).

1365. Article 159/2 PA.

1366. Article 159/3 PA.

1367. In order to acquire ownership by acquisitive prescription, possession must be uninterrupted, and the time limit for acquisitive prescription starts on the day independent possession begins, and it ends on the last day necessary for prescription to apply (Art. 160/1 PA). The rules of the law on civil obligations regarding the termination of the limitation period apply accordingly to the termination of the period of acquisitive prescription (Art. 160/6 PA).

1368. In order to acquire ownership by acquisitive prescription on the things owned by the Republic of Croatia, the counties, local self-government units, the Church and other legal entities serving various charity or other generally useful purposes, the period of time for acquisitive prescription is twice the period of time (Art. 159/4 PA).

1369. Article 160/1 PA.

1370. With respect to property which was under social ownership, the period of time started running on 8 Oct. 1991 (Art. 388/4 PA).

1371. With respect to a fair possessor whose possession is not lawful and truthful, when the time period over which his predecessor had possession of the thing lawfully, fairly and truthfully is included in the time period for acquisitive prescription, ownership is acquired by acquisitive prescription on the expiration of the time period needed for a fair possessor to acquire a thing by acquisitive prescription (Art. 160/4 PA). When, with respect to a lawful, fair and truthful possessor, the time period over which his predecessor had fair possession of the thing is included in the time period for acquisitive prescription, ownership is acquired on the expiration of the time period needed for a fair possessor to acquire ownership by acquisitive prescription (Art. 160/5 PA). An heir becomes

for acquisition by acquisitive prescription. When ownership of an immovable is acquired by acquisitive prescription, the acquisition does not require registration in the land register. Registration of ownership acquired by acquisitive prescription is only of a declaratory and public nature, and it is carried out on the basis of an enforceable court decision by which it is established that ownership has been acquired by acquisitive prescription.

§3. Acquisition of Easements on the Basis of Law

369. Real easement on the basis of law is acquired by acquisitive prescription when the possessor of a dominant immovable exercises the content of real easement for a period of twenty years, and the owner of the servient immovable has not opposed it.[1372] Real easement may not be acquired by acquisitive prescription if its content is exercised by abuse of trust, by force, covertly, or on request until revocation, i.e., when the exercise of the right of real easement is false.[1373] A real easement is acquired by means of the period necessary for the acquisitive prescription without an entry in the land register. An entry in the land register takes place on the proposal of the owner of the dominant immovable and on the basis of a court decision establishing that the real easement is acquired by acquisitive prescription. Before such an easement acquired by acquisitive prescription is entered in the land register, the land register status is incomplete, and the legal effects of the protection in trust in the completeness of the land register may be set in favour of a fair acquirer. The unregistered real easement may not be contrary to the right of a fair acquirer who entered his right on the same immovable in good faith; it will terminate on account of the operation of the principle of the protection in trust in the completeness of the land register.[1374,1375]

§4. Acquisition of Real Burdens on the Basis of Law

370. Real burdens of public law are established on the basis of law by the fulfilment of the conditions laid down by law (public real burdens).[1376] The law lays down when a public real burden is well-founded, which immovables it encumbers, who the beneficiary of the burden is and what the criteria for the determination of obligations arising from the public real burden are. Concrete obligations arising

a fair possessor from the moment of death of the testator, even if the testator was an unfair possessor, and the heir did not know it or could not have been aware of it (Art. 160/3 PA).

1372. Article 229 PA. Possession of the right of real easement is factual enforcement of the content of this right regarding particular real property (Art. 10/5 PA).

1373. If easement, by its nature, may only rarely be enforced, a person claiming that the easement was established in favour of his immovable by acquisitive prescription must prove that in a period of not less than twenty years the situation of enforcement of such easement occurred at least three times, and that he or his predecessor each time enforced its content (Art. 229/3 PA).

1374. For more details, *see* Part I, Ch. 2, §2. III. The Protection of Trust.

1375. Stipković in *Property Law II*, 22; Klarić / Vedriš in *Civil Law*, 328.

1376. Article 266/1 PA.

from public real burdens may also be determined by a decision of public authorities (e.g., by virtue of a decision issued by a competent authority) rendered on the basis of law.[1377] Public real burdens are effective for any third person by virtue of law without being entered in the land register.[1378]

§5. Acquisition of Liens on the Basis of Law

371. Liens are acquired on the basis of law at the moment all the conditions stipulated by a separate act are fulfilled.[1379] A statutory lien may exist on movables and immovables. When a statutory lien is acquired on immovables, it is entered in the land register at the request of the lienee.[1380]

372. The acquisition of a lien is provided for in the PA but also in many other regulations. The PA lays down that co-owners have a statutory lien on a thing where, as a result of the dissolution of co-ownership, the thing comes under the ownership of a co-owner. Until the payment of the values of their co-owned part, other co-owners have statutory liens on the thing.[1381] The same rule applies in cases where a community of heirs is dissolved in inheritance proceedings – a statutory lien is assigned to the heirs to secure the payment of their claims against the heir who acquires the entire inherited thing.[1382] A statutory lien is also provided for in various separate regulations. The OA, in its provisions on various contracts, lays down that a party to the contract, in order to secure its claims and costs against the other party, has, by virtue of law, a lien on particular things belonging to the other party to the contract. The statutory lien exists in favour of a lessor on the lessee's things,[1383] a haulier on the things entrusted to him to be transported,[1384] a warehouseman on the things entrusted to him for safekeeping,[1385] an agent on the movables surrendered to him by the principal,[1386] a commissioner on the things received under commission,[1387] a dispatcher on the things given to be dispatched.[1388] The CHA lays down that public bodies which have invested their funds for the protection of immovable cultural goods have statutory liens on immovables against their owners to secure their claims for the return of the invested funds.[1389]

1377. Gavella in *Property Law II*, 57.
1378. Article 266/2 PA.
1379. Article 314/1 PA.
1380. Article 314/2 PA.
1381. Article 51/2 PA.
1382. Article 143/3 IA.
1383. Article 565 OA.
1384. Article 692 OA.
1385. Article 750 OA.
1386. Article 777 OA.
1387. Article 800 OA.
1388. Article 868 OA.
1389. Article 31 of the Cultural Heritage Act.

Part IV. Insolvency

§1. Concept

373. In the Republic of Croatia, bankruptcy (*stečaj*) is regulated by the Bankruptcy Act (hereinafter 'BA').[1390] Under Croatian law, bankruptcy proceedings (*stečajni postupak*) may be enforced against a legal person as well as against the assets of an individual trader or craftsman.[1391] Bankruptcy proceedings may also be enforced against other individuals (consumers). Personal consumer bankruptcy is regulated by Consumer Bankruptcy Act.[1392] These proceedings may not be enforced against the Republic of Croatia, funds financed from the state budget, pension and invalidity funds, the Croatian Institute for Health Insurance or local self-government units.[1393,1394]

374. Bankruptcy proceedings may be initiated only for reasons laid down in the law. These reasons include illiquidity and balance-sheet insolvency.[1395,1396] A debtor is illiquid if according to the Register of Order of Payments kept by the Financial Agency (*Financijska agencija*/FINA), he has one or several outstanding debts over a period of more than sixty days or if he has failed to pay three consecutive salaries to an employee. [1397] A debtor is considered to be balance-sheet insolvent if his assets do not cover the existing obligations.[1398]

§2. General Information on Bankruptcy Proceedings

375. The commercial court in whose territory the debtor has headquarters has jurisdiction over his bankruptcy proceedings.[1399,1400] The bodies involved in

1390. Bankruptcy Act, OG 71/5, 104/17, 36/22.
1391. Article 3/1 BA.
1392. Consumer Bankruptcy Act, OG, 100/15, 67/18, 36/22.
1393. Article 3/2 BA.
1394. If the law excludes the possibility of bankruptcy against a legal person's property, its founders or members have joint and several liability for the arising obligations (Article 3/4 BA).
1395. Article 5/2 BA.
1396. A debtor may himself propose the opening of bankruptcy proceedings if he shows that it is probable that he will be incapable of fulfilling his pending obligations when they become due – the threat of incapacity to execute payments (Art. 5/3BA).
1397. Article 6/2 BA.
1398. Article 7 BA.
1399. Article 8 BA.

bankruptcy proceedings are a bankruptcy judge (*stečajni sudac*), a bankruptcy administrator (*stečajni upravitelj*), the creditors' assembly (*skupština vjerovnika*) and the creditors' committee (*odbor vjerovnika*).[1401] The bankruptcy judge decides on the initiation of bankruptcy proceedings, appoints and dismisses the bankruptcy administrator, supervises the work of the creditors' committee and renders a decision on the termination and cancellation of bankruptcy proceedings, etc.[1402] The bankruptcy administrator has the rights and obligations of the legal person's body of debtors. The bankruptcy administrator performs the activities of the bankruptcy debtor and acts as his representative.[1403,1404] A committee of creditors may be established by the bankruptcy judge if it is necessary to protect the creditors' interests in bankruptcy proceedings.[1405] The creditors' committee monitors the work of the bankruptcy administrator and assists him in performing his activities, analyses the bankruptcy administrator's reports, inspects the business books and gives an opinion on the encashment of the debtor's assets.[1406] The creditors' assembly is convened by the bankruptcy judge.[1407] It decides on the encashment of the bankruptcy estate and renders other important decisions concerning the implementation and termination of bankruptcy proceedings.

376. Bankruptcy proceedings are initiated on the proposal of an authorized person. Persons authorized to make a petition for the initiation of bankruptcy proceedings are a creditor and a debtor. The creditor is authorized to propose the initiation of bankruptcy proceedings if he shows in all probability that he has a claim and that any of the grounds for bankruptcy exist (incapacity to pay debts, over-indebtedness). A petition for the initiation of bankruptcy proceedings may be made by creditors entitled to so-called separate satisfaction (creditors with separate satisfaction rights), but only if they can show that it is likely that their claims cannot be settled in full against the things on which they have separate satisfaction rights (e.g., liens). Proposals for the initiation of bankruptcy proceedings may be made on behalf of the debtor by any persons authorized for the representation of a legal person.[1408] A petition for the initiation of bankruptcy proceedings must be submitted by the Financial Agency if a legal person, according to the Register of Order of Payments, has outstanding debts over an uninterrupted period of 120 days. A proposal for bankruptcy proceedings must be made not later than 21 days from the day of the existence of the grounds for bankruptcy by a person authorised by law to represent

1400. Bankruptcy proceedings are conducted as emergency proceedings under the rules governing a civil procedure conducted before commercial courts (Arts 11/2 of BA).
1401. Article 75 BA.
1402. Article 76 BA.
1403. Article 88, 89 BA.
1404. The bankruptcy administrator may be a natural person with a university degree who has passed the examination for bankruptcy administrators and whose name is on the list of qualified bankruptcy administrators (Art. 79 BA). A list of bankruptcy administrators is drawn up by the Minister of Justice and is published in the Official Gazette (Art. 78 BA).
1405. Articles 96,97 BA.
1406. Article 98BA.
1407. Article 103 BA.
1408. Article 109 BA.

the debtor, a member of the management board of the joint-stock company, a liquidator, a member of the debtor's supervisory board or a member of a limited liability company.[1409]

377. On the basis of a petition for the initiation of bankruptcy proceedings, a bankruptcy judge renders a decision on the initiation of proceedings to establish the conditions for the initiation of bankruptcy proceedings (preliminary proceedings). Preliminary proceedings may last no longer than sixty days from the decision on their initiation unless there are particular circumstances requiring a longer period of time.[1410,1411] The bankruptcy judge renders a decision on the initiation of bankruptcy proceedings after the conditions for their opening have been discussed.[1412] In his decision on the initiation of bankruptcy proceedings, the bankruptcy judge, among other things, appoints a bankruptcy administrator.[1413] With the decision on the initiation of bankruptcy proceedings, the creditors are invited to communicate their claims against the debtor to the bankruptcy administrator.[1414] A separate hearing is also scheduled to examine the communicated claims, as well as a hearing where the schedule of bankruptcy proceedings is decided.[1415,1416,1417]

378. The legal consequences of the initiation of bankruptcy proceedings are regulated in the BA.[1418] They come into play when the announcement is placed on the e-Notice board of the courts.[1419] At the moment of the initiation of bankruptcy proceedings, the rights of the debtor's management bodies are transferred to the bankruptcy administrator,[1420] and the rights acquired by enforcement or security during the last sixty days before the filing of the petition for the initiation of bankruptcy proceedings cease to exist.[1421] After the initiation of bankruptcy proceedings, enforcement against the debtor's assets constituting the bankruptcy estate may not be carried out.[1422] The debtor's contractual obligations, which have not been fulfilled at the moment of the initiation of bankruptcy proceedings, are to be met by the bankruptcy administrators.[1423] Leases and rentals of immovables or premises do

1409. Article 110. BA.
1410. Article 115BA.
1411. In preliminary proceedings, the bankruptcy administrator may order measures to prevent a decrease in the debtor's assets, to appoint a temporary bankruptcy administrator, to prohibit the disposition of the debtor's assets and payments from the debtor's account (Art. 118 BA).
1412. Article 128/6 BA.
1413. Article 129BA.
1414. Article 129 BA.
1415. Article 130. BA.
1416. An announcement is placed on the e- Notice board of the courts . Creditors are invited to file their claims within a given time limit (Art. 129/3 BA).
1417. A decision on the initiation of bankruptcy proceedings is sent, among other bodies, to the bodies keeping public registers (e.g., land register) where the debtor's assets are entered in order to make a recordation of the opening of bankruptcy proceedings (Art. 129/2 BA).
1418. Articles 158-215 BA.
1419. Article 158/1 BA.
1420. Article 159 BA.
1421. Article 168 BA.
1422. Article 169/1 BA.
1423. Article 181/1 BA.

not terminate on the initiation of bankruptcy proceedings.[1424] Labour contracts entered into with the debtor as an employer do not terminate.[1425] Offers made to the debtor, or by the debtor, cease to be valid on the day of the opening of bankruptcy proceedings.[1426] On the day of the opening of bankruptcy proceedings, the debtor's accounts are closed, and the rights of persons authorized to dispose of the debtor's assets in these accounts also terminate.[1427]

379. Separate rules apply to the status of the legal actions taken by the debtor before the initiation of bankruptcy proceedings by which the equal settlement of bankruptcy creditors is disturbed or by which individual bankruptcy creditors are put in a more favourable position (preferential treatment of creditors). Such actions may be refuted by a special action (*action pauliana*). They may be challenged by the bankruptcy administrator or bankruptcy creditors.[1428] The conditions and the time limits for their challenge are determined differently depending on the type of legal action and its consequences. A legal transaction which offers the creditor security or a settlement of the claim in a way, in a time and in accordance with the content of his right (congruent discharge), carried out in the three months immediately before the petition in bankruptcy was communicated, may be refuted if at that time the debtor was incapable of paying and the creditor knew about this incapacity.[1429] A legal transaction by which a bankruptcy creditor is given or is provided with security or a settlement which he was not entitled to request (incongruent discharge) may be refuted if the legal transaction had been undertaken in the last month before the petition in bankruptcy was communicated or afterwards, or if it had been undertaken during the third or the second month before the petition and the debtor was at that time incapable of paying,[1430] or if the creditor knew that with this transaction damage would be caused to creditors.[1431] Legal transactions by which creditors are directly damaged may be refuted if they were done three months before the petition in bankruptcy was communicated, if the debtor was incapable of paying and the other party knew of such incapacity,[1432] or if a legal transaction was done after the petition in bankruptcy had been communicated, and the other party knew of the debtor's incapacity to pay, or knew of the petition in bankruptcy.[1433] It is also possible to refute a legal transaction carried out by the debtor in the last ten years before the petition in bankruptcy was communicated, or subsequently, if it had been done with the intention of harming the creditors or if the other party knew of the debtor's intention.[1434] An action to refute must be filed within two years from the initiation

1424. Article 187 BA.
1425. Article 191 BA.
1426. Article 194 BA.
1427. Articles 193,196 BA.
1428. Article 198/1 BA.
1429. Article 199/1 BA.
1430. Article 200/1/2 BA.
1431. Article 200/1/3 BA.
1432. Article 201/1/1 BA.
1433. Article 201/1/2 BA.
1434. Article 202/1 BA.

of bankruptcy proceedings.[1435] The effects of such a refutation are that the objects of legal transactions are returned to the bankruptcy estate in order for the claims of all the creditors to be settled under the rules of bankruptcy proceedings.[1436]

380. Several categories of the debtor's creditors take part in bankruptcy proceedings – creditors in bankruptcy (*stečajni vjerovnici*), creditors with a right to separate settlement (*razlučni vjerovnici*), creditors with exclusion rights (izlučni vjerovnici) and creditors in bankruptcy (*vjerovnici stečajne mase*). For each of these categories, there are separate rules providing for the settlement of their claims. Creditors in bankruptcy are personal creditors of the debtor who, at the time of the initiation of bankruptcy proceedings, have a claim against the debtor.[1437] They may realize their claims against the debtor only in bankruptcy proceedings.[1438] In accordance with their claims, creditors in bankruptcy are classified according to the order of priority. The claims of lower-priority creditors may be settled only after the claims of creditors of higher priority have been fully settled.[1439] [1440] Creditors with exclusion rights are persons who, on the basis of their real or personal rights, can prove that a particular thing does not belong to the bankruptcy estate. They are entitled to exclude such a thing from the bankruptcy estate.[1441] Creditors with the right to separate settlement are those who are entitled to a separate settlement against a thing or a right because they have established a lien or another security right.[1442] Creditors in bankruptcy are creditors whose claims against the debtor came into existence after the bankruptcy proceedings had already started. Their claims are settled against the bankruptcy estate.[1443]

381. The main purpose of bankruptcy proceedings is the joint satisfaction of all creditors' claims through the encashment of the debtor's assets and their distribution among creditors.[1444] Therefore, one of the most important issues connected with bankruptcy proceedings is what constitutes the bankruptcy estate against which the claims of the debtor's creditors are settled. The bankruptcy estate includes all the debtor's assets existing at the time of the initiation of bankruptcy proceedings, as well as the assets acquired in the course of the bankruptcy proceedings.[1445] The bankruptcy estate is used to settle the claims of the debtor's creditors, the cost of

1435. Article 212/2 BA.
1436. Article 212/5 BA.
1437. Articles 138,139 BA.
1438. Article 96 BA.
1439. Article 70/2 BA.
1440. Claims of the highest order of priority are the claims of employees and former employees of the debtor which had come into being as a result of employment before the initiation of bankruptcy proceedings (salaries, severance payments, compensation for damages). All other claims against the debtor are classified as claims of higher priority (Art. 138/1,2 BA). Interest, costs and fees are claims of lower priority (Art. 139 BA).
1441. Article 147 BA.
1442. Article 149 BA.
1443. Article 154 BA.
1444. Article 2/1 BA.
1445. Article 134/1 BA.

the bankruptcy proceedings and the settlement of the claims secured by some security rights against the debtor's assets, such as liens.[1446,1447] Upon the initiation of the bankruptcy proceedings, the bankruptcy administrator collects all the debtor's assets and manages them.[1448] The bankruptcy administrator must make a list of all the objects of the bankruptcy estate[1449] and a list of all the debtor's creditors.[1450] The bankruptcy administrator converts into cash the entire assets constituting the bankruptcy estate by taking into account the decisions of the creditors' assembly and the creditors' committee.[1451] After all the communicated claims are determined in a special hearing, the settlement of creditors begins. This is carried out on the basis of a distribution list made by the bankruptcy administrator.[1452] Bankruptcy creditors are settled in accordance with their orders of priority in such a way that the claims of the creditors belonging to the same order of priority are settled in proportion to their claims. When the distribution is completed, a decision on the termination of bankruptcy proceedings is made.[1453,1454]

382. Separate rules apply to the encashment of objects on which there is a creditor's right to separate settlement or on which there is a lien or some other security right.[1455] The basic rule is that the claims of creditors with rights to separate settlement are settled on the basis of the rules on enforcement proceedings as if there were no bankruptcy proceedings against the debtor.[1456] They are settled against the value of the secured thing after it has been sold according to the rules of enforcement proceedings. The immovable is sold by the bankruptcy judge on the proposal of the bankruptcy administrator or creditor, who has the right to separate settlement.[1457,1458] The bankruptcy judge then establishes the value of the immovable and the modality and the conditions for sale.[1459] After the immovable on which there is a security right has been converted into cash and the costs of the proceedings are covered, the money resulting from the sale is returned to the bankruptcy assets.[1460]

1446. Article 134/2 BA.
1447. When bankruptcy proceedings are conducted against an individual trader or a craftsman, objects that are excluded from enforcement do not belong to the bankruptcy estate (Art. 135 BA).
1448. Article 216BA.
1449. Article 221/1 BA.
1450. Article 222 BA.
1451. Article 229 BA.
1452. Article 273 BA.
1453. Article 286/1 BA.
1454. It is possible to depart from the rules on the encashment and distribution of the bankruptcy estate if the creditors have made a bankruptcy plan (Arts 303 et seq. BA). The bankruptcy plan may provide for all the assets to be left with the debtor in order for operations to continue, for some changes in the debtor's status, for only a part of his assets to be sold, or for payments to creditors to be postponed. All the categories of a debtor's creditors are responsible for the development of such a plan. After the decision on the approval of the bankruptcy plan becomes final, bankruptcy proceedings terminate (Art. 344/1 BA).
1455. Articles 247 et seq. BA.
1456. Article 149 BA.
1457. Article 247/1 BA.
1458. The rules of enforcement proceedings are applied accordingly.
1459. Article 247/3 BA.
1460. Article 248, 254 BA.

The bankruptcy judge first separates 5% of the obtained amount and then settles the creditor with the right to separate settlement. The remaining amount is given to the bankruptcy assets.[1461] A movable on which there is a right to separate settlement is converted into cash by the bankruptcy administrator in accordance with the rules on enforcement or by way of a free bargain.[1462]

1461. Article 254/2 BA.
1462. Article 249 BA.

Part V. Trust and Fiduciary Mechanisms

Chapter 1. General

383. In Croatian law, there is no legal institution of trust as in Anglo-Saxon law. The Republic of Croatia is not a party to The Hague Convention on the Law Applicable to Trusts and on their Recognition of 1 July 1985. However, Croatian law provides for some fiduciary mechanisms by which ownership is transferred to another person under a particular condition or a time limit. The reasons for such a transfer of ownership may differ. This is most frequently a fiduciary transfer of ownership aimed at securing a particular claim, but there are also other possibilities.[1463] In fact, what is at issue here are special limitations to ownership under particular conditions or time limits based on a legal transaction, i.e., the transfer of ownership under special conditions or time limits.[1464]

1463. Gavella in *Property Law I*, 798.
1464. Article 34 PA.

Chapter 2. Fiduciary Transfer of Ownership

§1. Transfer of Ownership by Limitation in the Form of Conditions or Time Limits

384. The owner of a thing (an immovable/movable) may transfer his ownership to another with a limitation in the form of a postponement of a time limit or a suspended condition.[1465] Specific legal relations are then created between the seller and the acquirer. The seller remains the owner of the thing until the time limit or the conditions are met. Such an owner is bound to act with consideration towards the acquirer, who becomes the owner only upon the expiry of the time limit or the fulfilment of a condition. Until the conditions are met, the mutual relationship of the seller and acquirer regarding the thing whose ownership is transferred with limitation in the form of a condition or a time limit is regulated by the rules on usufruct.[1466,1467]

385. All other relations between a seller and an acquirer depend on whether the limitation by a condition or time limit applies only between the parties (*inter partes*) or also towards third persons (*contra omnes*). The limitation by a condition or time limit is effective only between parties if it is agreed upon at the moment of the transfer of ownership without being publicized in any way. If the limitation by a condition or time limit is entered in the land register, or any other public register, it is also effective against any third person.[1468] If the limitation by a condition or time limit is effective only between the parties, then the owner of the thing is actually the seller, who must transfer ownership to the acquirer when the time limit expires or when the condition is fulfilled.[1469] However, if the seller transfers ownership to the acquirer after the expiry of the time limit or the fulfilment of the condition, the acquirer is considered to be the owner from the very beginning, i.e., from the moment the transfer agreement was made, limited by a condition, or a time limit. When such a limitation is entered in the land register, the acquirer becomes the owner on the expiry of the time limit or on the fulfilment of the condition, i.e., from the moment the agreement on the transfer of ownership by limitation was entered into. In such a case, during the continuation of a time limit or until the fulfilment of a condition, both the seller and the acquirer exercise the right of ownership over the same thing: the seller as the previous owner and the acquirer as the subsequent one. They are both authorized to dispose of their previous or subsequent ownership, but such dispositions depend on the expiry of the time limit or the fulfilment of the conditions limiting the transfer of ownership.[1470]

1465. Article 34/4 PA.
1466. Article 34/4 PA.
1467. For further details on personal easement of usufruct, *see* Part I, Ch. 5, III. Personal easements.
1468. Article 34/4 PA.
1469. Article 34/4 PA.
1470. Gavella in *Property Law I*, 802–806.

§2. Transfer of Ownership for Security

386. The transfer of ownership for the purpose of security is a way to secure the fulfilment of a claim when the debtor transfers ownership of his thing to secure the fulfilment of a particular claim. The transfer of ownership for security is the transfer of ownership to the creditor by way of limitation in the form of a condition.[1471] Ownership is transferred to the creditor, but when the claim is settled, ownership is returned to the debtor. The creditor must immediately cease using and disposing of the thing, except for the purpose of settling the claim. If the claim is not settled upon its maturity, the creditor is entitled to enforce his claim against the value of the thing in conformity with the rules on the enforcement of claims secured by liens in out-of-court proceedings.[1472,1473]

§3. Judicial and Notarial Security of Claims by Transfer of Ownership

387. Judicial or notarial fiduciary transfers of ownership or rights are regulated in Articles 309–327 of the EA. These are special forms of the fiduciary transfer of ownership that occurs in the procedure of security carried out by the court or a notary public. After the transfer of ownership for security under the provisions of the EA, the creditor becomes the unconditional owner of the thing. The creditor is authorized to alienate the thing upon the maturity of the secured claim.[1474] He may alienate the thing even before the claim matures and is liable to the debtor for the damage thus inflicted.[1475,1476] The creditor is bound to return ownership to the debtor after the secured claim is settled.[1477,1478]

1471. Gavella in *Property Law I*, 799–802.
1472. Article 34/5 PA.
1473. For further details, *see* Part VI. Security Rights.
1474. Article 316/1 EA.
1475. Article 316/2 EA.
1476. Such dispositions are legally valid but they do not exclude the creditor's criminal liability for the alienation (Art. 316/5 EA).
1477. Article 323 EA.
1478. For further details, *see* Part VI. Security Rights.

Chapter 3. Administration of Property

§1. Commission Agent: Commissioner

388. Separate rules on the administration of property apply when a commission agreement is entered into. With a commission agreement, the commission agent is bound to perform one or more commission jobs in his name and for the account of the principal.[1479] If the commission agent sells a thing belonging to the principal, he has special obligations regarding its maintenance and safety. The principal then surrenders some of his things to the commission agent for sale with the due diligence of a conscientious businessman.[1480] He is liable for the accidental perishing or damage sustained if he failed to insure it when he ought to have done in accordance with the mandate.[1481] The commission agent must notify the principal of any changes to the goods that might cause their depreciation.[1482] In the case of bankruptcy of the commission agent, the principal may request the separation from the bankruptcy estate of the things he handed over to the commission agent for sale for his account and also of the things that the commission agent has acquired for his account.[1483] The commission agent's creditors may not take enforcement measures in respect of the things of the principal that the commission agent keeps for sale in order to settle the commission agent's debts.[1484] However, the commission agent has a lien on the things that are the objects of the commission agreement aimed at settling claims against the principal, such as commission fees, costs, advance payments, and the like.[1485,1486]

§2. Notarial Deposits

389. A notary public may accept cash, bills of exchange, cheques, public bonds and other types of securities and valuables for safekeeping.[1487] Notaries public are bound to take such things over when they are given to them for the purpose of drawing up a notarial act in order to give them to a particular person or to deposit them with a public administration body.[1488] Notaries public are bound to keep such things separate from their own cash and securities. The entrusted money must be kept in a separate bank account. If a notary public cannot perform the requested surrender

1479. Article 785 OA.
1480. Article 790/1 OA.
1481. Article 790/2 OA.
1482. Article 792 OA.
1483. Article 803 OA.
1484. Article 802 OA.
1485. Article 800 OA.
1486. For more details on commission contracts, *see* Klarić / Vedriš in *Civil Law*, 564–568.
1487. Article 109/1 NPA.
1488. Article 109/1 NPA.

of things upon the expiry of the time limit, he must return them without delay to the client or, if that is not possible, hand things over to the court for safekeeping and inform the seller accordingly.[1489,1490]

§3. Administration of Inherited Property

390. In inheritance proceedings, the court may appoint a temporary testamentary administrator.[1491] A testamentary administrator is appointed when the heirs are unknown, their place of abode is not known if they are inaccessible, or in other cases, if applicable.[1492,1493] A temporary testamentary administrator is appointed for the security of inheritance. On behalf of the heirs, a temporary testamentary administrator may sue and be sued, settle claims, pay debts and represent the heirs.[1494] Other rights and duties of a testamentary administrator are established by the inheritance court in a separate decision on the appointment of testamentary administrators.[1495,1496]

391. A testator may, in his testament, specify one or more persons as executors of the will.[1497,1498] If the testator has not specified differently, the executor's duty is to take care of and undertake all the necessary measures on behalf and for the account of the heir to preserve the legacy. The executor of the will administers the legacy on behalf and for the account of the heir, and he does all that is necessary for the payment of debts and legacies.[1499,1500] The executor of the will is accountable to the court for his work and is liable for damages.[1501] The executor of a will is entitled to compensation of costs and a fee payable from the legacy.[1502] He may be dismissed on the proposal of the client or ex officio if his work is not in conformity with the testator's will or the law.[1503,1504]

1489. Article 112 NPA.
1490. A deposit made with a notary public has the effect of a court deposit. These provisions apply accordingly in cases where a notary public, as the court's commissioner, has taken over inheritance documents, money, securities or valuables (Art. 113 NPA).
1491. Article 128 IA.
1492. Article 128/1 IA.
1493. A temporary testamentary administrator is appointed by the inheritance court. Prior to the appointment, the court will seek an opinion from the persons who are the probable heirs regarding the appointment of the temporary testamentary administrator (Art. 200 IA).
1494. Article 128/1 IA.
1495. Article 128/2 IA.
1496. For more details, *see* Gavella/Belaj in *Inheritance Law*, 471.
1497. Article 60/1 IA.
1498. An executor of the will may be any person possessing business capacity or any legal person (Art. 60/2 IA). The person specified as the executor of the will is not obliged to accept this duty (Art. 60/3 IA).
1499. Article 61/1 IA.
1500. If there are more executors of the will, they jointly perform their duties, unless the testator has specified differently (Art. 61/3 IA).
1501. Article 62/1 IA.
1502. Article 62/2 IA.
1503. Article 63/1 IA.

§4. Administration of Assets of Interest to the Republic of Croatia

392. Many assets of interest to the Republic of Croatia are privately owned.[1505] In order to protect the interests of the Republic of Croatia, various obligations are imposed on the owners of such things (movables/immovables).[1506,1507] If the owners do not act in accordance with these obligations, they may not be forced to undertake any particular measures aimed at protecting the assets of interest to the Republic of Croatia. However, by a decision of a public authority (a local self-government unit), it is legal to establish temporary administration of these things.[1508] The rules on temporary inheritance administrators apply accordingly to such administration when the heirs are unknown[1509] or if their place of abode is unknown. In the enforcement of temporary administration, the thing may be leased to a third person.[1510,1511] A lease contract is made for an indefinite period, and the owner is entitled to have the thing returned into his possession if he is ready to fulfil the obligations for its maintenance.[1512]

§5. Administration of Cultural Goods

393. The Act on the Protection and Preservation of Cultural Goods (APPCG) specifically provides for the management of a cultural good when its owner does not act with due care and in line with the obligations arising from the provisions of the Act providing for the administration, maintenance and utilization of a cultural good. If there is a danger of damage or destruction of a cultural good, the mayor is bound to appoint a temporary administrator of the particular cultural good.[1513,1514] A temporary administrator is bound to undertake measures of protection and preservation of a cultural good on behalf and at the expense of the owner.[1515] A temporary administrator is entitled to compensation for the work and costs which must be covered by the owner.[1516] On the proposal of a body responsible for the protection of cultural good, the mayor will cancel a decision on the appointment of a temporary administrator when the reasons for his appointment cease to exist.[1517,1518]

1504. For more details, *see* Gavella/Belaj in *Inheritance Law*, 171.
1505. Article 52 of the Constitution of the Republic of Croatia.
1506. Article 32/3 PA.
1507. For more details, *see* Part I, Ch. 7. Special Legal Regimes Regulating Immovable Property.
1508. Article 32/3 PA.
1509. For more details, *see* Part V, Ch. 3, §3. Administration of Inherited Property.
1510. Article 32/4 PA.
1511. Rent may only be used for the maintenance of the thing or for the fulfilment of other obligations because of which temporary administration has been established (Art. 32/6 PA).
1512. Article 32/7 PA.
1513. Article 31/1 of Act on the Protection and Preservation of Cultural Goods [hereinafter *APPCG*].
1514. A temporary administrator is also appointed in the case of inheritance or other proceedings whose subject matter is a cultural good (Art. 31/2 APPCG).
1515. Article 31/4 APPCG.
1516. A temporary administrator has a statutory lien on the cultural good as security for his claims against the owner of a cultural good (Art. 31/5 APPCG).
1517. Article 31/7 APPCG.
1518. For more details, *see* Josipović in *Property law III*, 384.

Part VI. Security Rights

Chapter 1. Introduction

394. In Croatian law, there are several types of security rights for securing creditors' claims. Security rights are property rights on things (immovables, movables) and on patrimonial rights by which claims are secured, ensuing from different legal obligations and arising from the relationships between creditors and debtors (loan contracts, contracts of sale, etc.). By security rights, creditors secure their claims against debtors. The advantages of security rights, compared to other instruments on securing claims (guarantees, bills of exchange, bank guarantees, and the like), primarily lie in the fact that by being property rights, they are absolute and have effects towards all third parties (*erga omnes*). The object of the security rights are movables, immovables and patrimonial rights. Security rights are inseparably connected with their objects. Therefore, a creditor may realize his claim on the charged thing regardless of who the owner is. A creditor may also realize such a claim secured by security right in relation to any subsequent owner of the thing, or holder of the right, and not only against the person who was the owner of the thing at the time when the security right was established. In addition, a creditor may protect his right arising from such security right in relation to all third persons and require them to respect his security right. However, the everyday owner of a charged thing is liable for the claim only with the charged thing and not with his entire property.[1519]

395. Security rights are regulated by the PA, the EA, the Notaries Public Act, the Financial Collateral Act, the Register Act, etc. However, the basic source of rules regarding security rights is the PA. Most provisions on security rights are those on liens.[1520] They deal with all types of liens, regardless of the object (a movable, an immovable, a patrimonial right). The PA contains special provisions on the conditions of acquisition and enforcement depending on the type and object of the liens. In practice, the PA provisions on liens have even wider applications. They apply accordingly to other types of security rights unless expressly provided otherwise in the PA or in any other act.[1521] The PA provisions on liens thus apply subsidiarily to

1519. However, if the owner of the charged thing is at the same time a personal debtor, he will be liable for the claim with his whole assets. In that case, the creditor alone decides whether to realize his claim from the thing charged by security right or from the debtor's entire assets.

1520. Articles 297–353 PA.

1521. Article 297/2 PA.

all other types of security rights if there are no separate rules governing their particular aspects.[1522] Security rights may be liens on movables, immovables or patrimonial rights,[1523] the retention of the ownership to secure a claim[1524] and the transfer of ownership for security of claims.[1525]

1522. The rules regulating the principles of liens apply accordingly to all securities. For more details, *see* Part VI, Ch. 2. Section Principles of Liens.
1523. Articles 297–353 PA.
1524. Article 34/5 PA.
1525. Article 34/5 PA, Arts 309–327 of EA.

Chapter 2. Liens

§1. Concept

396. A lien (*založno pravo*) is a limited property right on a particular thing (liened property; *zalog*) which authorizes its holder (lienor; *založni vjerovnik*) to enforce a matured claim against the value of the thing. An everyday owner (lienee; *založni dužnik*), i.e., the person who is the owner of a thing at the moment of the enforcement of a matured claim, is bound to sufferance.[1526,1527] The object of a lien (liened property) may be an individual movable or an immovable which may be converted into money[1528] and proportional shares of these things.[1529] The object of liens may also be patrimonial rights that are suitable for the settlement of the creditor's claim.[1530] The essential content of a lien is the right of enforcement against the value of the liened property. Due to the fact that liens, like all other rights, have an absolute effect, the enforcement of the claim against the value of the liened property must be suffered by any person who owns the liened property at the time of the enforcement.[1531] A claim secured by a lien has priority over all other claims not secured by liens charged to the liened property.[1532] A claim secured by a lien has priority in enforcement against the value of the liened thing with regard to all other claims subsequently secured by liens on the same thing, which come later in the order of priority.[1533] There is only one type of lien in Croatian law.[1534,1535] However, there are a large number of different subtypes of liens which differ with respect to their object,[1536] legal titles[1537] and content.[1538]

§2. Principles of Liens

I. Principle of Accessoriness

397. According to the principle of accessoriness, the existence of a lien depends on the existence and validity of the claim whose settlement it secures. A lien has the

1526. Article 297/1 PA.
1527. Gavella in *Property Law II*, 121–122; Klarić / Vedriš in *Civil Law*, 335.
1528. Objects of liens (the liened property) may only be things in circulation, i.e., which can be sold and converted into money, or patrimonial rights having a pecuniary value. Beside the thing itself, the liened property also includes all its appurtenances (particle, fruits, accretions and accessories).
1529. Article 298/1 PA.
1530. Article 298/2 PA.
1531. Gavella in *Property Law II*, 126.
1532. Article 302/1 PA.
1533. Article 302/2 PA.
1534. Articles 1/1, 297/1 PA.
1535. Gavella in *Property Law II*, 141.
1536. According to their objects, liens may be the following: liens on movables, liens on immovables and liens on patrimonial rights.
1537. According to the legal foundation of its existence, a lien may be: voluntary, judicial/notarial, compulsory and statutory.
1538. According to the content, or depending on whether or not the lienor is entitled to the possession of the thing, a lien may be: *pignus* and hypothek/mortgage (registered lien).

characteristics of accessoriness because it exists due to the claim, and it secures its settlement against the value of the liened property. A secured claim is the main right, and the lien is a secondary (accessory) right.[1539] The legal destiny of a lien depends on the destiny of the secured claim. When a secured claim ceases to exist, the lien also terminates because it simply does not exist if there is no claim to be secured. Therefore, liens terminate simultaneously with the termination of secured claims and any accessory claims regarding interests and costs.[1540] This rule applies regardless of whether a claim has terminated by fulfilment, setoff, dissolution, annulment, or in any other way. When a secured claim passes to another person by any legal title (cession, succession, etc.), the lien is also transferred to the same person without any particular legal title, or modus of acquisition, unless provided otherwise by law.[1541]

398. In the Croatian legal order, a lien is always an accessory in relation to the claim that it secures.[1542] There are no non-accessory securities in Croatian law, such as land debt in German law (*Grundschuld*), for example. There are only separate rules governing liens charged immovables according to which an owner may dispose of an undeleted lien or of the rank of priority of an undeleted lien.[1543]

II. Principle of Speciality

399. According to the principle of speciality at the moment of establishing liens, the claim secured by a lien and the object of the lien (the liened property) must be individualized and precisely determined.[1544,1545] A claim is precisely determined when the lienor and the lienee are specified and when the legal basis of the claim and its amount, or at least the maximum amount up to which it is secured by lien, are also specified.[1546] In addition, a claim must also be determined in accordance with the rules on foreign currency or index clauses.[1547] These rules on the determination of claims also apply when a future claim is secured by lien, i.e., a claim that

1539. Gavella in *Property Law II*, 727; Klarić / Vedriš in *Civil Law*, 327.
1540. Article 346 PA.
1541. Article 319 PA.
1542. Gavella in *Property Law II*, 733.
1543. For more details, *see* Part VI, Ch. 4, §4. III. Priority of Mortgage.
1544. Gavella in *Property Law II*, 733; Klarić / Vedriš in *Civil Law*, 328.
1545. An exception to this rule is envisaged for the floating charge on movables. For more details, *see* Part VI, Ch. 5, II. C. Floating Charge.
1546. Article 301/1 PA.
1547. In the Croatian legal order, the basic rule is that pecuniary obligations must be expressed in the national currency – *hrvatska kuna/HRK* (Art. 21 of OA). A provision is allowed, however, according to which the amount of the obligation in the currency of the Republic of Croatia is calculated on the basis of the price of gold, or the exchange rate of the currency used in the Republic of Croatia in relation to foreign currency (foreign currency clause, Art. 22 of OA). The extent of the pecuniary obligation in domestic currency may depend on changes in the prices of goods, commodities or services expressed by the price index established by an authorized entity (index clause, Art. 23 of OA).

will come into being after a certain period of time or upon the fulfilment of a condition resulting from a given loan, assumed management, or as a guarantee or compensation for damages.[1548] The modality of determining the object of a lien depends on whether movables or immovables are at issue.[1549]

III. Principle of Inseparability

400. A lien may not be separated from the liened property (a movable, an immovable), which is charged by a lien.[1550,1551] The inseparability of the lien and the liened property results in two important consequences. A lien is a right connected with the liened property, and whoever, on any legal foundation, acquires ownership of the liened property (by inheritance, legal transaction, *ex lege*) acquires it charged with the lien.[1552] Liens may not be transferred from one object to the other unless this is provided otherwise.[1553] Exemptions from the principle of the inseparability of liens are provided by law. For example, if the liened property is destroyed and replaced by a right coming in its stead (the right to compensation, the right to a secured amount, and the like), the lien continues to exist on such a right.[1554]

IV. Principle of Indivisibility

401. The principle of indivisibility means that liens are indivisible with regard to the secured claim against the liened property.[1555] A lien secures the claim as a whole, including all accessory claims.[1556] Charge by a lien is not reduced if the claim decreases unless otherwise stipulated by law. The indivisibility of a lien against the liened property is provided for in Article 301/4 of PA, according to which the settlement of a claim is secured by the liened property as a whole, including all its component parts (portions of a thing, inseparable fruits, appurtenances).[1557] A decrease or a division of a thing encumbered by a lien does not have any impact on its termination. A lien continues to exist even when the liened property has been divided into several parts or when a part has been separated from it. In such a case, the lien continues to charge all the parts ensuing from the partition

1548. Article 301/2 PA.
1549. A movable is determined as an object of a lien when it is individualized in such a way that it can be distinguished from other movables of the same order of priority and the same qualities. An immovable is determined as the object of a lien when it is marked according to the data in the land register. A patrimonial right is determined as the subject of a lien when it is individualized in such a way that it can be distinguished from other rights of the same kind.
1550. Article 299/1 PA.
1551. Gavella in *Property Law II*, 139–140; Klarić / Vedriš in *Civil Law*, 339.
1552. Article 299/1 PA.
1553. Article 299/2 PA.
1554. Article 301/4 PA.
1555. Gavella in *Property Law II*, 140–141.
1556. Article 301/5 PA.
1557. Article 5 PA.

or separation.[1558] A lien terminates only when the liened property is destroyed and when no other thing, or right, takes its place, whereby the claim continues to exist.[1559]

V. Principle of Judicial Enforcement

402. According to the principle of judicial enforcement, a lienor realizes his right to settlement against the value of the liened property through the court.[1560] The settlement is carried out under the rules of enforcement.[1561] The law expressly provides for cases where out-of-court enforcement is also possible.[1562] Out-of-court enforcement is possible when the object of a lien is a movable transferred into the lienor's possession. Such an enforcement is possible if the lienee has agreed to it[1563] or if the secured claim arises from a mercantile contract and the lienee has not expressly excluded out-of-court enforcement.[1564] The right to out-of-court enforcement is realized by the lienor in a public auction.[1565] The settlement of a claim secured by a lien on an immovable is possible only through the court conducting enforcement proceedings according to the rules laid down in the EA.

VI. Principle of Publicity

403. In order for a lien to be effective against all third persons, it must be appropriately publicized. The system of publication of liens depends, on the one hand, on the subject of the lien and, on the other hand, on the legal title of the acquisition of the lien. Liens on immovables, regardless of the legal foundation of acquisition, are always publicized by being entered in the land register. Liens on movables are publicized in various ways depending on the legal title of acquisition. For example, a voluntary lien on a movable is publicized by its transfer into the possession of the lienor. A judicial, or a notarial, voluntary lien on a movable is publicized by its entry in the special Register of Security Rights in Movables and Patrimonial Rights. A lien on a patrimonial right is publicized in various ways depending on whether it is a lien equated with an immovable (e.g., the right to build) or whether it is equated with a movable (e.g., claims). The model of publicizing liens is of special importance for the protection of bona fide acquirers and for the acquisition of a lien from a person who is not the owner of the liened property.

1558. Article 301/4 PA.
1559. Article 343 PA.
1560. Gavella in *Property Law II*, 144–145; Klarić / Vedriš in *Civil Law*, 338.
1561. Article 336/2 PA.
1562. Article 337 PA.
1563. Article 337/1 PA.
1564. Article 337/3 PA.
1565. Article 337/3 PA.

§3. Objects of Liens (Liened Property)

404. Objects of liens (liened property) may be individual movables or immovables that can be converted into money or the proportional shares of such things.[1566] A lien may also be established on individual patrimonial rights suitable for the collection of the creditor's claim.[1567] Objects of liens may be all things that are subject to a legal transaction.[1568] A lien may be established on several immovables as if all of them were one and the same thing (a simultaneous mortgage, *simultana hipoteka*),[1569] as well as on the whole of several movables (a floating charge).[1570] The object of a lien may also be the right to the fruits that a thing produces as the result of a legal relationship (rent, lease rental).[1571] In principle, the object of a lien may be anything owned by private or public entities. However, a lien may not be established on state-owned things, which, by operation of law, may not be alienated from the ownership of the state (e.g., forests and forest land, public roads) because such things cannot be sold to settle a claim.[1572]

405. There are several reasons why it is important for the legal position of the lienor to distinguish the object of a lien (liened property). First, the liened property determines the conditions that must be fulfilled for the acquisition of the lien. Second, the publicity of a lien depends on the type of liened property. The liened property is also important for the powers that the lienor has until the maturity of the secured claim as opposed to those after the maturity of the claim. The liened property also determines how the lienor must be compensated against the value of the liened property or of the right.

§4. Secured Claims

406. Liens are established to secure monetary claims or claims whose value is expressed in money.[1573] A lien may also secure a future claim, i.e., a claim which will only exist after a certain period of time or after the fulfilment of a particular condition.[1574] In order for such a future claim to be sufficiently determined when a lien is established, it is necessary that, at its establishment, at least the highest amount is determined up to which it is secured by the liened property. Besides the

1566. Article 298/1 PA.
1567. Article 298/2 PA.
1568. Objects of liens (liened property) may only be things that may be subject to legal transactions and that can be converted into money, or patrimonial rights that have a monetary value. Besides the thing itself, the object of a lien are all its particle, e.g. portions, fruits, accretions, appurtenances (Art. 298/4 PA).
1569. For further details, *see* Part VI, Ch. 4, §1. Mortgage (Lien on Immovables).
1570. For further details, *see* Part VI, Ch. 5, §1. Pledge C. Floating Charge.
1571. Common goods may not be the objects of liens, because of their natural characteristics, or due to a statutory provision, such goods may not be objects of ownership, or and other property rights including liens (Art. 3/1,2 PA).
1572. For more, *see* Gavella in *Property Law II*, 145–152; Klarić / Vedriš in *Civil Law*, 340–341.
1573. Article 301/1 PA.
1574. Article 301/2 PA.

principle claim, a lien is established to secure all accessory claims and interests (statutory and contractual), as well as all litigation and enforcement expenses arising when the claim is settled against the value of the liened property.[1575,1576]

§5. Acquisition of a Lien

407. A lien may be acquired on the basis of several legal titles – by lien contract, a court decision, or by law. There are three basic conditions for the acquisition of a lien: ownership of the liened property by the lienee, the legal title (*titulus*) for the acquisition and the corresponding modality of acquisition (*modus*). Depending on the legal title of the acquisition of a lien and its modality, it is possible to distinguish the following: voluntary liens, voluntary judicial or notarial liens, compulsory liens and statutory liens. Each of these liens may be established on any kind of liened property (immovables, movables, patrimonial rights).

§6. Protection of Liens

408. The protection of liens is realized in court proceedings. Claims made and realized by the lienor primarily depend on whether they are made against the lienee (owner of the liened property/holder of the patrimonial right) or against third persons, but also on the liened property involved (immovables, movables or patrimonial rights). A lienor whose claim is secured by a lien on an immovable is entitled to request, against all third persons, the protection of the lien according to the rules on the protection of rights registered in the land register.[1577] The lienor is also entitled to request that the lienee, or a third person, does not perform anything on the immovable that would endanger or diminish its value.[1578] A lienor whose claim is secured by a lien on a movable is entitled to request the surrender of the charged movable into his possession or the termination of activities interfering with his possession of the liened movable. The lienor is entitled to request the lienee to surrender another movable as liened property if the first liened movable has hidden defects and can request the sale of the movable prior to the maturity of the secured claim if the movable has lost its value.[1579] The lienor whose claim is secured by a lien on patrimonial right is entitled to bring an action against the lienee and seek the payment of any due interest and request from the lienee for the performance of the liened claim.[1580]

1575. Article 301/3 PA, Art. 42/1 LRA.
1576. For more, *see* Gavella in *Property Law II*, 129–135.
1577. Article 150 LRA.
1578. Article 332 PA.
1579. Article 328 PA.
1580. Article 335 PA.

§7. Termination of Liens

409. A lien may terminate in various ways. The most frequent way is the termination of the secured claim.[1581] Due to the fact that the lien is an accessory right and depends on the existence of a valid claim, the termination of the claim on any basis (payment, setoff, and the like) automatically leads to the termination of the lien.[1582] A lien ceases to exist by the destruction of the liened property if no other thing or right has taken its place.[1583,1584] A lien also ceases to exist with the lienor's waiver.[1585,1586,1587] A lien limited by a term or by a termination clause terminates on the expiration of the term or on the fulfilment of the condition.[1588,1589] A lien also terminates on the termination of the lienor who has no legal successor.[1590] A lien on an immovable also terminates on a court decision on the revocation of the lien.[1591,1592] Finally, a lien terminates on a decision of an administrative body rendered in accordance with a separate law.[1593,1594]

§8. The Position of Lienors in Enforcement and Bankruptcy Proceedings

410. When enforcement is carried out on a liened property, the claims of lienors who have not proposed enforcement are also settled in enforcement proceedings.[1595] In settlement against the value realized in the sale resulting from enforcement proceedings, priority is given to the lienor who first acquired the lien on the same liened property. Lienors' claims are settled against the value of the liened

1581. Article 346 PA.
1582. A lien on an immovable terminates, however, only when deleted in the land register. The deletion may occur upon the written assent of the lienor (Art. 347/1 PA).
1583. Article 343 PA.
1584. For example, if a secured liened movable is destroyed, the lien is transferred to the insurance premium to which the lienee (the owner of the destroyed movable) is entitled. However, with the destruction of the liened property, the secured claim does not cease to exist (Art. 343 PA).
1585. The lienor is deemed to have waived the lien if he unconditionally surrenders possession of the liened movable to the lienee. However, the loss of possession of the liened movable does not lead to the termination of the lien. If the lienor has unlawfully been deprived of possession of the liened movable, he is entitled to seek its surrender into his possession (Art. 328 PA).
1586. A lien on an immovable is deemed to have terminated by a waiver only upon its deletion in the land register as the result of a written waiver (Art. 344/5 PA).
1587. Article 344/1 PA.
1588. Article 345/1 PA.
1589. A lien on an immovable based on the expiry of a term or the fulfilment of a condition terminates only upon its deletion in the land register (Art. 345/1 PA).
1590. Article 350 PA.
1591. Article 351 PA.
1592. A decision on revocation is rendered by the land register court if the lien has been registered for more than thirty years and neither the lienor nor the lienor's successors can be found, and no new registration regarding the lien has been requested for more than thirty years (Art. 162 LRA).
1593. Article 352 PA.
1594. For example, in expropriation proceedings, the lien on an immovable that is subject to expropriation terminates.
1595. Article 86 EA.

property in the order of the acquisition of the liens after the priority claims have been settled (costs of enforcement proceedings, taxes, maintenance claims, and the like).[1596] More claims of the same order of priority secured by liens are settled in proportion to their amounts if the amounts obtained by sale are not sufficient for the full settlement of the claims of all lienors.[1597]

411. In bankruptcy proceedings, the lienor has the position of a creditor with a right to separate enforcement. The claims of a lienor who has acquired a lien on a thing belonging to a lienee prior to the opening of bankruptcy proceedings will be separately enforced in these proceedings in accordance with enforcement law provisions.[1598] The lienor's claim is settled against the value achieved as a result of the sale of the liened property in the full amount of the secured claim. A lienor taking part in bankruptcy proceedings is entitled to priority enforcement from the value of the liened thing before other lienors of the bankruptcy debtor are satisfied.

1596. Article 113 EA.
1597. Article 116 EA.
1598. Article 149 of BA.

Chapter 3. Other Types of Security Rights

§1. General

412. In the Croatian legal order, besides liens, there are also other ways of security rights. In order to secure a claim, parties may agree that the alienator retains the right of ownership of a thing (*pridržaj vlasništva*).[1599] The parties may also agree on the transfer of ownership aimed at securing the claim (*prijenos vlasništva radi osiguranja*).[1600] An agreement on the transfer of ownership with the aim of securing a claim may be made before the court in the form of court minutes or before a notary public in the form of a notarial act: the judicial or notarial security of a claim by the transfer of ownership (*sudsko/javnobilježno osiguranje prijenosom vlasništva/prava*).[1601] All these security rights are based on the general rule that ownership resulting from a legal transaction may be limited by time limits or conditions and that such limitation of ownership has an effect on third persons if it is entered in a public register.[1602] Through the limitation of ownership by time limits or conditions, until the time limit expires or a condition is fulfilled, two persons participate in the ownership of the same thing – one as the previous and the other as the contingent owner,[1603] but the content of the right of ownership is not divided between them.[1604] All these forms of security rights have the same objective as in the case of liens: to secure the enforcement of a claim. Therefore, in Article 297/2, the PA expressly provides that what is laid down for liens applies accordingly to the transfer of ownership for security, as well as to any other form of security rights, unless otherwise provided by law. This is a safeguard against situations where, by contracting various property securities, the rules on liens, conceived to protect both the lienee and the lienor, are not circumvented.

§2. Reservation of Ownership

413. Reservation of title (*pridržaj vlasništva*) for the purpose of security is the transfer of ownership of a particular thing from the alienator to the acquirer whereby the alienator retains the ownership of the thing until the acquirer fulfils a particular claim.[1605] By retaining the ownership, the settlement of a particular alienator's claim against the acquirer is secured, ensuing from the legal transaction of the alienation of the thing. The ownership of a thing is transferred to the acquirer only after the acquirer has fulfilled a particular claim. The alienator remains the owner, and the acquirer becomes the owner only after the claim has been fulfilled. The owner who has retained ownership for security is bound not to use, or dispose of, the thing

1599. Article 34/5 PA.
1600. Article 34/5 PA.
1601. Articles 309–327 EA.
1602. Article 34/1, 34/3 PA.
1603. Article 34/4, 34/5 PA.
1604. Gavella in *Property Law II*, 478–479.
1605. Gavella in *Property Law II*, 551–561.

except in order to settle the secured claim.[1606] If the claim is not paid on its maturity, the owner will settle his claim against the value of the thing in accordance with the rules on the enforcement of secured claims from liens in out-of-court proceedings.[1607,1608] The transfer of ownership by reservation of title to secure the claim, i.e., ownership transferred within the time limit or a condition of postponement, has an effect on third parties only if it is entered in the public register where things with retained ownership are registered.[1609] Reservation of title on immovables is thus entered in the land register in favour of the acquirer, who becomes the owner when the time limit expires or when a condition is fulfilled.[1610,1611] Reservation of title on a movable, if it lasts longer than a year, is entered in the Register Act.[1612,1613]

§3. Fiduciary Transfer of Ownership

414. Transfer of ownership for security (*prijenos vlasništva radi osiguranja*) is a model of securing a claim when a debtor transfers ownership of his thing to a creditor to secure the settlement of a claim. The transfer of ownership as security is the transfer of ownership to the creditor limited by the condition of cancellation.[1614] Ownership is transferred to the creditor, but when his claim is fulfilled, ownership returns to the debtor. Legal relationships between creditors and debtors are organized in the same way as in the case of reservation of title for security.[1615] The creditor is bound to cease using and disposing of a thing except for the settlement of a claim. If the claim is not settled upon its maturity, the creditor is authorized to settle it against the value of the thing in accordance with the rules on the enforcement of claims secured by liens in out-of-court proceedings.[1616] The transfer of ownership as security has an effect on third parties only if it is entered in a public register where charged things are entered. The transfer of ownership as security is entered in the land register.[1617] This is very rare in practice since security through a judicial or notarial transfer of claim for security provided for in the EA is more frequently used.

1606. Article 34/5 PA.
1607. Article 34/5 PA.
1608. Separate rules on the sale with reservation of title are provided for in Arts 462–473 of the OA.
1609. Article 32/4 PA.
1610. Article 3/4 LRA.
1611. For further details on the legal effects of such an entry, *see* Gavella in *Property Law II*, 559; Josipović in *Land Registration Law*, 156–159.
1612. Article 6/1/7 of Register Act.
1613. A separate rule applies if, after a sale with reservation of title, the buyer goes bankrupt, or enforcement proceedings are conducted against him. In such cases, reservation of title on a movable has an effect on the buyer's creditors only if made in the form of a certified public document drawn up before the buyer's bankruptcy, i.e., prior to the initiation of enforcement proceedings. In other words, if reservation of title is not contracted in such a document, the buyer's creditors will be able to settle their claims against the value of the sold thing on which there is reservation of title in favour of the seller.
1614. Gavella in *Property Law II*, 469–551.
1615. For more details, *see* Part VI, Ch. 3, §2. Reservation of Title.
1616. Article 34/5 OA.
1617. Article 36/5 LRA.

§4. Judicial or Notarial Security Claims by Transfer of Ownership/Rights

415. Judicial or notarial fiduciary transfers of ownership/rights (*sudski ili javnobilježnički prijenos vlasništva/prava radi osiguranja*) are regulated in Articles 309–327 of the EA. This is a special form of fiduciary transfer of ownership, which is performed in security proceedings regulated in EA and conducted by the court or a notary public.[1618] The legal title for the judicial fiduciary transfer of ownership/right is an agreement between the creditor and the owner or the holder of a right to secure a claim by fiduciary transfer of ownership/right. The agreement must be made before the competent court in the form of court protocol (the so-called judicial fiduciary transfer of ownership/rights).[1619] The court protocol has the effect of a court settlement.[1620] The agreement may also be made in the form of a notarial act – a notarial fiduciary transfer of ownership/rights.[1621,1622] The modus of establishing judicial fiduciary ownership on an immovable is its registration in favour of the creditor with a recordation that the transfer is made for security reasons.[1623] A model of establishing judicial or notarial fiduciary ownership on a movable/right for security is registration in the Register of Security Rights on Movables and Patrimonial Rights.[1624] The creditor, in whose favour ownership is transferred for security, settles the secured claim in separate out-of-court proceedings conducted by a notary public.

§5. Right of Retention

416. The right of retention (Lat. *ius retentionis*; *pravo zadržanja*) is the right of a creditor of the matured claim, who possesses the thing belonging to the debtor, to keep it in his possession and to settle the claim against the value of the thing.[1625] The right of retention is regulated by Articles 286–289 of the OA. The creditor may keep the debtor's thing that is in his possession until his claim is paid[1626] or until the debtor provides a corresponding security.[1627] Objects of the right of retention may be movables or immovables capable of being converted into money. The claim to be secured and the thing on which the right of retention is exercised do not need to result from the same legal transaction.[1628] In Croatian law, the right of retention empowers the creditor to realize his claim against the value of the retained thing in

1618. Dika in *Enforcement Law*, 784–822; Gavella in *Property Law II*, 496–551.
1619. Article 310/1 EA.
1620. Article 310/4 EA.
1621. Article 327/2 EA.
1622. The provisions of Arts 310–326 of EA on the judicial fiduciary transfer of ownership/rights apply accordingly to the notarial fiduciary transfer of ownership/rights.
1623. Article 312 EA.
1624. Articles 6/3,4 of the Register Act.
1625. Gavella in *Property Law II*, 898.
1626. Article 286/1 OA.
1627. Article 288 OA.
1628. Klarić / Vedriš in *Civil Law*, 418.

the same way as the lienor.[1629] The creditor is under the obligation to inform the debtor in a timely manner of his intention.[1630] The right of retention terminates with the termination of the claim or with the loss of the actual possession of the thing.

1629. Article 289 OA.
1630. Article 289 OA.

Chapter 4. Security Rights on Immovable Property

§1. Mortgage: Lien on Immovables (Mortgage)

I. Concept

417. A lien on an immovable (mortgage; *hipoteka*) is a limited right on an individually specified immovable which empowers its holder (mortgage creditor, mortgagee; *hipotekarni vjerovnik*) to settle the matured claim against the value of the immovable. A mortgage on an immovable is established without transferring it into the mortgagee's possession.[1631] The object of a mortgage may be the following:

- individually specified immovable capable of being converted into money,[1632,1633] i.e., a plot with what is reasonably permanently attached to it, on or under its surface, together with what is built onto the immovable, added to it or joined to it, or in any other way permanently connected to it.[1634] Besides the immovable, all its appurtenances are also encumbered unless otherwise specified by law;[1635]
- the right to build since this is legally equal to the immovable.[1636] Then, the object of the mortgage will be the right to build together with the building erected on the plot encumbered with the right to build;[1637,1638,1639]
- an ideal share of the immovable;[1640,1641]
- an ideal share of the immovable which is connoted with the ownership of an individual part of the immovable (condominium);[1642,1643]

1631. Article 304/1 PA.
1632. Article 298/1 PA, Art. 40/1 LRA.
1633. Objects of mortgage may only be immovables that can be sold on the market. Immovables which may not be subject to enforcement according to the rules of the EA may not be objects of liens, such as objects used for defence (Art. 4/6 of EA). Immovables exempted from enforcement, or where enforcement is limited, may not be subject to compulsory liens (Arts 75, 76, 91/1, 241/2 of EA). However, immovables on which, according to the EA, enforcement is exempted or limited may be subject to voluntary mortgage established by mortgage contract (Arts 77, 305/5 of EA).
1634. Article 9 PA.
1635. Article 298/4 PA.
1636. Article 280/2 PA.
1637. Articles 280/3, 285/2,3 PA.
1638. The mortgage will then be entered as a charge to the right to build in the land register file where the right to build is registered as if it was an immovable. When the right to build terminates, the mortgage charged the right to build charges the compensation that the owner of the land owes the person whose right to build has terminated (Art. 206/2 PA).
1639. Pursuant to Art. 81/3 EA, the right to build may be an independent object of enforcement to which the rules on the enforcement of immovables of that Act apply accordingly.
1640. Article 298/1 PA, Art. 39/1 LRA.
1641. Each co-owner may independently dispose of his proportional share of an immovable according to the rules applicable to the owner's legal disposition of things, provided that by doing so other persons' rights are not infringed (Art. 37/5 PA). A co-owner may, therefore, mortgage his co-owned part of an immovable. It will be entered in the land register as an encumbrance of the proportional share of that particular co-owner (Art. 35/1 PA). Enforcement of the payment of the secured claim will be carried out on the proportional share of the immovable as an independent object of enforcement according to the rules on enforcement on immovables (Art. 81/2 of EA).
1642. Article 69/1 PA.

- several immovables as a joint mortgage (simultana hipoteka);[1644,1645]
- the right to fruits derived from an immovable as the result of a legal relationship such as rent, lease rental.[1646,1647]

II. Types of Mortgages

A. *Voluntary Mortgage*

418. A voluntary mortgage is a mortgage established on the basis of a contract aimed at establishing it on an immovable (mortgage contract) in the way stipulated by law.[1648] A mortgage contract is entered into by the mortgagor (the owner of an immovable) and the mortgagee (creditor). By virtue of a mortgage contract, the mortgagor voluntarily charges his immovable with a mortgage. A voluntary mortgage may be acquired on any immovables suitable to be converted into money, including immovables which, according to the rules of the EA, are exempted from enforcement, or when enforcement is limited on them for the protection of the mortgagor.[1649,1650]

419. The conditions for the acquisition of voluntary liens on immovables are the following:

1643. The object of the lien will then be the co-owned part of the immovable with which ownership of the individual part of immovable is connected, including all the accessory parts to which the ownership of the separate part extends (Art. 67/3,5 PA). Enforcement for the payment of the claim secured by a mortgage will be carried out on the co-owned part with which ownership of the individual part of the immovable is connected, and all limitations arising from the ownership of the separate part of the immovable will be transferred to the buyer (Art. 69/3 PA).
1644. Article 298/3 PA, Art. 41 LRA.
1645. In the case of a joint mortgage, all immovables are taken together to secure the claim as if they were a single thing or an integrated piece of liened property. The joint mortgage is entered in the land register undivided as a mortgage on two or more immovables in all land register units where charged immovables are registered. The procedure of entering a joint mortgage is regulated in Arts 151-161LRA. When registering a joint mortgage, one land register file is marked as the main file and all others as auxiliary files (Art. 151/1 LRA). A creditor whose claim is secured by a joint mortgage may freely choose against which immovable to settle his claim unless this is otherwise established (Art. 301/6 PA). A creditor may choose whether to settle the claim secured by a joint mortgage against all immovables, against only one, or several of them (Art. 41/2,3,4 LRA).
1646. Article 298/5 PA.
1647. When a mortgage is established only on fruits, this must be expressly specified in the land register (Art. 39/2 LRA). A creditor in whose favour a mortgage is established on fruits is entitled to collect these fruits (Art. 331/1 PA). The value of the collected fruits is set off against the creditor's claim (Art. 331/2 PA). The settlement of the secured claim is against the value of the fruits and consequently the immovable is placed under temporary management. *See* Gavella in *Property Law II, 418-419.*
1648. Article 306/1 PA.
1649. Articles 77, 305/5 EA.
1650. Dika in *Enforcement Law*, 755–756; Gavella in *Property Law II*, 313–360.

- the mortgagor's ownership of the immovable.[1651] Due to the fact that mortgages are derived from the ownership of an immovable, a mortgage may only be established by the owner of the immovable. The owner of an immovable given as the mortgaged property may be a personal debtor, but it can also be a third person not owing any claim to the lienor. The owner of an immovable is the person who is entered in the land register as the owner. The registered owner is presumed to be the actual owner of the immovable who is authorized to dispose of it. In order for a mortgage to be established, the registered person must be the actual (real) owner of the immovable;[1652]
- a valid mortgage contract,[1653] which is the legal title (titulus) for the establishment of a mortgage on an immovable. This is an agreement by which a debtor or a third person obliges himself to allow the mortgagee, in order for the claim to be secured, to enter the mortgage in the land register as a charge on the immovable. The mortgagee is obliged to let the mortgage be deleted from the land register as soon as the claim secured by the mortgage terminates.[1654,1655] In order for a mortgage contract to be valid, it must be made in written form.[1656] The PA also contains explicit rules on the content of a mortgage contract whereby some specific provisions are not allowed. Such provisions of a mortgage contract are null and void and do not have any legal effects. These provisions are contrary to the nature of a mortgage because both the mortgagee and mortgagor are unnecessarily limited in exercising their rights;[1657]
- a valid modus of acquisition.[1658] An entry in the land register is a modus for the acquisition of a voluntary lien on an immovable. Registration is of a constitutive nature when it comes to the acquisition of a voluntary mortgage, and it is considered as acquired only when it is entered into the land register. A mortgage is entered in the land register by registration or conditional registration as a charge

1651. Article 306/1 PA.
1652. When an immovable is co-owned or jointly owned, all co-owners or joint owners must provide mutual assent for the establishment of a mortgage on the entire immovable (Arts 306/2, 41/1, 61 PA). When a co-owner establishes a mortgage against only his co-owned part of the immovable, he does not need to have the consent of the other co-owners (Art. 306/2 PA).
1653. Articles 306/1, 307 PA.
1654. Article 307/1 PA.
1655. A mortgage contract is a two-sided obligation in a legal transaction, a causal legal transaction which comes into being when the parties (mortgagor and mortgagee) have agreed on the essential elements of the agreement (Art. 247 of OA). A mortgage contract may be entered into as an independent legal transaction. It is possible that the provisions of such an agreement become the component part of a contract from which a claim arises that is secured by a mortgage.
1656. Article 307/6 PA.
1657. Inadmissible provisions of a lien contract are the following: provisions that are contrary to the nature of the liened property and the claim to be secured by the lien (Art. 307/3 PA); provisions laying down that the liened property will be transferred to the creditor's ownership if the debt is not paid within the specified time limit (Art. 307/4 PA); provisions stating that the lienor may not redeem the liened property (Art. 307/4 PA); a provision that the lienor may not allow anyone else to establish a lien on the same liened property (Art. 307/4 PA); a provision that the lienee may not request the liened property to be sold, not even after the maturity of the secured claim (Art. 307/4 PA); a provision laying down that the lienee may, on his own will, or at a predetermined price, alienate the liened property, or keep it (Art. 307/5 PA).
1658. Article 309 PA, Arts 48,49, 57-61 LRA.

on the mortgaged immovable.[1659,1660] When an immovable is not entered in the land register, the mortgage is established by depositing a legalized document with the court that has territorial jurisdiction over the immovable on which a mortgage is established.[1661,1662]

420. A voluntary mortgage on an immovable may be acquired from non-owners under the rules on the protection of trust in the truthfulness and completeness of the land register. When the situation in the land register differs from the actual legal status of an immovable because the actual owner is not entered as the owner of the immovable, the mortgage may be acquired from the registered owner (predecessor) under the rules on the protection of trust in the truthfulness and completeness of the land register.[1663] The rules on the acquisition of ownership of an immovable on the basis of trust in the land register apply accordingly to the acquisition of mortgages from non-owners, i.e., from a person who is entered in the land register as the owner although not being the actual owner of the immovable.[1664] In order to acquire a voluntary mortgage on the basis of the protection of trust in the land register, a bona fide mortgagee must make a valid mortgage contract with the registered owner and enter the mortgage in the land register. The protection of trust is effective only in favour of a bona fide mortgagee. A mortgagee is considered as being bona fide only if he did not know or did not have sufficient reason to doubt that the registered immovable belonged to the registered owner.[1665] When the legal effects of the protection of trust in the truthfulness of the land register are established in favour of a bona fide mortgagee, the acquisition of the lien cannot be denied because the registration of the owner is inaccurate. However, such legal effects of the protection of trust come into play only when the time limits have expired, within which the deletion of an invalid predecessor's registration may have been sought even against a fair acquirer by way of a suit for release.[1666] When the legal effects of the protection of trust in the completeness of the land register become operative in favour of a bona fide mortgagee, the acquisition of a mortgage can no longer be denied because the registered owner is not the actual owner and because some other person has acquired the immovable and has not yet registered as the owner.

421. A mortgagee in whose favour a voluntary mortgage is established is not entitled to the possession of the mortgaged property.[1667] Such a mortgagee does not

1659. Articles 309/1,2 PA.
1660. A claim secured by a mortgage is entered in the land register by specifying the amount of money determined in accordance with the rules on foreign currency or index clauses (Art. 40/1 LRA). When entering a mortgage up to the highest amount, the highest amount of the principal is entered (Art. 40/4 LRA).
1661. Article 309/3 PA.
1662. The rules on the acquisition of a voluntary mortgage through an entry in the land register apply accordingly to the changes and termination of a mortgage resulting from a legal transaction (Art. 309/4 PA).
1663. Article 318 PA.
1664. Articles 122–125 PA.
1665. Article 122/2 PA.
1666. Article 150/2 LRA.
1667. Article 329/1 PA.

have the right to collect fruits and other benefits from the immovable.[1668,1669] The right to the possession of the immovable, its use and collection of fruits and other benefits remains with the mortgagor. The main rights belonging to the mortgagee prior to the maturity of the secured claim are limited to requests addressed to the mortgagor to preserve the value of the immovable.[1670] The objective of such a request is to maintain the value of the immovable so that upon the maturity of the claim, the mortgagee can settle it against the value of the immovable. The mortgagee is entitled to request the mortgagor to refrain from any actions that would endanger or diminish the value of the immovable encumbered by a mortgage.[1671] If the mortgagor fails to act in accordance with the mortgagee's request, the latter may request a compulsory enforcement of the claim secured by a lien even before its maturity.[1672,1673]

B. Voluntary Judicial or Notarial Mortgage

422. Voluntary judicial or notarial mortgage is a type of voluntary mortgage on immovables acquired on the basis of a mortgage contract made in the form of court protocol or a notarial act.[1674] A mortgage is then established by the court in proceedings aimed at securing a claim based on the parties' agreement according to the rules of the EA[1675] or before a notary public.[1676] The proceedings of establishing a mortgage are initiated by a mutual proposal of the mortgagor and the mortgagee to the court or to a notary public to determine and establish the mortgage as security of the mortgagee's monetary claim by registering a mortgage on the mortgagor's immovable.[1677] A judicial or notarial voluntary mortgage may be acquired on all immovables on which a voluntary mortgage may be acquired, i.e., on all immovables suitable to be converted into money, including immovables which, pursuant to the rules of the EA, are exempted from enforcement, or where their enforcement is limited.[1678]

1668. Article 329/1 PA.
1669. The provision of an agreement contrary to the rule that the mortgagor does not have the right to possession of the mortgaged immovable would be null and void unless otherwise stipulated by law (Art. 329/2 PA).
1670. Article 330 PA.
1671. Article 330/1 PA.
1672. Article 330/1 PA.
1673. However, the mortgagor's actions by which the value of an immovable is endangered or diminished do not entitle the mortgagee to dissolve the relationship of obligation resulting in a claim secured by a mortgage (Art. 330/2 PA).
1674. Dika in *Enforcement Law*, 746–782; Gavella in *Property Law II*, 371–378.
1675. Articles 299–306 EA. Territorial jurisdiction for decisions on the establishment of mortgage and its implementation lies with the court that would be competent for enforcement regarding the settlement of the monetary claim on the immovable on which a voluntary court mortgage is established (Art. 299 EA).
1676. Article 307 EA.
1677. Article 300/item 1 EA.
1678. Articles 77, 305/5 EA.

423. The conditions for the establishment of voluntary judicial or notarial liens on immovables are the following:

- the mortgagor's ownership of an immovable.[1679] All the rules on the derivation of voluntary mortgage from the ownership of immovables apply accordingly to judicial or notarial voluntary mortgage;[1680]
- a valid mortgage contract made before the court in the form of a court protocol,[1681] or in the form of a notarial act.[1682,1683] At the hearing, the court or a notary public establishes the existence of the parties' agreement regarding the mortgagee's claim, its amount, its legal basis and the period of its maturity, as well as their consent that it should be secured by a mortgage.[1684,1685] A signed agreement in the form of a court protocol/notarial act on the establishment of a mortgage has the force of a court settlement;[1686]
- a valid modus of acquisition – registration of a judicial or notarial voluntary mortgage in the land register.[1687] Registration is of a constitutive nature. A judicial or notarial voluntary mortgage is entered in the land register as a charge on the mortgaged immovable.

424. The mortgagor's and mortgagee's rights and obligations arising from a voluntary judicial or notarial mortgage on an immovable are the same as in the case of a voluntary mortgage on an immovable. The mortgagee is not entitled to the possession of an immovable or the collection of fruits or benefits. The mortgagor continues to possess the immovable.

425. The crucial difference between a voluntary mortgage and a judicial or notarial mortgage on immovables is the rules on the enforcement of the secured claim against the value of the mortgaged property. The enforcement procedure in the case of voluntary, judicial or notarial mortgage is much shorter. A court protocol or a notarial act containing a mortgage contract has the force of an enforcement document from the moment of maturity of the secured claim. From the maturity of the secured claim, the mortgagee disposes of the enforcement document on the basis

1679. Article 306/1 PA.
1680. For further details, *see* Part VI, Ch. 4, §1. II. A. Voluntary Mortgage.
1681. Article 213/1 PA, Art. 301 EA.
1682. Notarial acts are documents on legal transactions and statements drawn up by notaries public (Art. 3/1 of Notaries Public Act). Notarial acts have the force of public documents (Art. 3/2 of Notaries Public Act). A notarial act, which contains a mortgagor's statement expressing his consent that on the basis of that document, in order to enforce due performance and upon the maturity of the obligation, enforcement will directly be carried out (*clausula exequendi*), has the force of an enforcement document (Art. 54/1 of the Notaries Public Act).
1683. Article 307 EA.
1684. Articles 301/1, 307 EA.
1685. In their agreement, the parties may determine the value of the immovable which will be the basis for the establishment of the value of the object of security in enforcement proceedings aimed at it being converted into money (Art. 301/1 EA).
1686. Article 301/2 EA.
1687. Article 305 EA.

of which he may request the sale of the mortgaged immovable by the court.[1688] Therefore, a voluntary judicial or notarial mortgage is a much more favourable means of security for a creditor, and it is more frequently used in practice than a voluntary mortgage on immovables.[1689]

C. Compulsory Mortgage

426. Compulsory mortgage is established against the will of mortgagor (the owner of an immovable) in proceedings for the compulsory security of the claim.[1690,1691] Compulsory mortgage is established in the way laid down in the statutory provisions on enforcement and compulsory security.[1692] Detailed rules on the establishment of compulsory mortgage are laid down in the EA.[1693,1694] Compulsory mortgage may be established on immovables whose value may be converted into money. However, as opposed to voluntary mortgage, the object of a compulsory mortgage may not be immovables which, for social reasons, are exempted from enforcement or where enforcement on them is limited (protection of the debtor and his family).[1695,1696]

427. The conditions for the establishment of compulsory mortgage depend on whether a mortgage is established for the security of a monetary claim established in an enforcement decision or a mortgage established for the security of a claim in the final judgment (which has not become enforceable).[1697] The conditions for the establishment of compulsory liens to secure claims specified in an enforcement judgment are the following:

1688. For further details *see* Part VI, Ch. 4, §1. V. Settlement.
1689. The establishment of voluntary judicial or notarial mortgages on immovables requires higher expenses because it involves court proceedings where fees and costs arise depending on the amount of the secured claim. However, the advantages and the benefits of such mortgages for creditors are such that they significantly exceed the initial costs for their establishment.
1690. Article 311/1 PA.
1691. Compulsory mortgage are always established on an immovable of the mortgagor who is a personal debtor and who is obliged to pay the mortgagee's claim. Compulsory mortgage may not be established on immovables owned by a third person who is not at the same time a personal debtor.
1692. Articles 311/1,2 PA.
1693. Articles 295–298, 328–330 EA.
1694. The rules on the establishment of compulsory mortgages are incorporated in separate acts, such as the General Tax Act and the Prevention of Corruption and Organised Crime Act.
1695. Articles 75/1, 91, 241/2 EA.
1696. Dika in *Enforcement Law*, 742–746; Gavella in *Property Law II*, 360–371.
1697. A judgment is final when no ordinary legal remedies (appeals) may be lodged, or when the second-instance court has already decided on an appeal. A judgment is enforceable when the time limit has expired within which the defendant (debtor) could voluntarily, after the finality of the judgment, meet his obligation from the judgment.

- ownership of an immovable in favour of a personal debtor, i.e., the person against whom an enforcement document is drawn up. This person must be entered in the land register as the owner of the immovable charged with a compulsory mortgage;
- court decision on the determination of a security measure for a monetary claim specified in an enforcement judgment. The measure consists of the compulsory establishment of a mortgage on the mortgagor's immovable.[1698] This decision is a legal title for the establishment of a mortgage. It is made by the court, which keeps the ledger where the immovable to be charged by a mortgage is entered.[1699] The decision is made on the creditor's proposal on the basis of an enforcement document establishing the claim whose security is requested;[1700]
- registration of compulsory mortgage in the land register.[1701] The registration is modus of establishment of a compulsory mortgage. It is constitutive for the establishment of a compulsory mortgage.

428. The conditions for the establishment of compulsory mortgage to secure claims established in the final judgment are the following:

- ownership of an immovable in favour of a personal debtor, i.e., a person against whom a final document is written. This person must be entered in the land register as the owner of the immovable encumbered with a compulsory mortgage;
- court decision on the determination of a security measure of a monetary claim specified in the final judgment.[1702] This decision is the legal title for the establishment of a compulsory mortgage. Such a security measure will be allowed on the proposal of the creditor who indicates a probable danger that without such a security measure, the enforcement of the claim established in the final judgment would be made impossible or more difficult;[1703]
- the conditional registration of a compulsory mortgage in the land register;[1704] this is a modus of establishing a compulsory mortgage whereby a mortgage is acquired under the condition of subsequent justification. Conditional registration will be justified when the judgment becomes enforceable. Then, entry will be entered, stating that a claim is enforceable.[1705] With such justification, conditional registration becomes the unconditional registration of a compulsory mortgage.[1706,1707]

1698. Article 296 EA.
1699. Article 295/1 EA.
1700. Article 296 EA.
1701. Article 297/1 EA.
1702. Articles 284–286, 328–330 EA.
1703. Article 328/2 EA.
1704. Article 335/1/1 EA.
1705. Article 297/3 EA.
1706. Article 64LRA.
1707. When a claim becomes enforceable, i.e., when the conditions for enforcement are met, the creditor/mortgagee must, within fifteen days, seek justification of the conditional registration or enforcement. The creditor must submit to the court proof that the judgment has become enforceable. If the creditor fails to do so, on the mortgagee's proposal the conditional registration of the compulsory mortgage will be deleted (Art. 339 EA).

429. The mortgagee, in whose favour a compulsory mortgage on an immovable has been established, is not entitled to the possession of the immovable, nor may he collect the fruits or enjoy any benefits from the immovable.[1708] The mortgagor remains in possession of the immovable even after the establishment of the compulsory mortgage. The same rules applying to the establishment of a voluntary mortgage also apply to the legal relationship between the mortgagee and the mortgagor regarding an immovable encumbered with a compulsory mortgage.[1709]

D. Statutory Mortgages

430. Statutory mortgages are established by the fulfilment of the conditions laid down in a separate law.[1710] They are entered in the land register at the request of a mortgagee.[1711] The entry is of declaratory nature because statutory mortgages are acquired at the moment of the fulfilment of the conditions specified in the law for their existence. By entering a statutory mortgage in the land register, the mortgagee is protected from the possibility of losing it through the operation of the protection of trust in the land register. Pursuant to Article 349 of the PA, a mortgage not entered in the land register terminates when an immovable is acquired by a person who did not know or had no reason to know that a mortgage existed. Therefore, it is beneficial for the mortgagee to request the mortgage to be entered into the land register as soon as all statutory conditions for its acquisition are fulfilled. The entry will be made on the basis of a document proving that the mortgage is acquired on the basis of law.

431. Statutory mortgages on immovables exist only in cases expressly laid down in a separate law. Such cases are very rare in the Croatian legal order. A statutory mortgage exists in the case of co-owners of an immovable acquired as the result of a dissolution of a co-ownership community whereby one co-owner acquires it through the execution of payment for the security of their claims to pay them the values of their co-ownership shares.[1712] The same right is exercised by heirs at the time of the dissolution of a community of heirs by way of payment.[1713]

III. Priority of Mortgages

432. An immovable may be encumbered with several mortgages. When an immovable is encumbered with several mortgages, their mutual relationship is regulated under special rules providing for the priority of the mortgages. This is determined in accordance with the time of the establishment of a mortgage, i.e., the

1708. Article 329/1 PA.
1709. Articles 329–332 et seq. PA.
1710. Article 341/1 PA.
1711. Article 314/2 PA.
1712. Article 51/2 OA.
1713. Gavella in *Property Law II*, 852.

moment when an entry of the mortgage in the land register is sought.[1714,1715,1716] When the same immovable is encumbered with several mortgages, after it is sold, the claims secured by the mortgages will be settled against its value in the order of their establishment. An earlier mortgage, i.e., a mortgage of a higher priority, will take precedence over subsequently established mortgages.[1717] The claim secured by a mortgage established before all other mortgages will have priority of enforcement. Only when a claim secured by a mortgage of the highest priority is settled in full will the claim secured by a mortgage of the next highest priority be settled, and so on.

IV. Transfer of Mortgage

433. In compliance with the principle of accessoriness, a mortgage may not be separated from the claim it secures. When a claim secured by a mortgage is transferred to another person on the basis of any legal title (cession, succession or the like), the mortgage by which the claim is secured also passes to that person.[1718] The mortgage is automatically transferred in favour of the person to whom the claim has been transferred without any particular legal title and without any particular modality of acquisition unless provided otherwise.[1719,1720] The person becomes the new creditor/mortgagee of the claim secured by it without being entered in the land register because the claim has been transferred in his favour. However, in order for the new mortgagee to be able to exercise his rights based on the mortgage transferred together with the claim, the mortgage must first be entered in the land register in his favour.[1721,1722] Prior to requesting an enforcement sale of an immovable in order to have his matured claims settled, the new mortgagee will have to request registration of the mortgage in his favour.[1723]

1714. Article 302/3 PA, Art. 50/1 LRA.
1715. An entry is considered requested when the land register court has received a proposal for registration (Art. 45/1 LRA).
1716. When the land register court receives several proposals for registration of several liens at the same time, all these liens will be of the same rank and will be enforced proportionally (Art. 50/2, 129 LRA).
1717. Article 302/2 PA.
1718. Article 319 PA, Art. 81 OA.
1719. Article 319 PA.
1720. The transfer of the entire secured claim is allowed, as well as its individual particle calculated as a fraction or an amount (Art. /3 LRA). When only one part of the claim is transferred to a new creditor, the creditor will also become the mortgagee whose mortgage secures the part of the claim transferred to him. A mortgage will also continue to exist in favour of the previous mortgagee, but it will secure only the remaining part of the claim not having been transferred.
1721. Article 320/2 PA.
1722. An entry in favour of the new mortgagee has only effects of publicity: it is declared that by the virtue of law, a change of the mortgagee has occurred. Therefore, registration of the new mortgagee does not lead to a change of the mortgage priority. The mortgage continues to have the rank acquired at the time when the first mortgagee was registered, i.e., the priority acquired at the time of the establishment of the mortgage.
1723. Registration will be carried out on the basis of a document proving that the claim secured by a mortgage has been transferred in favour of a new mortgagee (e.g., a contract of cession, a decision on inheritance, etc.).

V. Settlement of a Secured Claim

434. A mortgagee may request the enforcement of a claim against the value of the mortgaged immovable when the claim matures.[1724] The enforcement is carried out against the monetary value achieved by the sale of the mortgaged immovable. The sale of the mortgaged immovable is always carried out by the court (principle of officiality). This rule applies regardless of the type of mortgage. Every mortgage is exercised in court proceedings. The enforcement occurs by a court sale under the rules of the EA, providing for enforcement aimed at settling all monetary claims.[1725] The mortgagee must initiate enforcement proceedings and request that the court sells the immovable. In order to carry our enforcement by the sale of an immovable, it is necessary for the mortgagee to have an enforcement document establishing his claim because enforcement proceedings may only be initiated on the basis of an enforcement document.

435. When an immovable is charged by a voluntary mortgage, at the moment of maturity of the secured claim, the mortgagee does not yet have an enforcement document on the basis of which he could request enforcement against the value of the mortgaged immovable. There are two ways of obtaining an enforcement document. By being at the same time a personal creditor, the mortgagee may sue his debtor and request the payment of the due claim. On the basis of an enforcement judgment by which a personal debtor is ordered to pay a debt, the mortgagee may request settlement against the value of the mortgaged immovable.[1726] Another possibility is that the mortgagee brings a mortgage action against the mortgagor, i.e., an action by which the mortgagor (the owner of the immovable) is requested to settle the secured claim against the value of the immovable.[1727,1728] Through a mortgage action, the mortgagee exercises his right to enforcement against the value of the mortgaged property.[1729] On the basis of an enforcement judgment rendered on the basis of a final and enforceable judgment resulting from a mortgage action, the mortgagee may request enforcement by way of selling the immovable.[1730]

1724. Article 336/1 PA.
1725. Article 336/2 PA, Arts 79–132 EA.
1726. However, this will be possible only if the personal debtor is at the same time also the mortgagor, i.e., if he was the owner of the mortgaged immovable at the time when enforcement was requested.
1727. Article 338/1 PA.
1728. When bringing an action, the mortgagee may request its recordation in the land register file where the mortgaged immovable is entered (Art. 338 PA, Arts 83-85 LRA).
1729. A mortgage action is brought against the person registered as the owner of the mortgaged immovable at the moment the action is brought. If the personal debtor and the mortgagor are not the same person, the mortgagee's only option is to bring a mortgage action in order to obtain an enforcement document on the basis of which enforcement on the immovable may be required.
1730. Enforcement is carried out by means of recordation of enforcement in the land register, by the establishment of the value of the immovable, by its sale and by paying the mortgagee from the amount obtained by the sale (Art. 80 of EA). Any mortgagees who have not initiated enforcement are also satisfied in enforcement proceedings (Art. 86/1 of EA). The value of the immovable involved is established on the basis of an expert's evaluation and on other facts regarding the amount of its market price on the day of assessment (Arts 92/3, 93 of EA). The sale of the mortgaged immovable is carried out in an electronic public auction (Art. 97/1 of EA).

436. When an immovable is charged by a voluntary judicial or notarial mortgage, the mortgagee disposes of an enforcement document from the moment of maturity of the secured claim. An agreement between the mortgagee and the mortgagor on the existence and maturity of the claim secured by a voluntary judicial or notarial mortgage drawn up in the form of a court protocol has the effects of an enforcement document from the moment of maturity of the secured claim.[1731] A notarial act, or a solemnized private document by which a voluntary notarial mortgage is established, has the force of an enforcement document on the day of maturity of the secured claim. Therefore, on the basis of court protocol or a notarial act, the mortgagee may directly request enforcement to settle the secured claim against the value of the mortgaged immovable. The mortgagee need not bring a mortgage action or initiate litigation in order to obtain an enforcement document which is normally the case when voluntary mortgages on immovables are involved. At the moment of maturity of the secured claim, the mortgagee may request the sale of the immovable in enforcement proceedings. On the proposal of the mortgagee, the court will first establish that the parties' agreement has become enforceable and then issue an enforcement decision for the immovable on which a voluntary court/notarial mortgage was established.[1732] The procedure of the court sale of the immovable is carried out under the same rules which apply when a claim secured by a voluntary mortgage is settled.

VI. Termination of Mortgage

437. A mortgage on an immovable may terminate for all the reasons laid down in the PA regarding the termination of any liens. The basic rule is that regardless of the reason for the termination of the mortgage, it terminates when deleted from the land register, i.e., when the registration or conditional registration of deletion is carried out.[1733] The reasons for the deletion of a mortgage may be the destruction of the mortgaged immovable,[1734,1735] a valid waiver by the mortgagee,[1736] the expiration of the time limit or fulfilment of a dissolution condition,[1737] the termination of the secured claim,[1738] the termination of the mortgagee – a legal person without a universal legal successor,[1739] revocation in the depreciation procedure,[1740] relief by

1731. Articles 301/2, 305/1, 308/1 of EA.
1732. Article 305/1 of EA.
1733. Articles 344/5, 345/1, 347/1, 350, 351/2, 352/2, 353 PA.
1734. Article 343 PA.
1735. This reason for the termination of a mortgage is not very likely because an immovable as a land parcel, together with all that is reasonably permanently connected with it, cannot be destroyed. It is possible, however, that an immovable on which a mortgage is established is removed from circulation and can no longer be an object of mortgage. Then the mortgage will be transferred to the compensation the owner of the immovable is entitled to because the immovable has been removed from circulation (Arts 33/2, 301/4 PA).
1736. Article 344 PA.
1737. Article 345 PA.
1738. Article 346 PA.
1739. Article 350 PA.
1740. Article 351 PA.

operation of law or by the decision of an administrative authority,[1741] the finality of a decision revoking the security measures for the establishment of a compulsory mortgage,[1742] the termination of the circumstances due to which a statutory mortgage was established,[1743] and the protection of the trust of another.[1744,1745]

438. The deletion of mortgage is carried out at the request of authorized persons (mortgagee, mortgagor). It is carried out on the basis of a document by which it is proven that all the circumstances have been fulfilled for the termination of a mortgage. When a mortgage is deleted because a claim has terminated, it will be deleted on the basis of a document by which the mortgagee has agreed to its deletion (so-called declaration of deletion). Before the mortgagee agrees to deletion, there can be no registration of deletion, but a conditional registration will be entered on the basis of a document proving that an appropriate amount has been deposited with the court.[1746] A conditional registration of deletion will be justified by the document containing or replacing the mortgagee's assent to the deletion of the mortgage or by a final judgment justifying the conditional registration.[1747]

§2. Judicial or Notarial Security of Claims by Transfer of Ownership

439. The judicial or notarial security of a claim by transfer of ownership is a fiduciary transfer of ownership of an immovable to the creditor to secure his claim.[1748] Ownership is transferred for security before the court or a notary public pursuant to the provisions of Articles 309–327 EA. Compared to other property securities on immovables, this modality of securing claims has a number of advantages which provide for a faster settlement of creditors' claims. Therefore, besides voluntary judicial or notarial mortgages on immovables, the judicial or notarial fiduciary transfer of ownership of an immovable is the most frequent way to ensure property security of claims in Croatian business practice.

440. The judicial or notarial fiduciary transfer of ownership of immovables is carried out on the basis of an agreement between the creditor and the owner of an immovable by which the parties agree that ownership of an immovable will be transferred to the creditor in order to secure a particular claim against the owner of the immovable or any third person.[1749] Such an agreement must be made before the

1741. Article 352 PA.
1742. Article 353/1 PA.
1743. Article 353/2 PA.
1744. Article 349 PA.
1745. A mortgage not entered in the land register terminates when the charged immovable is acquired by a person who did not know and had no sufficient reason to know of its existence.
1746. Article 61LRA.
1747. Article 66 LRA.
1748. Dika in *Enforcement Law*, 784–822; Gavella in *Property Law II*, 496–551.
1749. Dika in *Enforcement Law*, 795; Gavella in *Property Law II*, 528.

competent court in the form of court protocol (judicial fiduciary transfer of ownership)[1750] or in the form of a notarial act (notarial transfer of ownership).[1751] The modus of acquiring fiduciary ownership is the registration of the transfer of ownership to the creditor with a recordation that the transfer is made for the purpose of security.[1752]

441. By entering the fiduciary transfer of ownership, the creditor unconditionally acquires ownership of the immovable which has been transferred. Unless otherwise specified in the agreement, the owner of the immovable is entitled to use the immovable even after the fiduciary transfer of ownership.[1753] The creditor is not entitled to the possession of the immovable whose ownership is transferred to him for security.[1754] If the debtor fulfils his obligation within the time limit, the creditor is obliged to return ownership of the immovable without delay.[1755] The creditor is then bound to issue a document by which he agrees that the fiduciary ownership be deleted and the person who transferred ownership to the creditor for security be entered again as the owner.

442. The advantages of this modality of securing claims become particularly clear when, upon maturity, the creditors' secured claims are not settled. After the maturity of the claim, the creditor does not need to initiate any lawsuit in order to obtain an enforcement document on the basis of which to settle the claim against the value of the immovable. As in the case of a voluntary, judicial or notarial mortgage on immovables, an agreement on the fiduciary transfer of ownership at the time of maturity of a secured claim has the force of an enforcement document on the basis of which the creditor may request enforcement of the claim. However, the settlement proceedings are completely different from those in the case of mortgages. In the case of the fiduciary transfer of ownership, for the settlement of the creditor's claim, the principle of officiality does not apply, according to which a creditor's claim must be settled in court proceedings. In the settlement procedure, an important role is played by a notary public. The creditor and the debtor inform each other through a notary public about their requests, and the notary public is authorized to convert the immovable into money.[1756] If the debtor is late with the fulfilment of the secured claim, the creditor is entitled to ask the debtor to inform him within sixty days whether he agrees for the immovable to be sold through a notary public.[1757] If the debtor does not act in accordance with the creditor's request, or if the notary public does not succeed in selling the immovable within

---

1750. Article 310/1 EA.
1751. Article 327 EA.
1752. Article 312 EA.
1753. Article 315 EA.
1754. The parties may agree that creditor is entitled to possess and use the immovable. Art. 274e/2 EA.
1755. Article 323 EA.
1756. Gavella in *Property Law II*, 534.
1757. Article 322 EA.

three months, the creditor will be deemed to have become the unconditional owner of the immovable for the price which corresponds to the amount of the secured claim with interest and expenses added to it.[1758] By becoming the owner of the immovable, the creditor will actually have settled the claim.

1758. Article 322 EA.

Chapter 5. Security Rights in Movable Property

§1. Pledge (Lien on Movable Property)

I. Concept

443. A pledge is a limited property right on an individual movable which authorizes its holder (pledgee; *založni vjerovnik*) to settle his matured claim against the value of the movable. A pledge may be established as a possessory pledge or a non-possessory pledge. The object of a pledge may be the following:

- an individual movable that may be converted into money,[1759] together with all its appurtenances;[1760]
- proportional (ideal) shares of a movable;[1761,1762]
- the right to fruits derived from a movable by means of a legal relationship (rent, lease);[1763]
- the totality of movables located in a particular space, such as various types of commodities, supplies, spare particles, equipment, tools, etc.[1764,1765]

II. Types of Pledges

A. *Voluntary Pledge (Possessory Pledge)*

444. The voluntary pledge (*ručni zalog*) is established on the basis of a contract aimed at establishing a pledge (a pledge contract; *založni ugovor*) according to the modality laid down by law.[1766,1767] By virtue of a pledge contract, the owner of a movable (pledger; *založni dužnik*) voluntarily charged his movable with a pledge to secure the pledgee's claim against him or a third person. A voluntary pledge may be established on any movables suitable to be converted into money, including movables which, according to the EA, are exempted from enforcement or when enforcement on them is limited.[1768]

1759. Article 298/1 PA.
1760. Article 298/4 PA.
1761. Article 298/1 PA.
1762. Each co-owner of a movable may independently dispose of his proportional share of the movable according to the rules applicable to the owner's legal dispositions of things (Art. 37/5 PA). An owner may thus pledge his proportional share of a movable. Enforcement aimed at the settlement of a secured claim is then carried out on the proportional share of the movable.
1763. Article 298/5 PA.
1764. Article 38 RA.
1765. For further details, *see* Gavella in *Property Law II*, 179–309; Klarić / Vedriš in *Civil Law*, 335, Dika in *Enforcement Law*, 742.
1766. Article 306/1 PA.
1767. Gavella in *Property Law II*, 182–231; Klarić / Vedriš in *Civil Law*, 343–347.
1768. Articles 77, 135 EA.

445. The conditions for the acquisition of a voluntary pledge on movables are the following:

- the pledger's ownership of the movable.[1769] The owner of a movable (pledger) may be a personal debtor, i.e., a person on whom a pledgee has a claim that is secured by a pledged item. The owner of a movable (pledger) may also be a third person who gives his movable as a pledge to secure a debt owed to the pledgee by another person. A person possessing a movable is considered to be its owner.[1770] The possessor is assumed to be the real owner of the movable and is entitled to dispose it off. In order to establish the pledge on a movable, the person who possesses the movable must be its real owner;[1771]
- a valid pledge contract[1772] which is the legal title (titulus) for the establishment of a pledge. It is entered into by the owner of a movable (pledger) and a pledgee. Through a pledge contract, a pledger is bound to surrender a movable into the pledgee's possession, and the pledgee is obliged to keep the movable and return it to the pledger when the claim terminates.[1773] No special form is required for the pledge contract to become valid. A pledge contract is also valid if made orally. Unpermitted stipulations which are contrary to the nature of a pledge may not be incorporated into a pledge contract;[1774]
- the surrender of a movable into the pledgee's possession:[1775] this is a modus of acquisition of a voluntary pledge on a movable. All modalities of the derivative acquisition of the possession of a movable are possible.[1776] Normally, this is the surrender of a movable into the pledgee's direct possession.[1777]

446. A voluntary pledge of a movable may be acquired from a non-owner by the appropriate application of the provisions of the PA on the acquisition of ownership from non-owners.[1778] A pledgee acquires a pledge from a person who possesses

---

1769. Article 306/1 PA.
1770. Article 11/3 PA.
1771. When a movable is co-owned or jointly owned, the pledge of the entire movable may be established only with the consent of all co-owners or joint owners (Art. 306/2 PA). When a co-owner pledges his proportional share of a movable, he does not need the consent of other co-owners (Art. 306/2 PA).
1772. Articles 306/1, 307 PA.
1773. Article 307/1 PA.
1774. For further details on unpermitted stipulations in pledge agreements, *see* the part on voluntary mortgages on immovables. Part VI, Ch. 4, §1. II. A. Voluntary Mortgage.
1775. Article 308/1 PA.
1776. Articles 14, 15 PA.
1777. If a movable is already pledged in favour of another pledgee and surrendered into his possession, a new pledge is acquired in such a way that the pledger informs the first pledgee about the new pledge. Upon the termination of the first pledge, the first pledgee is bound to surrender the movable into the possession of the second pledgee (Art. 308/2 PA). In such a case, the second pledgee acquires the pledge from the moment the first pledgee was informed about the establishment of the second pledge.
1778. Articles 118, 317/1 PA. For more details, *see* Part III, Ch. 2, §4. III. Acquisition of Ownership from Non-owners.

another person's movable if he has entered into a valid pledge contract with that person and if he has acted as a bona fide pledgee (he did not know or did not have sufficient reason to doubt that the possessor was not the owner of the movable). A pledge is acquired from a possessor who is a non-owner at the moment the movable is surrendered into the pledgee's direct possession.

447. Prior to the maturity of the secured claim, the pledgee is entitled to immediate possession of the pledged movable.[1779] The pledgee is bound to maintain the movable.[1780,1781] In principle, the pledgee is not entitled to use the pledged movable unless the pledger has expressly allowed him to do so.[1782,1783] If the pledged movable has some deficiencies due to which its value is insufficient to settle the secured claim, the pledgee may request the pledger to pledge another movable.[1784] The pledgee is entitled to protect his pledge against all third persons. If someone deprives the pledgee of his movable, he is authorized to initiate a lawsuit for its return.[1785] When the claim terminates, the pledgee must without delay return the movable to the pledger.[1786]

B. *Voluntary Judicial or Notarial Pledge (Registered Pledge, Non-possessory Pledge)*

448. A voluntary judicial or notarial pledge (*sudsko ili javno bilježničko dobrovoljno založno pravo na pokretnini*) is a type of voluntary pledge acquired by virtue of a pledge agreement made in the form of court minutes or a notarial act.[1787] A pledge is established in the procedure of judicial security of a monetary claim through the establishment of a pledge based on the parties' agreement under the rules of the EA[1788] or before a notary public.[1789] A voluntary judicial or notarial pledge may be acquired on all movables on which a voluntary pledge may be acquired.

449. The conditions for the establishment of a voluntary judicial or notarial pledge are the following:

1779. Article 321 PA.
1780. Article 322/1 PA.
1781. The pledgee is entitled to compensation of costs for the maintenance of the thing (Art. 322/5 PA).
1782. Article 322/2 PA.
1783. If the pledgee does not properly maintain the pledged movable or uses is illicitly, the pledger may request that the movable be taken away from the pledgee and be given to a third person for maintenance (Art. 324 PA).
1784. Article 326 PA.
1785. Article 328 PA.
1786. Article 322/3 PA.
1787. Gavella in *Property Law II*, 268–283; Klarić / Vedriš in *Civil Law*, 343–347., Dika in *Enforcement Law*, 756–768.
1788. Articles 299–306 EA.
1789. Article 307 EA.

- the pledger's ownership of a movable.[1790] The rules on the derivation of a voluntary pledge from the ownership of a movable apply accordingly to a voluntary judicial or notarial pledge;[1791]
- a pledge contract made in the form of court protocol[1792] or in the form of a notarial act.[1793] This means that a pledge contract must always be made in writing and in the form of a public document. A court protocol or a notarial act has the force of court enforcement;[1794]
- registration of the pledge in the Register of Security Rights in Movables and Patrimonial Rights before a Court or a Notary Public.[1795] An entry in the Register is of a constitutive nature so that a pledge is acquired only after it has been registered.[1796,1797]

450. In the case of a voluntary judicial or notarial pledge, the pledged movable remains in the possession of the pledger (owner of the movable). The pledgee is not entitled to possession of the movable. The provisions of the PA on the legal position of the pledgee in whose favour a voluntary mortgage on an immovable is established apply accordingly to the legal position of the pledgee.[1798] This means that the pledger is entitled to continued possession and use of the pledged movable. The pledger is bound to maintain its value so that upon the maturity of the claim, the pledgee can settle the claim against its value.[1799] However, the pledgee is entitled to protect the pledge against any third person. He may initiate a lawsuit to request that the pledger or any third person avoid actions which diminish the value of the pledged thing.[1800]

451. Voluntary judicial or notarial pledges on movables have a number of practical advantages compared to voluntary pledges on movables. These advantages are expressed both in the phase before the maturity of the claim as well as after it. Before the maturity of the claim, the pledger is in the possession of the pledged movable. He may use the movable, exploit it economically and, in such a way,

1790. Article 306/1 PA.
1791. For more details *see* Part VI, Ch. 5, §1. II. A. Voluntary Pledge (Possessory Pledge).
1792. Articles 312/1 PA, 301 EA.
1793. Article 307 EA.
1794. Article 301/2 EA.
1795. Articles 6/1/1, 17 RA.
1796. The Register of Security Rights in Movables and Patrimonial Rights is maintained by the Financial Agency (FINA). Data on FINA are available at www.fina.hr. The Register is organized as a debtor-based registration system. However, since the Register is kept in electronic form, a search is possible both according to debtors and the encumbered movables and/or rights. Access to the Register is unlimited and is available online at http://zaloznaprava.fina.hr. The Register is based on the filing system of the relevant documentation and a procedure requiring the registrar to verify the legal position publicized through registration and to decide in the form of a court decision on the registration. After an entry has been made in the Register, third parties may not claim ignorance regarding the existence of such registration (Art. 21/4 RA).
1797. A pledge is deemed to have been acquired at the time (day, hour, minute) a proposal for registration is received by the Register (Art. 17/ RA).
1798. Article 329/3 PA.
1799. Article 330 PA.
1800. Article 332 PA.

secure the funds for paying back the debt. The pledgee is not entitled to possession of the movable. He need not take any actions to maintain the pledge, preserve its value, ensure a suitable place for its keeping, and the like. In brief, the pledgee does not bear any costs regarding the pledged thing because all the maintenance costs are borne by the pledger who possesses it. Another important advantage of voluntary judicial or notarial pledges is seen in the phase of the settlement of the matured claim. A pledge agreement made in the form of court protocol or a notarial act, upon the maturity of the claim, has the force of an enforcement document, and the pledgee may immediately, on the basis of that document, request enforcement, i.e., the sale of the pledged item. In such a way, the procedure of the settlement of the secured claim is significantly shortened, and it is not necessary to conduct litigation aimed at obtaining an enforcement document.[1801]

C. Floating Charge

452. The object of voluntary judicial or notarial pledges may be the totality of all movables located in a particular space (floating charge; *lebdeće založno pravo*).[1802,1803] The object of such a pledge is the totality of movables (e.g., a particular kind of commodities, supplies, operating materials, spare particles, furniture, equipment, tools, and the like) located in a particular space (e.g., warehouse, storehouse, silo, plant, business premises, and the like). The pledge is established under the same conditions which apply to the voluntary judicial or notarial pledge of a particular movable.[1804] The pledge is established with an entry in the Register of Security Rights in Movables and Patrimonial Rights,[1805] where it is not necessary to specify individual things but only to give the data on the type of totality of movables and their location.[1806]

453. Movables that are the objects of a pledge remain in the possession of the pledger. He is entitled to alienate individual things from the totality of the movables. The pledge ceases to exist on individual movables that are subject to disposition after they are surrendered to a third person or after they have been removed from the place where they were located.[1807] However, the pledger is bound to replace the alienated or removed movables in order to maintain the value of the totality of the things from which the pledgee will settle his claim.[1808] Upon the maturity of the claim secured with a floating charge, the pledgee's claim is settled

1801. For more details, *see* Part VI, Ch. 5, §1. IV. Settlement.
1802. Article 38 of Register Act.
1803. Gavella in *Property Law II*, 283–294; Klarić / Vedriš in *Civil Law*, 343–347.
1804. For more details *see* Part VI, Ch. 5, §1. II. B. Voluntary Judicial or Notarial Pledge (Registered Pledge, Non-possessory Pledge).
1805. Articles 6/1/2, 38/3 Register Act.
1806. Article 38/2 Register Act.
1807. Article 38/4 Register Act.
1808. Article 38/5 Register Act.

against the value of the thing which, at the time of enforcement, is located in a certain space.[1809] The pledgee always settles his claim against the value of the totality of movables pledged with a floating charge in enforcement proceedings.[1810]

D. Compulsory Pledge

454. A compulsory pledge is established on the basis of an enforcement decision on the enforcement debtor's movables rendered to settle a monetary claim[1811] or on the basis of a decision on the imposition of a preliminary measure to secure a monetary claim.[1812] A compulsory pledge may be established only on movables owned by a personal debtor or a person who is bound to pay the creditor's claim. A compulsory pledge may not be acquired on movables which are excluded from enforcement for the sake of the protection of the pledger's basic needs.[1813] The conditions for the establishment of compulsory pledges depend on whether they are established on the basis of an enforcement decision or as a separate measure of securing a monetary claim established by a final judgment.[1814]

455. The conditions for establishing a compulsory pledge on the basis of an enforcement decision are the following:

(1) ownership of a movable by a personal debtor against whom the creditor has initiated enforcement proceedings for the settlement of a monetary claim.[1815] One of the enforcement activities in enforcement proceedings conducted for the settlement of a monetary claim (including claims not secured by a pledge) is the establishment of a compulsory pledge of a movable that will be sold in enforcement proceedings in order for the claim of the pledgee to be settled;
(2) an enforcement decision on the pledger's movables aimed at the enforcement of a monetary claim;[1816] this decision is the legal title (titulus) for the establishment of a pledge. It is rendered on the proposal of the creditor who seeks enforcement of a claim from the sale of the debtor's movables; and
(3) seizure of a movable that will be sold in enforcement proceedings: with the seizure of a movable, the creditor who has initiated enforcement proceedings

1809. Article 38/6 Register Act.
1810. In the case of the bankruptcy of the pledger, the pledgee has a separate satisfaction right on the pledged totality of things, i.e., the right to a separate settlement before bankruptcy creditors (Art. 38/7 Register Act).
1811. Article 311 PA, Art. 161 EA.
1812. Articles 322, 335 EA.
1813. Article 135 EA.
1814. Dika in *Enforcement Law*, 483–529; Gavella in *Property Law II*, 235–266.
1815. The pledger is deemed to be the owner of movables that are located in his immovable property, flat or business premises (Art. 138/4 EA). Spouses are deemed to be the co-owners of identical particle of all movables found in their house, business premises or any other immovable property (Art. 138/5 EA).
1816. Article 41 EA.

acquires a compulsory pledge on the movable.[1817,1818,1819] Seizure is considered to be a modus for the acquisition of a pledge. On the proposal of the creditor/pledgee, a compulsory pledge is entered in the Register of Security Rights in Movables and Patrimonial Rights.[1820] The entry is only of a declarative nature because the pledge is already acquired from the moment of seizure.

456. The conditions for the establishment of compulsory pledges to secure monetary claims established by final judgments are the following:

- ownership of a movable by a personal debtor against whom a final judgment has been rendered ordering the obligation to repay the debt;
- decision on the imposition of a measure aimed at securing a monetary claim established in a final judgment.[1821] This decision is the legal title for the establishment of a compulsory pledge. It is rendered on the proposal of the creditor who indicates the probable danger that without the establishment of the compulsory pledge, the settlement of his claim would be impossible or significantly more difficult;[1822]
- seizure of a movable[1823] carried out in accordance with the rules on enforcement against movables: seizure is a modus for the acquisition of a compulsory pledge. On the proposal of the creditor/pledgee, a compulsory pledge is entered in the Register of Security Rights in Movables and Proprietary Rights.[1824] The entry is only of a declaratory nature because a pledge is acquired at the moment of seizure.

E. Statutory Pledge

457. A statutory pledge on movables is established with the fulfilment of the conditions laid down in a separate act.[1825] A statutory pledge is acquired only exceptionally. For example, when a community of co-owners is dissolved by way of settlement, the co-owners who must be paid in proportion to their co-ownership shares have a statutory pledge on a thing which belongs to the co-owner seeking termination until the payment is executed.[1826] A statutory pledge does not authorize

1817. Articles 135–143 EA.
1818. Listed movables are taken from the debtor's/pledger's possession and given to the creditor/pledgee or a third person for safekeeping (Art. 140 EA).
1819. If enforcement is conducted on a motor vehicle, a compulsory pledge is acquired with the registration of enforcement in the register of motor vehicles kept by the police administration (Art. 161/4 EA).
1820. Articles 6/1/1, 16 Register Act.
1821. Articles 331–339 EA.
1822. Article 332/2 EA.
1823. Articles 335/1/2, 300/1/3 EA.
1824. Articles 6/1/1, Art. 16 Register Act.
1825. Article 314 PA.
1826. Article 51/2 PA.

its holder to have possession of the movable. Possession of the pledged movable remains with the pledger even after the establishment of the statutory pledge.[1827,1828]

III. Priority of Pledges

458. The mutual relationship of several pledges of the same movable is determined according to the order of their establishment. A pledge obtains its rank of priority at the moment of establishment or when all the conditions required for its establishment are met.[1829] The order of establishment of pledges involving the same movable is also important for the enforcement of claims secured by pledges. The enforcement of secured claims against the value of a movable will be made in the order of their establishment. Priority in enforcement is given to the claim for which a pledge is established before all others.[1830] All pledges, regardless of the legal title of their establishment and regardless of whether they are possessory or non-possessory, registered or non-registered pledges, have a common order of priority.

IV. Enforcement

459. According to the principle of officiality, the conversion of the pledged movable into money for the enforcement of the claim is carried out in court proceedings according to the rules on enforcement involving movables.[1831] The sale of movables is carried out in accordance with the rules referred to in Articles 148–165 of the EA. For the purpose of the sale of a pledged movable, the pledgee must have an enforcement document ordering the pledger to pay the secured claim. In the case of a voluntary pledge, the pledgee will first have to initiate a lawsuit to receive a judgment on the basis of which enforcement proceedings can be conducted to settle the secured claim against the value of the pledged movable. In the case of a voluntary judicial or a notarial pledge, the pledgee disposes of an enforcement document from the moment the secured claim matures. A pledge agreement made in the form of a judicial or a notarial document has the force of an enforcement document from the moment the secured claim matures.[1832] Therefore, the pledgee may not directly request an enforcement sale on the basis of a judicial or notarial document containing a pledge agreement. The procedure of settlement in the case of a voluntary judicial or notarial pledge is thus much shorter and faster. This is why a voluntary judicial or notarial pledge is, in practice, the most frequent property security on movables.

1827. Article 321/4 PA.
1828. For more details, *see* Gavella in *Property Law II*, 294–303.
1829. Article 302/3 PA.
1830. Article 302/2 PA.
1831. Article 336/2 PA, Arts 133–170 EA.
1832. Articles 300/2, 305, 308 EA.

460. The settlement of a claim against the value of a pledged item may exceptionally also be conducted out of court. An out-of-court settlement is carried out in cases where the voluntary pledge is established and where the pledger, at the moment of the establishment of a pledge or later, expressly agrees in writing to an out-of-court settlement.[1833] If the secured claim arises from a commercial contract, the pledger does not need to expressly agree to an out-of-court settlement. In that case, the pledgee is already entitled by law to sell the movable in an out-of-court auction. However, the pledger may expressly exclude such a settlement at the moment of the establishment of a pledge.[1834] When a pledgee is entitled to settle his claim out of court, he must organize a public auction.[1835] The public auction does not need to be organized if the movable has its stock market or market price. In that case, the pledgee may sell the movable through a person authorized to sell things on the stock market or to sell such things on the market.[1836]

V. Termination

461. A pledge terminates with the destruction of the movable,[1837] with the pledgee's waiver,[1838] with the termination of the secured claim,[1839] with the expiry or fulfilment of conditions,[1840] with the termination of a pledgee who does not have a legal successor,[1841] or with a decision abolishing the security measures imposed in enforcement proceedings.[1842] In any case, when a pledge terminates, an obligation arises for the pledgee to return the movable which is in his possession to the pledger (e.g., in the case of a voluntary pledge) or to agree to the removal of the pledge from the Register (e.g., in the case of a voluntary judicial or notarial pledge).[1843]

§2. Judicial or Notarial Security of Claims by Transfer of Ownership (Registered Fiduciary Transfer of the Ownership of Movables)

462. Judicial or notarial security by means of the transfer of ownership of a movable is the fiduciary transfer of ownership of a movable aimed at securing a pledgee's claim. The same rules laid down in the EA regulating the fiduciary transfer of ownership of immovables also apply to the fiduciary transfer of ownership of

1833. Article 337/1 PA.
1834. Article 337/2 PA.
1835. Article 337/ PA.
1836. Article 337/4 PA.
1837. Article 343 PA.
1838. The pledgee is deemed to have waived the pledge when he unconditionally returns the pledged movable to the pledger (Art. 344/2 PA).
1839. Article 346 PA.
1840. Article 345 PA.
1841. Article 350 PA.
1842. Article 353 PA.
1843. Article 36/1/2 Register Act.

movables.[1844] The judicial or notarial transfer of ownership of a movable for security is carried out on the basis of an agreement made between the pledgee and the owner of the movable (a personal debtor or a third person) in which the parties agree that ownership of a particular movable is transferred to the pledgee to secure his claim. The agreement must be made in the form of court protocol or a notarial act.[1845] The object of a fiduciary transfer may be any movable that may be an object of sale, including movables that are exempted from enforcement. On the basis of such an agreement, fiduciary ownership is acquired by an entry of the transfer of ownership in favour of the pledgee in the Register of Security Rights in Movables and Patrimonial Rights.[1846] Entry in the Register is of a constitutive nature for the acquisition of fiduciary ownership.[1847]

463. After the ownership of a movable for the purpose of security has been transferred to a pledgee, the pledgee becomes the unconditional owner of the movable, and the pledger retains possession of it. The pledger is entitled to continue possessing and using the movable.[1848,1849] When the pledger settles the claim, the pledgee is bound to return the ownership of the movable. It is returned in such a way that fiduciary ownership is deleted from the Register. The pledgee is bound to agree that his fiduciary ownership will be deleted from the Register.[1850]

464. The legal position of a creditor to whom ownership of a movable is transferred to secure a monetary claim is significantly more favourable than the legal position of a pledgee. Once the claim secured by the fiduciary transfer of ownership of a movable matures, the creditor settles his claim out of court through a notary public. The settlement may be requested immediately upon the maturity of the claim. The judicial or notarial document regulating the fiduciary transfer of ownership has the force of a court enforcement, and, at the moment of maturity, it becomes an enforcement document on the basis of which enforcement may be sought.[1851] Enforcement is carried out under the same rules that apply to the settlement of a creditor to whom ownership of an immovable is transferred as security.[1852] If a notary public does not succeed in selling the movable in three months, the pledgee becomes the rightful owner of the movable[1853] and the secured claim is settled.[1854]

1844. Articles 309–327 EA.
1845. Articles 310, 327 EA.
1846. Article 6/1/3 Register Act.
1847. Dika in *Enforcement Law*, 783–822; Gavella in *Property Law II*, 496–551.
1848. Article 274e PA.
1849. However, the parties may expressly agree that the pledgee will possess and use the movable (Art. 315/1,2 EA). This is why an agreement needs to be made in the form of a public or a private document with the certified signature of the pledger.
1850. Article 36/1/2 Register Act.
1851. Article 310/4 EA.
1852. For more details *see* Part VI, Ch. 4, section Judicial od Notarial Security of Claim by Transfer of Ownership.
1853. Article 322/7 EA.
1854. For more details, *see* Dika in *Enforcement Law*, 783–822.

Chapter 6. Security Rights on Patrimonial Rights

§1. PLEDGES ON PATRIMONIAL RIGHTS

I. Concept

465. A pledge on a patrimonial right (*založno pravo na pravu*) is a limited property right authorizing its holder (pledgee) to settle a claim against the value of the patrimonial right which the holder (pledger) of that right is bound to suffer. In order for a patrimonial right to be the subject matter of a pledge, it must be a right that is in circulation and suitable to be converted into money so that the pledgee can settle his claims against its value.[1855] Rights, as objects of pledges, are equated with things, movables or immovables. The rules on pledges on movables, and mortgages on immovables, apply accordingly to pledges on rights unless it is otherwise stipulated for pledges on rights or unless it arises differently from their legal nature.

466. The object of a pledge may be the following:

- a patrimonial right which is suitable for the settlement of a monetary claim (claims, shares, stocks in companies, rights arising from securities, easements, usufruct, and the like);[1856]
- proportional shares of a patrimonial right;
- fruits arising from a patrimonial right by means of a legal transaction (e.g., interest on savings).[1857]

II. Types of Pledges on Rights

A. *Voluntary Pledges*

467. A voluntary pledge (*dobrovoljno založno pravo na pravu*) on a patrimonial right is established on the basis of a contract aimed at the establishment of a pledge on rights (a pledge contract) in the way prescribed by law.[1858,1859] With a pledge contract, the pledger (holder of a patrimonial right) voluntarily charged his patrimonial right with a pledge to secure the pledgee's claim against him or against a third person. The object of a voluntary pledge may be any patrimonial rights suitable to

1855. Gavella in *Property Law II*, 387–462.
1856. Besides the patrimonial right, the subject matters of the pledge are also all appurtenances to this right, as well as the right to the fruits derived by means of a legal relationship.
1857. Article 298/5 PA.
1858. Article 306/1, 310 PA.
1859. Gavella in *Property Law II*, 389–422; Klarić / Vedriš in *Civil Law*, 343–347, Dika in *Enforcement Law*, 756–768.

be converted into money, including those that, according to the EA, are excluded from enforcement or when their enforcement is limited for the sake of the protection of the pledger's basic needs.[1860]

468. The conditions for the establishment of voluntary pledges on rights are the following:

- a patrimonial right which belongs to the pledger; a pledge is derived from the patrimonial right of the pledger, as is the case with a pledge on a movable or a lien on an immovable derived from the ownership of a thing.[1861] A pledge on a patrimonial right may only be acquired from a person who is its holder;
- a valid pledge contract;[1862] a pledge agreement is the legal title (titulus) for the establishment of a pledge on the patrimonial right. It is entered into by the holder of a patrimonial right (pledger) and the pledgee. The pledger is bound by a pledge contract to transfer his right as security. The pledgee is bound to return the right to the pledger when the claim is settled.[1863] No special form is required to ensure the validity of a pledge contract concerning a patrimonial right which is equated with a movable. However, in order for a pledge contract concerning a patrimonial right equated with an immovable to be valid, a written form is required. It is not permitted to incorporate provisions which are contrary to the nature of a pledge;[1864]
- a corresponding modus of the acquisition of a pledge on a patrimonial right.[1865] The modus of the establishment of pledges on rights depends on the type of patrimonial right that is pledged and on whether the pledge is incorporated into the security. A pledge on a claim is established by the assignment of claim for reasons of security, with an obligation to inform the debtor's debtor about the assignment. A pledge on a right arising from securities issued to a particular name is established by assignment for reasons of security, and the debtor (cesus) must be informed about the assignment.[1866] A pledge on the right arising from securities made out to the holder is acquired by the transfer of that paper to the pledgee for security.[1867] A pledge on a right arising from a security made out on order is

1860. Articles 172, 173 EA.
1861. Article 306/1 PA.
1862. Articles 306/1, 307 PA.
1863. Article 307/1 PA.
1864. For more details *see* Part VI, Ch. 4, §1. II. A. Voluntary Mortgage.
1865. Article 310 PA.
1866. A contract of assignment is a contract by which a creditor transfers his alienable claim to another person. This is regulated in Arts 80–89 of the OA. Assignment for reasons of security is the assignment to secure the assignee's claim against the assignor. The assignee undertakes to take care, with the diligence of a conscientious businessman, of the collection of the assigned claim, and, having deducted the amount necessary for settling the secured claim, to deliver the excess to the assignor (Art. 89 OA).
1867. The rules of the OA on the transfer of the pledged movable to the possession of the pledgee apply accordingly.

acquired by endorsement.[1868] Pledges on other patrimonial rights equated with movables (patents, technical advancements, benefits arising from author's rights) are transferred in the way envisaged for the transfer of rights unless otherwise established by law. A pledge on rights arising from an entry in the public register where no security is issued (such as non-materialized securities) is acquired by an entry in the register.[1869] A pledge on the right on an immovable (the right to build) is acquired by an entry in the land register, i.e., by registration or conditional registration.[1870]

469. As a rule, a voluntary pledge on a patrimonial right may not be acquired from a person who is not its holder.[1871] Exceptions to this rule are envisaged for the acquisition of pledges on the rights arising from securities made out to the holder.[1872] In this case, the rules on the protection of trust in the acquisition of a pledge on movables from non-owners will be applied.[1873,1874] Another exception is the acquisition of a pledge on the right entered into a public register (e.g., the land register). The acquirers of pledges on rights entered in public register acquire pledges on registered rights also from a person who is not their holder, although entered as such in the public register. The protection of trust has an effect on a bona fide acquirer of a pledge on a registered right so that he acquires the pledge, although the registered holder of the pledged right is not its real holder.

470. The pledgee's rights in relation to pledged rights depend on the nature of this right. A pledgee who has a voluntary pledge on a right which is equal to a movable has in relation to that right the same powers as if he had a pledge on a movable.[1875] A pledgee who has a pledge on a right which is equal to the immovable has powers as if he had a mortgage on an immovable.[1876,1877] Separate rules are envisaged for the powers of a pledgee who has a pledge on the claim. The pledgee

1868. A pledge endorsement is a written statement given by the holder of a right arising from a security (e.g., a bill of exchange payable to order, a cheque payable to order) by which the right is transferred to the pledgee for pledging. Pledge endorsements are regulated by the Bills of Exchange Act (OG 74/94, 92/10) and the Cheques Act (OG No. 74/94).

1869. Non-materialized securities are an electronic record on the securities account in the computer system of the Central Depository Clearing Company Inc. (www.skdd.hr) by which the issuer is bound to fulfil the content of non-materialized securities in favour of the owner (Art. 531/1 of the Capital Market Act OG 65/18, 17/20). The Central Depository Clearing Company Inc. is a legal person authorized to carry out the activities of a depository of non-materialized securities. A pledge on non-materialized securities is established by a corresponding entry of the pledge on the account of non-materialized securities by virtue of a valid pledge contract. Only a single pledge may be acquired on a non-materialized security. The pledgee's claim is settled in out-of-court proceedings (Art. 531/2 of the Capital Market Act).

1870. All the rules of land register law on the entry of real rights on immovables in the land register apply accordingly to the entry of such a pledge.

1871. Gavella in *Property Law II*, 392.

1872. The holder of a security is presumed to be the authorised person for the rights incorporated in the security.

1873. Article 317/1 PA.

1874. Gavella in *Property Law II*, 401.

1875. Article 333/1 PA.

1876. Article 33/2 PA.

is bound to take the necessary measures for the protection of the pledged claim.[1878] If the pledged claim yields interest or some other occasional revenues, the pledgee is bound to collect them.[1879] When the pledged claim matures, the pledgee is entitled to and is bound to do what is necessary for its fulfilment and to receive the performance.[1880] The pledgee is entitled to request the fulfilment of the pledged claim.[1881] Upon the performance of the pledged claim, the lien passes to the thing used to perform the claim. When the pledgee receives money for the performance of the pledged claim, and the secured claim (a claim secured by a pledge on the patrimonial right) has not yet matured, the pledgee is bound to deposit the received money with the court.[1882]

471. When the claim secured by a pledge on a right is performed, or when the claim terminates in any other way, the pledgee is bound to return the pledged claim to the pledger. The claim is returned by so-called reverse assignment.[1883]

B. Voluntary Judicial or Notarial Pledges (Registered Pledges)

472. Voluntary judicial or notarial pledges on rights are voluntary pledges on patrimonial rights acquired on the basis of a pledge contract made in the form of a court protocol or a notarial act. A pledge is established in the procedure of the establishment of court security of a monetary claim on the basis of an agreement of the parties under the rules of the EA[1884] or before a notary public.[1885] Voluntary judicial or notarial pledges may be established on all patrimonial rights on which a voluntary pledge on a right is established, including the rights exempted from enforcement for the sake of the protection of the basic needs of the pledger.

473. The conditions for the establishment of voluntary judicial or notarial pledges are the following:

- a patrimonial right belonging to the pledger; the rules on the derivation of a voluntary pledge from the patrimonial right of the pledger apply accordingly;[1886]

1877. The rules regulating pledges on movables will thus apply accordingly to pledged claims (bank savings). Concerning lien on rights to build, the rules on mortgage on immovables apply accordingly because the right to build is equal to an immovable (Art. 280/2 PA).
1878. Article 334/1 PA.
1879. The value of the interest will be set off against the pledgee's costs, then against the interest owed to him by the pledgee, and finally against the principal (Art. 334/2 PA).
1880. Article 334/3 PA.
1881. Article 335/PA.
1882. Article 334/4 PA.
1883. Gavella in *Property Law II*, 409.
1884. Articles 299–306 EA.
1885. Article 307 EA.
1886. For more details, *see* Part VI, Ch. 6, §1. Voluntary Pledge.

- a valid pledge contract made in the form of court protocol[1887] or in the form of a notarial act;[1888] Regardless of whether the pledged right is equal to a movable or an immovable, a written form is always necessary;
- registration of the pledge in the Register of Security Rights in Movables and Patrimonial Rights before a Court or a Notary Public[1889] or in the Central Depository Clearing Company Inc.[1890] An entry into a public register is of a constitutive nature so that the pledge is established only upon registration.[1891]

C. Compulsory Pledges

474. A compulsory pledge on a right is established on the basis of a court decision in enforcement proceedings and in the proceedings of compulsory security under the rules of the EA.[1892] A court decision on the establishment of a compulsory pledge on a right is rendered against the will of the pledger.[1893] A compulsory pledge on a right may be established only on patrimonial rights whose holder is a person who is at the same time also a personal debtor of the creditor/pledgee whose claim is secured. The subject matter of the pledge may be any patrimonial right belonging to the debtor which is suitable for the compulsory settlement of the pledgee's claim (monetary claim, salary, a bank account claim, shares, non-materialized securities, and the like). A compulsory pledge may not be established on the debtor's rights that are exempted from enforcement under the rules of the EA.[1894]

475. The conditions for the establishment of a compulsory pledge in enforcement proceedings are the following:

- a patrimonial right which must belong to a personal debtor against whom the creditor/pledgee has an enforcement document for the settlement of a particular claim;
- an enforcement decision by which the court orders enforcement on a patrimonial right of the debtor for the settlement of the pledgee's claim.[1895] An enforcement decision is a legal title for the establishment of the pledge;
- seizure of the debtor's claim or of some other patrimonial right belonging to the debtor.[1896] By means of the seizure, the pledgee acquires a pledge on the debtor's claim, or on some other right. The modality of seizure depends on the type of the

1887. Article 313/1 PA, Art. 301 EA.
1888. Article 307 EA.
1889. Articles 6/1/1, 17 RA.
1890. Article 531 of the Capital Market Act.
1891. The pledge is deemed to have been established at the time (day, hour, minute) when a proposal for an entry is received at the Register (Art. 17/2 Register Act).
1892. Article 311 of OA, Arts 176/2, 335 EA.
1893. Dika in *Enforcement Law*, 529–559, 614–655; Gavella in *Property Law II*, 422–456.
1894. Articles 172, 173 EA.
1895. Article 41 EA.
1896. Articles 176/3, 183, 230/1, 235/1, 239 EA.

debtor's patrimonial right, which is subject to enforcement.[1897] Compulsory pledges on rights acquired in enforcement proceedings are entered in the Register of Security Rights in Movables and Patrimonial Rights before a Court or a Notary Public on the pledgee's proposal or by a court order,[1898] but such an entry is only of a declaratory nature.

476. The conditions for the establishment of compulsory pledges on rights in the security procedure are the following:

- a patrimonial right which belongs to a personal debtor against whom the creditor has a final document for the collection of a particular claim;
- a decision on the imposition of a security measure on a monetary claim established in a final judgment.[1899] This decision is the legal title for the establishment of a compulsory pledge on a right. It is rendered on the proposal of the creditor, who indicates the probable danger that the realization of the claim would be made impossible or significantly more difficult without such security;[1900]
  the seizure of the debtor's claim or any other patrimonial right.[1901] The modality of seizure differs and is carried out according to the rules governing seizure on the establishment of a compulsory pledge on a right on the basis of an enforcement decision.

477. The pledgee, in whose favour a compulsory pledge on a right is established, is not entitled to enforce the pledged right in any way. However, a compulsory pledge on a right imposes specific duties on the pledger's debtor, i.e., on the person who owes the pledged claim to the pledger. This person is prohibited from paying the due claim to the pledger or to any third person. The pledger is likewise prohibited from disposing of the pledged claim (e.g., transferring it to other persons).[1902,1903]

1897. For example, seizure of a claim is carried out by delivering the enforcement decision to the pledger's debtor, by which the fulfilment of the pledger's (debtor's) monetary claim is prohibited, and the pledger is prohibited from collecting the claim, or from otherwise disposing of a claim charged by a pledge (Art. 176/1 EA). The seizure of a claim secured by a lien entered in a public register is carried out by being entered in that register (Art. 183 EA).The seizure of a claim involving a bank account is carried out by delivering the enforcement decision to the bank (Art. 178 EA). The seizure of a share for which no document has been issued is carried out by delivering the enforcement decision to the joint-stock company which keeps the book of shares (Art. 230/1 EA). The seizure of a non-materialized security is carried out by delivering the enforcement decision to the Central Depository / Clearing Company Inc. (Art. 235/1 EA), etc.

1898. Articles 6/1/1, 16 Register Act.

1899. Articles 332–339 EA.

1900. Article 332/2 EA.

1901. Articles 335/1/2, 300/1/4-12 EA.

1902. For more details, *see* Dika in *Enforcement Law*, 534.

1903. Articles 176 et seq. EA.

D. Statutory Pledges on Rights

478. A statutory pledge on a right is established only when it is so regulated by a separate act. It is established upon the fulfilment of the conditions laid down in a separate act.[1904] For the establishment of such a pledge, no registration in a public register is necessary.

III. Priority of Pledges

479. The mutual relationship of several pledges on the same right is regulated by order of their establishment. A pledge on a right is given its rank of priority at the moment of establishment, i.e., when all the conditions for the establishment of pledges are fulfilled. These conditions vary and depend on the type of pledges on rights.[1905] A single order of priority is established for all pledges on the same rights regardless of the type of particular pledge. Pledges established on the same right are collected in the order of their establishment. No pledge on a right, regardless of its legal title, has priority of enforcement.

IV. Enforcement

480. When a claim secured by a pledge on a right matures, the pledgee is entitled to settle his claim against the value of the pledged right, against the proceeds of the right (interest and other occasional revenues), against the proceeds of the fulfilment of the right or against what is received as compensation for the right. The settlement of a pledgee‘s claim against the value of the pledged right is, as a rule, governed by the principle of officiality. The settlement is carried out in enforcement proceedings conducted by the court.[1906] Enforcement against the value of the pledged right by enforcement may be sought on the basis of an enforcement document (judgment) by which the pledger is ordered to suffer the settlement against the value of the pledged right. In the case of voluntary judicial or notarial pledges on rights, a pledge agreement is made in the form of a judicial or notarial document and has the force of a court enforcement.[1907] The pledgee does not need to initiate a lawsuit in order to obtain an enforcement document but may seek an enforcement sale based on a certificate showing that the parties‘ agreement on the establishment of the pledge has become enforceable. The modality of collection depends on the nature of the pledged right.[1908]

1904. Article 314 PA.
1905. Article 302/3 PA.
1906. Article 336/2 PA.
1907. Gavella in *Property Law II*, 461.
1908. A claim secured by a pledge on a monetary claim is settled by the transfer of the monetary claim to the pledgee, so-called enforcement assignment (Arts 184–197 EA). On the pledgee's request, the court may order a transfer of claim for collection or instead of payment (Art. 186/2 EA). With a transfer of claim for collection, the pledgee is entitled to request the pledger's debtor to pay the amount specified in the enforcement decision (Art. 189 EA). With the transfer of claim instead of

481. An out-of-court settlement against the value of pledges is possible only in exceptional cases. A voluntary pledge on a right which is made equal to a movable may be enforced by an out-of-court settlement if all the conditions are fulfilled under which an out-of-court settlement may be carried out on a pledged movable.[1909,1910] When a monetary claim is the object of a pledge, the claim of the pledgee may be settled out of court against the money received for the purpose of settlement of the pledged claim. Once the pledgee's monetary claim subject to the pledge is paid by the pledger's debtor, the pledgee is entitled to keep the amount of money owed to him.[1911]

V. Termination

482. A pledge on a right terminates on the basis of the same legal foundations as in the case of any other pledges, such as the pledgee's waiver,[1912] the expiration of the time limit for the fulfilment of conditions,[1913] the termination of the secured claim,[1914] the termination of the pledgee who loses legal personality and does not have a legal successor,[1915] and a decision abolishing the security measures imposed in enforcement proceedings.[1916] If the pledge on a right is entered in a public register, it will terminate only upon deletion from the register.[1917] When a voluntary pledge on a right transferred to the pledgee has terminated, the pledgee is bound to return the pledged right to the pledger (reverse assignment).

§2. JUDICIAL OR NOTARIAL SECURITY BY TRANSFER OF RIGHTS (REGISTERED FIDUCIARY TRANSFER OF RIGHTS)

483. Judicial or notarial security by the transfer of rights is a fiduciary transfer of rights to secure a particular creditor's claim.[1918] The same rules apply as in the

payment, the pledgee acquires the debtor's claim (Art. 195 EA). A claim secured by a pledge on a salary or other monetary income is settled by issuing an order to the employer to pay the pledgee the amount for which enforcement is determined (Art. 197 EA). A claim secured by a pledge on a claim involving a bank account by ordering that a certain amount be paid to the pledgee is regulated in Arts 3/1/7 and 11 of the Act on the Execution of Enforcement on Financial Means (OG No. 91/2010). The enforcement of a claim secured by a pledge on non-materialized securities is performed by the sale of non-materialized securities (Art. 234 EA).

1909. Article 337 PA.
1910. For more details *see* Part VI, Ch. 5, §1. IV. Enforcement.
1911. Article 334/4/sentence 2 PA.
1912. Article 344 PA.
1913. Article 345 PA.
1914. Article 346 PA.
1915. Article 350 PA.
1916. Article 353 PA.
1917. Article 36 RA.
1918. Dika in *Enforcement Law*, 784–822; Gavella in *Property Law II*, 496–551.

case of the fiduciary transfer of ownership of immovables or movables.[1919] The judicial or notarial transfer of rights for security is carried out on the basis of an agreement made between the creditor and the holder of a right (a personal debtor or a third person) whereby the parties agree that a particular right is transferred to the creditor to secure a particular claim. The agreement must be made in the form of a court protocol or a notarial act.[1920] The object of a fiduciary transfer of rights may be all patrimonial rights that may be converted into money, including rights excluded from enforcement. Monetary claims, financial means in bank accounts, and stocks and shares in companies may also be the objects of a fiduciary transfer of rights. A creditor acquires security through a fiduciary transfer of a right at the moment of registration in the Register of Security Rights in Movables and Patrimonial Rights Before a Court or a Notary Public.[1921]

484. After a claim has been transferred to a creditor, the creditor is bound to take measures necessary for the maintenance of the transferred claim and collect any interest or other occasional claims.[1922,1923] The creditor is bound to collect the transferred claim upon its maturity.[1924,1925] When stocks or shares of a joint-stock company are transferred to the creditor, the debtor does not lose the right to vote or the right to share in the profit unless the parties have agreed otherwise.[1926] If the debtor pays the claim secured by a fiduciary transfer of right, the creditor is bound to return (re-transfer) the right to the debtor.[1927]

485. When a claim secured by a fiduciary transfer of right matures, the creditor settles his claim out of court through a notary public.[1928] The settlement may be requested immediately upon maturity of the secured claim by virtue of a pledge agreement made in the form of a court protocol or a notarial act because these documents are deemed to be enforcement documents from the moment the secured claim matures. The settlement is carried out under the same rules which regulate the settlement of a fiduciary owner of an immovable or a movable. If the notary public does not succeed in converting the right into money in three months, the creditor

1919. Articles 309–327 EA.
1920. Articles 310, 327 EA.
1921. Article 6/1/3 RA.
1922. Articles 320/1/1,2 EA.
1923. These claims are compensated against the amount of secured claim, interest or the expenses for its collection (Art. 320/1/2 EA).
1924. Article 320/1/3 EA.
1925. If the object of the claim is an immovable or a movable, the creditor is in the position of a creditor to whom ownership of the immovable or the movable is transferred as security. If the object of a claim is money, the creditor is bound to deposit the money with the court or a notary public. However, if the secured claim has matured, the creditor may keep the owed amount of money (Art. 320/3 EA).
1926. Article 326/3 EA.
1927. Article 323 EA.
1928. Article 322 EA.

becomes the unconditional holder of the right,[1929] and thereby, the settlement of the secured claim also occurs.[1930]

1929. Article /322/7 EA.
1930. For more details, *see* Dika in *Enforcement Law*, 783–822.

Selected Bibliography

Bagić, Snježana. Denationalization: Current Issues in Practice; Hrvatska gospodarska revija:časopis za ekonomiju i pravo: 47(1998), 7; pp. 872–880 (78–86) (original in Croatian).

Bagić, Snježana. The Law on Expropriation; Aktualnosti hrvatskog zakonodavstva i pravne prakse: (1999), 6; pp. 365–385 (original in Croatian).

Belaj, Vladimir. Establishment, Protection and Cessation of Right to Build; Pravni vjesnik: 19 (2003),1-2; pp. 9–24 (original in Croatian).

Belaj, Vladimir. Performance of Rights and Obligations on a Separate Part of Real Property; (original in Croatian) Zbornik Pravnog fakulteta Sveučilišta u Rijeci: 27(2006), 1; pp. 345–370.

Borić Tomislav. Ownership and Privatization in Croatia and Hungary, Berlin, 1996 (original in Croatian).

Brežanski, Jasna/ The Protection of Property Rights; Zbornik Pravnog fakulteta Sveučilišta u Rijeci: 23(2002), 1; pp. 295–333 (original in Croatian).

Brežanski, Jasna. Some Issues of Real Servitude and Neighboring Rights on Construction Land; Zbornik Pravnog fakulteta Sveučilišta u Rijeci: 18(1997),1; str.215–234.; (original in Croatian).

Brežanski, Jasna. Building on Another's Ground; Zbornik Pravnog fakulteta Sveučilišta u Rijeci: 19(1998), 2; pp. 505–525 (original in Croatian).

Brežanski, Jasna. Law on Lease and Sale of Business Premises-Aplication in Practice; Zbornik Pravnog fakulteta Sveučilišta u Rijeci: 26(2005), 1; pp. 527–587 (original in Croatian).

Brežanski, Jasna. Lease – a Protected Tenant Status: a Review of the Proposed Amendments to the Lease; Zbornik Pravnog fakulteta Sveučilišta u Rijeci: 25(2004),1; pp. 481-521 (original in Croatian).

Brežanski, Jasna. The New Law on Waters; Zbornik Pravnog fakulteta Sveučilišta u Rijeci: 31(2010), 1 (Dodatak); pp. 295–320 (original in Croatian).

Dika, Mihajlo. Civil Enforcement Law; Narodne novine, 2007 (original in Croatian).

Ernst, Hano. New conditions for the establishment of condominium ownership; Hrvatska pravna revija: 6 (2006), 11; pp. 4–14 (original in Croatian).

Ernst, Hano. Simultaneous Hypothec; Zaštita vjerovnika: Zagreb(2005); pp. 193–226 (original in Croatian).

Ernst, Hano, Josipović, Tatjana. The Role of Land Registers in Marital Property Transactions, in: Liber amicorum in honorem Jadranko Crnić, Zagreb, 2009, 547–592 (original in Croatian).

Selected Bibliography

Ernst, Hano. Objects of Condominium Ownership – Dilemmas and New Solutions; Objekti etažnog vlasništva – dileme i nova rješenja; Zbornik Pravnog fakulteta u Zagrebu: 57(2007), 1; pp. 169–216 (original in Croatian).

Ernst, Hano. Primary Establishment of Consent Between the Land Registry and Cadastre, Primarna uspostava suglasnosti zemljišne knjige i katastra; Liber amicorum Nikola Gavella: Zagreb (2007); pp. 177–226 (original in Croatian).

Ernst, Hano. Secondary Synchronization of Land Registration and Cadastral Data; Selected Topics in Civil and Family Law: Zagreb (2008); pp. 141–216 (original in Croatian).

Gavella Nikola, Josipović Tatjana. Transformation of Rights of Use and Disposition on Real Property after the Transformation of Right Holders into Companies as a Precondition of the Croatian Legal Order to the European Legal Order, Zbornik Pravnog fakulteta u Rijeci, Suppl. no. 3, 2003 (original in Croatian).

Gavella Nikola. Property Law in Croatia: Changes of Property Law and State Transition; Modernization of Croatian Property Law: Zagreb (2007); pp. 13–57 (original in Croatian).

Gavella, Nikola. Acquisition of Title Processing, Consolidation, Construction of Buildings and Separating the Fruit; Zbornik Pravnog fakulteta u Zagrebu, nos 1-2/1981, pp. 39–79 (original in Croatian).

Gavella, Nikola. New Croatian Property Law in Function of Adjustment of Croatian Law to European Law: Situation Existing at the Time of Entry into Force of the Constitution 1990.; Das Budapester Symposium: Beitraege zur Reform des Sachenrechts in den Staaten Suedosteuropas = Budimpeštanski simpozijum: doprinos reformi stvarnog prava u državama jugoistočne Evrope. - Bremen(2003); pp. 20–47 (original in Croatian).

Gavella, Nikola. Property Act – Key Novelties with Particular Emphasis on Land Accession; Pravo u gospodarstvu: 36 (1997), 6; pp. 912–934 (original in Croatian).

Gavella, Nikola. Restrictions on Ownership; Zbornik Pravnog fakulteta Sveučilišta u Rijeci: 19 (1998), 2; pp. 351–362 (original in Croatian).

Gavella, Nikola, Gliha, Igor, Belaj,Vlado, Stipković, Zlatan: Property Law, Vol. I. Zagreb, 2007 (original in Croatian).

Gavella, Nikola, Gliha, Igor, Belaj, Vlado, Stipković, Zlatan: Property Law, Vol. II. Zagreb, 2007 (original in Croatian).

Gavella, Nikola, Ernst, Hano, Belaj, Vlado, Jug, Jadranko, Nikšić, Saša, Gliha, Igor, Josipović, Tatjana., Radionov, Nikoleta, Marin, Jasenko, Baretić, Marko, Property Law – Special Property Regimes, Vol. III. Zagreb, 2011 (original in Croatian).

Gliha, Igor. Josipović Tatjana: The Impact of Uniform Laws on the Protection of Cultural Heritage and the Preservation of Cultural Heritage in the 21st Century, National Report Croatia, The Impact of Uniform Laws on the Protection of Cultural Heritage and the Preservation of Cultural Heritage in the 21st Century, ed. Toshiyuki Kono, Leiden-Boston, 2012.

Gliha, Igor. The New Arrangement of Neighbourly Relations in the Light of Adjustment of the Croatian Civil Law System to the European Law; Das Budapester Symposium: Bremen (2003); pp. 48–65 (original in Croatian).

Jelčić, Olga. Register of Judicial and Notarial Security Rights on Movables andIn-tangibles; Hrvatsko registarsko pravo: Zagreb(2006); pp. 83–115 (original in Croatian).
Jelčić, Olga. The Realization of the Right to Enforcement of Claims Secured by Mortgage and Fiduciary Ownership of Assets, Pravo u gospodarstvu: 44 (2005) 3; pp. 52–79 (original in Croatian).
Jelčić, Olga. Protection of Property Rights by Legal Means in the Process of Land registration: The Role of the Land Registry in Property Transactions Law: Zagreb (2004); pp. 81–110 (original in Croatian).
Jelčić, Olga. Acquisition of Ownership Through Building, Hrvatska pravna revija: 5 (2005), 3; pp. 12–24 (original in Croatian).
Jelčić, Olga. Claim in Litigation to Protect the Rights of Ownership – Ownership and Land Claims; Nekretnine kao objekti imovinskih prava: Zagreb (2007); pp. 125–157 (original in Croatian).
Jelčić, Olga. New Fiduciary Insurance Claims; Novela Ovršnog zakona iz 2005.: Zagreb (2005); pp. 243–278 (original in Croatian).
Josipović, Tatjana. Confidence in the Legal Protection of Real Property – Austrian Model of the Croatian Way, Öffnung und Wandel – Die internationale imension des Rechts II, Festschrift für Willibald Posch, Wien, 2011 (original in German).
Josipović, Tatjana. Financial Leasing in Croatia and its Unification by UNIDROIT, 271–290, Uniform Law Review, Vol XVI, 2011–2012.
Josipović, Tatjana. Land Registration and Cadastre in Croatia, Land Registration and Cadastre in selected European Countries, Wien – Graz, 2009.
Josipović, Tatjana. Legal Foundations for Establishing Apartment Ownership, in: Real Property as Objects of Patrimonial Rights, Zagreb, 2007 (original in Croatian).
Josipović, Tatjana. State and Public Ownership, Zbornik Pravnog fakulteta u Rijeci, 1/2001 (original in Croatian).
Josipović, Tatjana. Amendments to the Ownership and other Real Rights Act, in: Real Property Transactions, Zagreb, 2006 (original in Croatian).
Josipović, Tatjana. Building Right – Legal Aspects, in: Real Property Transactions, Zagreb, 2006 (original in Croatian).
Josipović, Tatjana. Disposing of Security Interests, in: Creditor Protection – Legal, Tax and Accounting Aspects, Zagreb, 2006 (original in Croatian).
Josipović, Tatjana. Extra-tabular Acquisition and Cessation of Proprietary Rights in Land (Adaptation of Land Register) in: Real Property as Objects of Patrimonial Rights, Zagreb, 2005 (original in Croatian).
Josipović, Tatjana. Flexibility of Mortgage in Europe I, National Report for Croatia, Berlin, 2006 (original in German).
Josipović, Tatjana. Harmonisation of Croatian Real Property Law with EU Law, Private Law Reform in South East Europe – Liber Amicorum Christa Jessel-Holst, Belgrade, 2010.
Josipović, Tatjana. Modernizing Proprietary Security, Round Table – Modernizing Croatian Property Law, Zagreb, 2007 (original in Croatian).
Josipović, Tatjana. Proprietary Security in Land – Legal and Economic Effects, in: Real Property Transactions – current questions in legislation and practice 2007, Zagreb, 2007 (original in Croatian).

Selected Bibliography

Josipović, Tatjana. Protection of Creditors According to the Financial Collateral Act, in: Protection of Creditors -Financial, Legal and Tax Aspects, Zagreb, 2007 (original in Croatian).

Josipović, Tatjana. Real Property Transactions According to the Accession and Stabilization Agreement and Other International Treaties, in: Real Property Transactions, Zagreb, 2004 (original in Croatian).

Josipović, Tatjana. Recodifying Private Law in Croatia, Codifying, Europeanization and Harmonization of Private Law, Bratislava, 2005 (original in German).

Josipović, Tatjana. The Hypothec, in: Creditor Protection – Proprietary, Contractual and Judicial Security, 2005 (original in Croatian).

Josipović, Tatjana. The Land Registration System in Croatia – Characteristics, Functions, Reform in: Das Cavtater Symposium 'Beiträge zur Reform der freiwilligen Gerichtsbarkeit in des Staaten Südosteuropas', Bremen, 2005 (original in Croatian).

Josipović, Tatjana. The Publicity Function of the Land Register in Croatian Law, Zeitschrift Wirtschaft- und Recht in Osteuropa, 4/2000 (original in German).

Josipović, Tatjana. The Rail Protocol and Croatian Secured Transactions Law, Uniform Law Review, 2007-3.

Josipović, Tatjana. The Role of Cadastre in Real Property Transactions, in: Conference Proceeding of the Third Croatian Cadastre Conference with International Participation, Zagreb, 2005 (original in Croatian).

Josipović, Tatjana. The Role of the Land Register in Condominium Transactions, in: The Role of the Land Register in Real Property Transactions, Zagreb, 2004. (original in Croatian).

Josipović, Tatjana. Conforming Croatian Civil Law to European Standards, in: Privatrechtsentwicklung in Zentral- und Osteuropa, Wien, 2008 (original in German).

Josipović, Tatjana. The Principle of Publicity, the Principle of Trust and the Principle of Vindicatio in Real Property Transactions; Zbornik Pravnog fakulteta u Zagrebu: 45 (1995), 4–5; pp. 455–482. (original in Croatian).

Josipović, Tatjana. ABGB in Croatia – Historical Significance and the Role of Croatian Legislation to the Present, 200 Jahre Allgemeines Bürgeliches Gesetzbuch (ABGB) und Europäisches Vertragsrecht, 23. Europäische Notarentage 2011, Georg E.Kodek (Hrsg) 2012 (original in German).

Josipović, Tatjana. New Security Interests in Croatia, in: Property Regimes in Transitional Countries – Current State and Perspectives, Zagreb, 2009 (original in Croatian).

Josipović, Tatjana. Commentary on the Land Registration Act (original in Croatian), Informator, Zagreb, 1998.

Josipović, Tatjana. Land Registration Law in (original in German and Croatian, bilingual ed.) Vienna, FOWI-Wirtschaftsuniversität, 1999.

Josipović, Tatjana. Land Registration Law in the Socialist Era/Changes in Land Registration, Chapter in: Gavella, N. et al.: Theoretical Foundations of Civil Law – Civil Law and the Position of the Croatian Legal System in the Continental-European Legal Circle, Zagreb, 2005 (original in Croatian).

Josipović, Tatjana. Land Registration Law, Informator, Zagreb 2001 (original in Croatian).

Josipović, Tatjana. Property Law in Croatia (original in German), Vienna, 2002.

Jug, Jadranko. The Procedure in Connection with Property that Has not Been Evaluated by the Conversion of Community Companies; Nekretnine u pravnom prometu – aktualna pitanja zakonodavstva i sudske prakse – 2007.: Zagreb, (2007); pp. 217–234 (original in Croatian).

Jug, Jadranko. Dissolution of Joint Ownership of Property; Pravo u gospodarstvu: 49 (2010), 1; pp. 123–165 (original in Croatian).

Kontrec, Damir. Connecting Land Registry and Registry on Deposit Contracts: de lege lata and de lege ferenda; Liber amicorum in honorem Jadranko Crnić: Zagreb(2009); pp. 495–513. (original in Croatian).

Kontrec, Damir. Foreigners as Property Owners in the Republic of Croatia (New Regulations, the Procedure to Validate a Contract); Pravo u gospodarstvu: 43 (2009), 3; pp. 794–809 (original in Croatian).

Kontrec, Damir. An Entry of Tenant Ownership (Ownership of a Separate Part of Property) into the Land Register) Paying Special Attention to Entries Executed Prior to the Law on Ownership and Other Property Rights Entering into Force, Dilemmas and Issues in Practice; Zbornik Pravnog fakulteta Sveučilišta u Rijeci: 30 (2009), 1; pp. 703–724 (original in Croatian).

Kontrec, Damir. Connecting the Land Registry and Registry on Deposit Contracts and the Registration of Ownership of a Special Part of Property – the New Role of the Property Manager; Pravo u gospodarstvu: 50 (2011), 1; pp. 73–106. (original in Croatian) Liber amicorum in honorem Jadranko Crnić: Zagreb (2009), pp. 463–494 (original in Croatian).

Matko-Ruždjak, Jožica. Notarial Security by Transfer of Things and Rights; Zaštita vjerovnika: Zagreb(2005); pp. 271–293 (original in Croatian).

Matko-Ruždjak, Jožica. Notarial Services and Insurance Claims on Real Property; Zbornik Pravnog fakulteta u Zagrebu: 59 (2009), 6; pp. 1321–1354 (original in Croatian).

Matko-Ruždjak, Jožica. Satisfaction of Fiduciary Secured Creditors by the Sale of Collaterals; Javni bilježnik: 12 (2008), 29; pp. 9–22 (original in Croatian).

Matuško-Antonić, Ljiljana. The Establishment of the Unity of Property on Constructed Construction Land; Liber amicorum in honorem Jadranko Crnić: Zagreb (2009), str. 463–494 (original in Croatian).

Mihelčić, Gabrijela. Authority of Mortgage Creditors in the Settlement of Mortgage Claims of Sequestration Properties de lege lata and de lege ferenda; Liber amicorum in honorem Jadranko Crnić: Zagreb (2009); pp. 405–428 (original in Croatian).

Mihelčić, Gabrijela. Legal Status of the Buyer / Owner of Property in the Mortgage Regime; Hrvatska pravna revija: 9 (2009), 6; pp. 6–14 (original in Croatian).

Mihelčić, Gabrijela. Legal Status of the Buyer / Owner of Property in the Mortgage Regime, Zbornik Pravnog fakulteta Sveučilišta u Rijeci: 30 (2009), 1; pp. 629–647 (original in Croatian).

Radišić, Nives. Land Register; Hrvatsko registarsko pravo: Zagreb (2006); pp. 61–77 (original in Croatian).

Šarčević Petar, Josipović Tatjana, Gliha Igor, Hlača Nenad, Kunda Ivana: Family and Succession Law (Suppl. 27, July 2005) in: International Encyclopedia of Laws, Kluwer, 2005.

Sessa, Đuro & Susjedska prava. Real Property in Legal Transactions – Current Issues of Legislation and Case Law – 2008.: Zagreb (2008); pp. 95–115 (original in Croatian).
Simonetti, Petar. Acquisition of Ownership by Adverse Possession and Confiscation of Public Property; Zbornik Pravnog fakulteta Sveučilišta u Rijeci: 29 (2008), 1; pp. 27–70 (original in Croatian).
Simonetti, Petar. Discussions on Proprietary Rights; Pravni fakultet Sveučilišta u Rijeci, 2001 (original in Croatian).
Simonetti, Petar. Legal Duality of Land and Buildings before the Establishment of the Legal Union of Property; Liber amicorum Nikola Gavella: Zagreb (2007); pp. 105–139 (original in Croatian).
Simonetti, Petar. The Right to Build – its Duration and Cessation; Zbornik radova Ekonomskog fakulteta u Rijeci: 32 (2011), 1; pp. 1–29 (original in Croatian).
Vedriš, Martin & Klarić, Petar. Civil Law, 12th edition Narodne novine, 2009 (original in Croatian).
Zbornik Pravnog fakulteta Sveučilišta u Rijeci: 18 (1997), 1; pp. 215–234 (original in Croatian).
Žuvela, Mladen. Acquisition of Property by Contract; Pravo u gospodarstvu: 39 (2000), 6; pp. 21–47 (original in Croatian).
Žuvela, Mladen. Acquisition of Property by Adverse Possession: 1 part; Informator: 57 (2009), 5800–5801; pp. 5–6 (original in Croatian).
Žuvela, Mladen. Boundaries – an Institution of Our Civil Law; Pravo i porezi: 9 (2000), 5; pp. 32–35 (original in Croatian).
Žuvela, Mladen. Establishing a Legal Unity of Real Property: Current Croatian Legislation and Legal Practice: Zagreb (2005); pp.175–210 (original in Croatian).
Žuvela, Mladen. Neighbours' Rights: Boundary Construction; Pravo u gospodarstvu: 40 (2001), 6; pp. 31–48 (original in Croatian).
Žuvela, Mladen. The Lease Contract; Hrvatska pravna revija: 9 (2009), 9; pp. 1–17 (original in Croatian).
Žuvela, Mladen. Warranty of Title – the Conceptual Definition of Property Rights – the Basic Rules of the Constitutional System of Property Ownership; Odvjetnik: 84 (2011), 11–12; pp. 23–28 (original in Croatian).

Index

The numbers given here refer to paragraph numbers.

Index

www.ingramcontent.com/pod-product-compliance
Ingram Content Group UK Ltd.
Pitfield, Milton Keynes, MK11 3LW, UK
UKHW020137290926
15471UKWH00003B/543

9 789403 523668